A Sugar Creek Chronicle

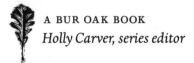

A BUR OAK BOOK

Holly Carver, series editor

CORNELIA F. MUTEL

A Sugar Creek Chronicle

*Observing Climate Change from
a Midwestern Woodland*

UNIVERSITY OF IOWA PRESS | IOWA CITY

University of Iowa Press, Iowa City 52242
Copyright © 2016 by the University of Iowa Press
www.uiowapress.org
Printed in the United States of America
Design by Sara T. Sauers

The University of Iowa Press is a member of Green Press Initiative and is committed to preserving natural resources.
Printed on acid-free paper

Library of Congress Cataloging-in-Publication Data
Names: Mutel, Cornelia Fleischer.
Title: A Sugar Creek chronicle : observing climate change from a midwestern woodland / Cornelia F. Mutel.
Description: Iowa City : University of Iowa Press, [2016] | Series: Bur oak books | Includes bibliographical references and index.
Identifiers: LCCN 2015033808 | ISBN 978-1-60938-395-4 (pbk) | ISBN 978-1-60938-396-1 (ebk)
Subjects: LCSH: Climatic changes—Iowa—History—20th century. | Meteorology—Iowa—Observations.
Classification: LCC QC903.2.I6 M88 2016 | DDC 577.3/276097776—dc23
LC record available at http://lccn.loc.gov/2015033808

ᕲ For my dear grandchildren
Sophia, Noah, Moses, Matvei, Ellie, and Will

CONTENTS

SINCE CHILDHOOD, I HAVE SOUGHT OUT NATURE'S HIDDEN pockets and worked to learn about their inhabitants, particularly their plants. As a young adult, my passion for the natural world expanded into a career of sharing my knowledge of botany and ecology with the general public. I have done so through teaching and through writing books on the integrity and necessity of healthy ecological systems. In recent years, my writing has increasingly addressed major environmental problems such as the loss of biodiversity, flooding, and now climate change.

In 2010, while editing a climate-change impacts report submitted to the Iowa general assembly, I became acutely aware of the escalating expressions of climate change and the urgent need to address its causes and results. I already knew the basics: climate change refers to a growing atmospheric blanket that prevents release of the planet's heat energy and thus raises Earth's average temperature. Even a deceptively small annual temperature change influences all of Earth's operating systems and plays havoc with our planet's lifeforms and elementary natural processes. The heat-trapping blanket is produced primarily by gases from the burning of fossil fuels.

But only after working on this report did I comprehend the magnitude and urgency of the problem and the stark diagnosis of climate change. I came to understand that it is happening now, manifesting itself faster than we had expected, and accelerating rapidly enough to challenge adaptation by humans and the natural world. That ongoing greenhouse-gas emissions are on a trajectory that could, within decades, propel us beyond irreversible, dangerous temperature limits. That such uncontrolled growth of greenhouse gases could set off reactions that could limit our ability to mitigate future disasters and restore the earth to health. If that occurs, for all human purposes, major destabilization of our climate will become permanent.

Climate change, I realized, has the power to redefine all other political, social, economic, cultural, and environmental realities, indeed everything we know about life on earth—*if* we don't do something to prevent this. The more I learned, the more I felt the need to contribute what I could to addressing this enormous and growing problem. And for me, that meant writing about it.

But how? Rather than compile a book of facts, I hoped to write something that would invite you, my readers, to consider the importance of climate change and to realize that we can—indeed that we must—rapidly take action to limit its expression. I wanted to use a personal approach, reaching out by sharing how my growing knowledge of the looming climate crisis was reshaping my own perceptions, life, and home. This book is the result of my deliberations. It began as a journal for my then-unborn granddaughter and grew into the current structure, one that interweaves climate-change science with personal memoir, natural history, and weather observations.

As I began assembling materials, my ideas on these subjects fell naturally into two timelines. The timelines define the structure of this book, which pairs four Weather and Climate Journal chapters about a single year in the Iowa woodland where I live with four Memoir chapters. In the four fast-moving Memoir chapters, I weave my own life story into that of our planet's environmental dilemmas, which have redefined our world during the years 1947 to 2012, my lifespan when I began this book. I also describe the problems that have touched my life during this same period, especially my experiences with cancer, which have dramatically altered my understanding of the world.

In the four interwoven quieter, slower-paced Weather and Climate Journal chapters, written for the seasons winter, spring, summer, and autumn, I bring you, the reader, into my home to watch the natural world of our woodland unfold through a single year, 2012. I also describe what turned out to be the tumultuous weather events of that year, which became perhaps the first year that the reality of climate change came home to the American public. During 2012, weather records were broken time and time again; I speculate about what those weather events may portend. Information about the science of climate change and its dramatic alteration of the planet is integrated into these chapters where appropriate.

With my heightened attention to weather and climate throughout 2012, I found it difficult to stop writing about these subjects when the calendar rolled over to 2013, and so I devote a chapter to summarizing the unusual weather events for that year. My final chapter suggests what can be done about climate change, how we can restore our planet to health, and how we all can contribute to the process.

If you are moved to delve deeper into climate change and keep up with its evolving expressions, as I hope you are, "Finding More Information" (at the book's end) lists some of the many excellent science-based information sources and gives suggestions for differentiating these from non-evidence-based sources (e.g., sources shaped by political or economic considerations). My sources of information for climate change are listed in the bibliographic essay, which also includes citations for specific climate data, notes on interpretation of key data, and references to important studies and reports mentioned in the book.

And finally, a note on the title. Our neighborhood is known as Sugar Bottom because of the maples that once grew here and were tapped for the making of maple syrup. Our woodland drains into an intermittent creek that flows past our land into a larger tributary of the Iowa River. Although that larger stream is not officially named, we call it Sugar Creek; hence, *A Sugar Creek Chronicle*.

By explaining Earth's climate system in a straightforward manner for a nonscientific audience, *A Sugar Creek Chronicle* challenges its readers to explore the many ramifications of a single major question: What happens if more heat energy enters than leaves Earth's atmosphere? Climate-science complexities are necessarily simplified and condensed; the book is neither a comprehensive treatise on climate change, nor is it an all-inclusive explanation of the unusual weather events of 2012. Even so, the concepts presented herein are based on thousands of peer-reviewed scientific articles and masses of scientific data examining how our delicate and complex planet is responding to a growing energy imbalance.

While climate change is a global phenomenon, it is expressed with distinct regional differences. My primary focus area has been the contiguous United States as well as the Arctic, which is important in shaping U.S. climate. Many examples and trends refer specifically to the Midwest, where I live. Occasionally I expand my discussion to North America, the northern hemisphere, or the entire globe.

Climate events are described as they were interpreted during the years chronicled in the book, 2012 and 2013; statistics are accurate for those years, although I have also included some later appraisals, such as those in the *Fifth Assessment Report of the Intergovernmental Panel on Climate Change* volumes published in 2014. In addition, I updated the Third National Climate Assessment's 2013 draft conclusions using the 2014 final report. As climate change intensifies, these statistics may become outdated. However, the trends outlined herein are expected to continue as described.

A word on weather and climate. Extreme weather and climate change are not synonymous. Simply put, climate is what we expect, while weather is what we get. Climate (and climate change) address major large-scale long-term trends, while weather describes daily events in one small area. While 2012's very hot March and Superstorm Sandy in October are indicative of what climate change may produce in coming years, climate scientists remain wary of attributing one-to-one causation. They point out that weather's natural variability helped to shape 2012 events. Many of these same scientists, however, also state that our changing climate may have raised the probability and magnified the intensity of the 2012 weather events.

On a similar note, you may be puzzled by the disparity between very high 2012 regional temperature extremes and much smaller global average temperature rises. The former may make the latter seem inconsequential. But these are two different entities, and they cannot be compared. The first refers to a single local weather event, while the second is changing climate—the long-term average rise in temperature in all seasons and around the globe.

Because my book is being published in the U.S., I have used Fahrenheit (rather than Celsius) temperatures. However, readers may already recognize a few important Celsius benchmarks. The temperature 2°C is accepted by most climate scientists as the global average temperature rise which, if exceeded, could produce dangerous interference with our climate system; discussions often focus on keeping the rise below this limit. In the text, that limit is given as 3.6°F. Again, 0.8°C defines our current global average rise, derived by comparing temperatures in recent years (2003 to 2012) to those of the period 1850 to 1900; in the book, I convert that 0.8°C increment to 1.4°F.

Climate change is a complex and dynamic process. As such, it will continue to manifest in new ways, and we will interpret its ramifications in new ways. This was already happening in 2014 and 2015, while this book was in its final preparation. In May of 2014, a large sector of the West Antarctic ice sheet was melting rapidly and appeared to be in unstoppable decline; that ice sector alone, which could take several centuries to melt, contains enough ice to raise the global sea level by four feet. Also, the Risky Business Project, which analyzes the economic risks of climate change for the U.S. business community, published its first report, which stated that climate change is already costing local economies billions of dollars.

Finally, a word of encouragement. Climate change is not an easy subject to deal with. If taken seriously, it can become overwhelming and depressing. I know. I have been there. While I was becoming intimate with the implications of climate change, I went through months of quiet despair. I mourned the possible uncertainties and miseries of future people, mentally ticking these off as I wrote: new health problems, uncertain provision of food and water, growing numbers of environmental refugees, and the inability to assume that a spring day will bring joy and abundance. I also mourned the inevitable loss of other species. At times, I believed that our ongoing business-as-usual lifestyles were a sign of societal insanity, and I felt that insanity penetrating my spirit. At other times, I grew jealous of people who seemed blissfully unaware of how ordinary human behavior is altering climate processes.

My husband's mental stability helped ground me during these times. Robert is an astronomer. He thinks of distant places and big time spans. Coming to grips with climate change has forced me to adopt his broader vision of time and place. I now understand, at a gut level, that all of human civilization developed in the past 10,000 years, the twinkling of an eye as far as our 4.6-billion-year-old planet is concerned. In that relatively short time span, humans have gone from being one life-form on par with 10 million other species to dominating Earth's flow of energy and resources and assuming that it is our right to do so. This shift has allowed us to distance ourselves from the natural world and from our responsibility for maintaining its health. But, as is often said, Mother Nature speaks last; if we do not reassess and preemptively reshape our use of the earth and its resources, climate change might be the natural world's final indictment of our species.

Like living with cancer and its implications, living intimately with my new climate-change awareness has led me to view my life in a different way. Many small problems, once important, now seem inconsequential. At the same time, the moment is often miraculous, and I treasure each small element of normalcy. I relish rising in the morning to feed the birds and listen to our dog, Sidney, chomp down her breakfast. I revel in the rising sun's rays streaming through the forest. I walk slowly. At my age, I give thanks for each step taken without pain or danger.

In summary, coming to grips with climate change has forced me to the mental place where I should have been all along: living more intensely and thoughtfully in each moment, while simultaneously considering the big picture and distant future of this planet and working to ensure its health and vitality.

I do hope that this book will draw you, my reader, further into thoughts about your own life and homeland. Beyond that, I hope you might consider how you could use your unique skills in your own chosen manner to help shape a more positive climate future. I believe that this is something we all can and must do because of our obligations to our children and grandchildren and others yet to be born; because of our dependence on a healthy and fully functioning planet; and because of all Earth's wonders that might disappear if we remain silent.

A Sugar Creek Chronicle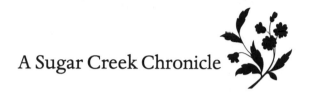

ONE

The Place I Call Home

I LIVE WITH MY HUSBAND, ROBERT, AND OUR DOG, SIDNEY, in the center of an eastern Iowa woodland, within the embracing arms of white, black, red, and bur oaks and shagbark hickories that wave in the wind a hundred feet over my head, large trees that have lived far longer than my 65 years and will, if conditions permit, thrive long after I am gone. Our three boys were rooted and raised here, roving the woods in search of baby squirrels, chasing toads as they leapt through the leaves, discovering insects and cocoons tucked into the crevices of bark, damming the rivulet below our house with sticks, and following that trickle down to Sugar Creek, which is large enough for a youngster's fishing expedition. Now, when they bring their children back to visit, our grown sons tell stories of the tree forts they built as kids, the fire crackers they lit near the pond, their secret naming of "winter wonderland" and other special woodland hideaways. I love listening to my sons' recounting of their collective past, although they do not often include our more tender moments together, the times that I remember. Yet, their stories tell me that this house, this plot of land remain their planet's center, a stable refuge, a dreamscape to which our sons mentally return when times get rough. Our home and the surrounding woods have nurtured them, protecting and providing stability for their spirits even after their bodies left to roam elsewhere.

I am a walker. Most days I roam our land and the trails and lanes defining neighboring woods, fields, and creek bottoms, observing their wild occupants and considering processes from long ago that continue today. When I proceed up our lane to the county road at the top of the hill, I peer across a series of flat ridgelines that stretch to the horizon. These ridges mark the plane formed by a glacier that leveled this landscape half-a-million or more years ago, ages before humans roamed North America's midcontinent. At that time, I could have hiked for miles in any direction across a uniform terrain dotted with rocks dropped from the glacier's melting ice. But not now. Time and running water have cut channels deep into the land, so that whenever I walk out our door, I must go uphill or down. The landscape and its inhabitants are constantly evolving, although usually in a slow and orderly fashion.

Going in the opposite direction, following a path that winds downhill to the far corner of our land, I pass the remains of the original settlers' summer kitchen, part of a larger homestead from the 1800s, a tiny rough structure built of heavy timbers. I find plants here that the settlers or perhaps their children collected from nearby riversides and native prairies and brought back to their home gardens—shooting star, obedient plant, creamy gentian. Despite landscape changes, this region undoubtedly cared well for these immigrant settlers, Iowa's rich soils growing grains, the wildlands yielding meat, our woods relinquishing logs for constructing and warming their crude homes.

Continuing from the summer kitchen down the lane, I pass the neighbor's pond, where our boys swam in the summer and skated in the winter, and then follow the road to an expanse of public land bordering a large reservoir. Meandering south a few miles along the reservoir, I approach circular Native American burial mounds on hilltops overlooking the Iowa River—places significant to peoples living in nearby villages a thousand years ago.

Crossing Sugar Creek and hiking a few miles in the opposite direction, I reach a cave where small groups of these same ancient residents camped in fall and winter while hunting deer, collecting mussels, and gathering nuts from surrounding forests, which provided diverse foods in abundance. Long before these food-gathering sessions, this same cave was occupied by other human wanderers of riverside forests who also sought warmth and shelter here. The message is clear: this eastern Iowa landscape has sustained human life for several thousand years, providing the food and shelter people needed to flourish.

I imagine that all these earlier residents lived through times of beauty and crisis, wonder and conflict, as I have. Surely their lives outlined stories of changes in the land and its means of provision. But on the whole, throughout human civilization's occupancy of our planet, natural changes have occurred slowly, within predictable limits. The land's dependability and integrity, its provision of fundamental resources and ecological services have remained for the most part intact.

This may now be changing. As a student of the natural world, I have traced our woodland's expression through several decades, monitoring the sequence of wildflowers emerging in spring, watching the fading of color in autumn, observing the migrating breeding birds arriving in May and disappearing with their broods in October. But I am starting to sense vagaries in the air and weather patterns, disruptive shifts that are influencing our woodland's occupants and seem to be accelerating. The first wildflowers used to bloom like clockwork on April 7. And ticks were a worry primarily in spring months. Now, with the winter's cold dissolving earlier and summertime's warmth persisting longer, the early wildflowers might bloom in March, perhaps before their pollinators emerge, and I sometimes find ticks in November. Meanwhile the well-regulated rains that previously characterized Iowa's rich growing season are shifting to intense downpours falling earlier in the year and eroding springtime's bare cropland soils. Similar symptoms have been documented across the country and around the world. Too many unusual changes are happening too fast. An unsettled feeling permeates the air. The climatic stability that has regulated our landscape and governed Earth's residents for thousands of years seems to be teetering.

As individuals and societies, we depend on the earth's constancy to order our days and give our years structure and direction. A beneficent climate is, like health, something elementary, something we tend to ignore until disturbing symptoms arise, something we assume will always be there like the sun rising in the morning. What if that regularity dissolves? Would we know how to pattern our lives?

For someone who likes the illusion of stability, fosters traditions, and shuns unplanned change, I was born at the wrong time. I arrived in 1947 on the coattails of World War II, a take-off period for many of the environmental challenges now plaguing our globe. Between then and now, the planet's natural features have been altered arguably more rapidly and profoundly than at any time in the past, except perhaps during dramatic geologic seizures such as massive volcanic eruptions or meteor strikes.

Consider the shifts that have occurred from 1950 to 2010, approximately my current lifespan. Tremendous increases in the human population, paired with increasing per-person consumption, have triggered the use of vastly more resources and products, use that was made possible by exploding industrialization fueled by increases in energy consumption, energy provided by large increases in the burning of natural gas and oil. The result: soaring rises in carbon dioxide emissions and other pollutants, along with decreases in wildlands available for Earth's perhaps 10 million other species, which are now experiencing species extinction at 100 to 1,000 times the normal rate. Inexpensive and readily available fossil fuels also have encouraged adoption of the car as the primary means of transportation, which has totally changed our lifestyles and expectations.

Humanity, while implementing all these changes, has accomplished something hitherto considered impossible. We have measurably and significantly altered two of the planet's largest physical entities: the oceans, making them warmer and more acidic, and the atmosphere, which is on average warmer and growing warmer still.

These changes have been so monumental that some have earned newly minted names. Today's human-induced loss of species is being called the sixth mass extinction, equating it with other extinctions during the last half-billion years that were triggered by natural causes such as massive volcanic eruptions, asteroid impacts, or glaciations. And the sum total of these changes, some say, is defining a new geologic epoch—the Anthropocene—a time when humans (rather than natural processes) are altering the entire global environment in a major way.

One of the Anthropocene's defining traits is an increase in the globe's average annual surface temperature by 1.4 degrees, with most of the rise occurring since 1980. [Note: Because this book is published in the U.S., temperatures throughout are given in Fahrenheit, not Celsius units. Readers may see Celsius temperatures used in scientific articles and elsewhere.] This seemingly small temperature rise embraces a suite of trends that have been defined by scientific measurements and are occurring around the world: increasing ocean heat content, rising sea levels, growing atmospheric moisture, shrinking ice and snow cover, poleward- and upward-climbing plant and animal ranges, shortening winters and earlier springs. All these factors contribute to the definition of climate change, which is also called global warming, although the phenomenon goes well beyond warmer temperatures. The process originates with the atmosphere's retention of greater heat energy, created primarily by increasing greenhouse-gas emissions produced when fossil fuels are burned. This process has been acknowledged by an estimated 97 to 98 percent of trained climate scientists and validated by thousands of peer-reviewed research studies.

While researching and writing this book, I learned a tremendous amount about climate-change science. I now understand how small invisible changes—parts-per-million increases in certain atmospheric gases—can upset the flow of heat energy into and out of the atmosphere. The consequences of this altered flow are profound and transformative. They include concerns about food production, water availability, emergency relief, military security, infrastructure integrity, society's stability, the economy, and ecological biodiversity and integrity. As greenhouse-gas emissions and average temperatures grow further, they will increasingly touch every aspect of global function and human life, from what and how much we eat, to where we live and how we die, to our basic economic, political, and societal stability. We are now entering a new reality.

I learned that a cascade of climate-induced changes is already reshaping life on Earth in multiple and diverse ways. And that the rate of these changes is too fast to allow nature's ready adaptation and fast enough to challenge human adaptation.

I learned that some expressions of climate change are appearing sooner than was predicted, and that we are just beginning to see their unveiling. Without a reduction in greenhouse-gas emissions, average temperatures are expected to climb considerably higher and multiply concerns during this century. At some point, if we do not restrain our current emissions' unchecked growth, they could trigger self-feeding tipping points that would make rising temperatures and their spinoffs impossible to halt. If we allow this to happen, climate change threatens to transform the human experience on Earth and potentially human survival as well.

And yet, I learned that *if* is a powerful word. *If* we let all this happen. *If* we do not address climate change soon and in a major fashion, the future will likely be shaped by increasingly severe and unpredictable weather and all its environmental and societal spinoffs. By contrast, *if* we take strong and rapid steps to mitigate greenhouse-gas production, we can put the worst climate-change ramifications into remission.

Hope for limiting climate change is not naïve. We can take definite steps to limit its repercussions even as we improve our economy and quality of life. Dozens of countries around the world are already doing so, as are large and small corporations and some states and cities in the U.S. Research institutions and individuals are working on creative solutions. And many concerned citizens are reordering their lives to reduce their carbon footprint—that is, they are cutting the amount of carbon dioxide they personally release into the atmosphere. If we all reduced our carbon footprint, our combined actions could make a large difference.

The coming months and years will determine our climate future and, through this, humanity's prognosis. If we take a proactive stance in dealing with climate change, the future could be a time of exhilarating challenge and attainment. The sooner we start acting, the easier and less expensive and more profound will be the results. We need to get going.

I remember well the moment that this book was conceived. Late one evening in December 2011, Robert and I were sitting at the kitchen table with our son and his wife when they shared the news that the next summer, we'd be welcoming a new grandchild into the family. We were overjoyed, as were they, and the four of us jubilantly chatted for some time about how this new life would affect future years.

As we talked, I felt something click deep within my mind. For the previous several months, I had been reading about the dangers of climate change and what it might do to the natural world and to human civilization. My growing knowledge had forced me to consider what sort of world I was leaving for my children and grandchildren and how I might employ my experience as an environmental writer to help others envision a healthier, more positive future. That evening, sitting at the table with my family as the night deepened, I realized that this grandchild-to-be could live through a dramatic reshaping of the planet's climate.

Within days of learning about the grandchild we now call Ellie, I had begun writing a journal that I hoped would someday tell her that I had understood the dangers of climate change and had done what I could to address them. The journal morphed as I wrote, taking on first one guise, then another, but with time my focus narrowed to a few goals: I wanted to introduce Ellie to the woodland where Robert and I now live and where her father grew up—a woodland that I hoped she too would come to love—tracing it through a single year of seasonal changes. During that year, 2012, I also dedicated myself to carefully observing weather events and learning more about climate-change science and including elements of these subjects in my woodland journal.

As I wrote, I realized that the climate-change story needs to be rooted in an understanding of the past, especially within the explosion of environmental problems since World War II. I thus decided to add a longer perspective to my writing and also to share some of my personal story. I wanted Ellie to know of my lifelong passion for wild places and native plants, a passion that sprouted when I was a child. I also wanted to share the challenges of my life, in particular my ongoing skirmishes with cancer, which took my mother's life in her middle age and also has threatened my life.

While writing, I became aware of the similarities between cancer in the human body and greenhouse gases in Earth's atmosphere. Both can distort healthy functions and ultimately lead to dramatic changes, and both are best treated by strong actions taken early, before they spin toward points of no return. This comparison, which may seem all too obvious to some readers, has informed my thought processes and my writing.

All these writings and wanderings eventually became this book, which intertwines the two timelines and story lines—the woodland journal chapters, written for the year 2012, intermixed with memoir chapters that consider the period 1947 to 2012.

With that introduction, I invite you to turn the page and join me for a conversation at my kitchen table, a cup of tea in hand, and then to walk with me through the seasons of my life and of our woodland, considering the slow, ongoing changes that bring health and resilience to such natural systems and the ways that today's accelerating climate changes might alter them.

My guess is that even if you have not lived in a rural woodland, our lives are in some ways similar. You too have loved family, treasured a special place, worried about illness, been touched by beauty and by loss, felt drawn to things nonhuman, wondered about our rapidly changing world, and worried about where the future is taking us. You too have wanted to leave a legacy of a better world.

I now invite you to come along as I share how these universal themes have played out in my life, how I have met changes and challenges, and how I have searched for health and wholeness during difficult times, a search that you too have surely made.

And so I begin.

PART I
Winter

TWO

Weather & Climate Journal
January–March, 2012

JANUARY 7 ◆ Saturday. A day when I can enjoy being in a warm bubble—my home—in the middle of a cold woodland. I love this winter sense of enclosure, of being held inside a wooden shell that contains me and the things that help define me: my books and journals, the houseplants I clip and water, the cherry cupboard made by my great-great-grandfather, the chipped dishes we eat from every day. Family and wedding photographs, pictures of our boys growing up here in the woods, now pictures of them with their own children. The casual clutter of daily life that warms my spirit, the fireplace that warms my body.

And outside a different world, one where the birds and mice and squirrels are at home and have their own amazing ways of keeping warm. So many lives, so many little miracles: roots weaving through frozen ground, insects hiding under flaps of bark, trees bending to winter's winds, birds gathering at my feeder. And all of us held between the planet's atmosphere and soils, part of a thin skin of life that encircles the globe, sustained by dependable patterns and processes: the cycling of water, of energy, of nitrogen and carbon, of decomposing wastes that are resurrected into new life. The cycling of love and warmth and traditions—ours and those of 7 billion other humans and 10 million or more other species. All with their own voices and visions, their own ways of knowing the world, their own contributions to keeping this planet functioning well. I think about this when sitting here in my quiet shelter, looking out the window at woods that look barren and dead but are really full of life and promise.

My kitchen is small, simple, and cozy, as is the entire house. It's a fraction of the size of many houses built in our area today. Yet our home feels expansive because of the woods that surround it, which stretch uninterrupted to the horizon on all sides. The massive trees never fail to awe me—even now, after having lived here for thirty-five years, most of my adult life. My husband, Robert, and I built this house ourselves, erecting the walls and shingling the roof, back when we were young and had more time than money. It has remained essentially unchanged since we built it, although we added a rec room in the basement when the kids were teenagers and stuck a walled-in sleeping porch surrounded by windows onto our bedroom. Here I can lie in any season and watch the trees waving in the wind. I spend a lot of time gazing out the window at the woods or, when weather permits, wandering through them, connecting with the creatures who live here with me, acknowledging that I am a part of their lives as they are a part of mine.

Our house is near Iowa City, Iowa, where Robert and I both work. Because we live near the Iowa River, the landscape is hilly and rugged, having been eroded by streams since the retreat of the last glaciers 14,000 years ago. This region is a land of rolling pastures and woods, of oaks and shagbark hickories, of scampering chipmunks and soaring raptors, of flowers and birdsong, a refuge from Iowa's 23 million uniform acres of corn and soybean fields. Our woodland is surrounded by the acreages of similar nature-lovers: my neighbors' pastures, hayfields, and gardens, restored prairies and woods, an old horse stable and a few rebuilt barns, together forming a patchwork quilt of beauty and a vision of constancy and abundance. Here, listening to towhees sing in summer and watching goldfinches flutter around the winter feeder, observing flowers that appear in orderly succession throughout the summer and leaves twinkling in the early morning sunshine, I feel at peace, as if all is right with the world. Once a visitor from Chicago said to me, "This is what heaven will look like." Heaven, yes—this is my heaven and my haven now, in this world and at this time, the home where I have lived most of my life, the place where I hope to reside until I die.

JANUARY 9 ⁓ I refilled our woodbox last night, piling logs stored in our shed onto a cart and hauling them inside the basement. The full moon painted nearby tree trunks and the woodshed a pale tannish yellow, while the more distant woodlands remained hidden in shadow. A slight breeze chilled my face, even though my body was hot from carrying the heavy logs. Between loads I rested, leaning against a tree, noting the silhouettes of distant trees and surrounding hills outlined against the moonlit sky. My world narrowed to a small, safe place defined by soft light, the touch of moving air, and the occasional hoot of a barred owl.

After the woodbox was full, I lit a fire in the furnace. Just like living successfully on our complex planet, building a good fire is more art than science. Select the first logs for their small size, the presence of fast-lighting slivers, and the absence of bark or decay. These traits help logs light more easily. Place three or four of these logs over a few pieces of kindling, allowing plenty of space for air movement. If the fire is well laid, a single piece of paper will ignite the kindling and logs simultaneously. The logs may sputter a bit, but once they crackle, the fire has caught. Leave this nascent fire for about five minutes and then return to collapse the blazing logs into a closely packed heap. Then pile on larger logs at will. Stoke the fire every few hours.

I like to think about how the energy heating our house comes from right here, in our woods. I guess in this one small way my family is a throwback to times before the Industrial Revolution, when energy was produced close to home and usually involved human sweat, using plants as fuel, harnessing animals, or capturing the power of water or wind. The trees that surround our house are living machines that catch the sun's energy, pull in carbon dioxide, and meld the two to produce long-chained carbon molecules. When we burn firewood, those carbon molecules are split apart and their stored energy is released as heat. The result: a warm home and a nice tight energy cycle. Because the released carbon dioxide was pulled from the atmosphere as the trees grew, it does not add to our atmosphere's net carbon burden in the long term.

Considering this process, I understand how fossil fuels differ dramatically from renewable energy sources such as wind power, solar energy, biofuels, or the firewood cut on our land. Fossil fuels come from plants or other living organisms that grew hundreds of millions of years ago and then were buried and transformed into coal, oil, or natural gas. Those plants pulled their carbon from an ancient atmosphere, but the carbon was then stashed deep within the earth. Starting around 1750 with the Industrial Revolution, quantities of fossil fuels were pulled back up to the ground surface and burned. They too released the energy stored in their long-chained carbon molecules, combining it with atmospheric oxygen to form carbon dioxide. This "fossil" carbon dioxide is a brand new addition to our modern atmosphere, one with the power to radically alter its composition and properties.

Fossil fuels are a relatively inexpensive and highly concentrated form of energy—a single gallon of gasoline holds the energy equivalent of fifty horses working for an hour. Once fossil fuels became readily available, they and the engines they powered rapidly supplanted the back-breaking labor and tedium that had characterized human life for millennia. Greater ease and new products improved ordinary lives, transforming human expectations and patterns of living. Today, thanks to fossil fuels, I drive to work ten miles from home, fly to see my grandchildren, visit distant friends with ease, wear clothes sewn in China of cotton grown in India, and eat apples flown in from New Zealand and pineapples from Hawaii. I use dozens of plastic objects, synthetic fibers, detergents, and other products transported by and manufactured from fossil fuels. Fossil fuels form the raw materials for the fertilizers and pesticides used to grow the foods that spill from our refrigerator, foods that are cooked in an oven and served in a well-lit, temperature-controlled dining room, all powered by fossil-fuel-generated electricity.

I grew up assuming that electric power, ready transportation, central heating, and an abundance of consumables were a part of my birthright. And that the energy providing all of these was synonymous with one fossil fuel or another. Fossil fuels have revolutionized human society so thoroughly and brought my family such comfort and ease that I cannot imagine life without them.

Living here in the woods, depending on trees rather than fossil fuels for heating our house, our family has managed to reduce in one small way our dependence on fossil fuels, while at the same time recreating a sense of self-reliance and reassuring family patterns similar to those of my childhood. Every fall Robert goes out to cut downed trees and cart them back to a work area near the garage. Once the pile is large enough, he rents a wood splitter and hauls the split logs down to the woodshed, where they dry until we start bringing the wood into the basement, a cartload at a time, to burn in the furnace. This last fall, our grown sons came back for the splitting and hauling. In two days, they had filled the woodshed to overflowing. The boys grew up with this routine. Fall Saturdays, when Dad got out the chainsaw or rented the splitter, other events had to be put aside. The boys griped about wood-gathering when they were younger, but now they remember those days with pleasure—the crisp air, the crunch of leaves underfoot, coming inside for a bowl of soup, and finally smelling smoke come from the chimney for the first time that season. They know that the house is warm and welcoming because of their efforts, not because of a truck that delivers fuel. Now our sons talk about coming back in the fall to help with the wood; it's become a tradition, and life doesn't feel quite right without it.

One year, when our son Andy was helping load a cart of wood, he cut off the tip of his middle finger in the tractor hitch. A quick amputation. We picked it up, wrapped it in a clean handkerchief, and raced him to the hospital where the fingertip was sewn back on. Today it works fine, but he says he still feels it sometimes. Heating with wood is not entirely risk-free.

But then nothing in life is free of possible danger or damage—nothing at all. Too often in my adult life, I have feared that the unexpected would bring calamity. However, all our children and grandchildren are still here and healthy. All our family's wounds, including my own, have healed, at least to some degree.

JANUARY 11 ❧ It snowed last night. Not much—just a few inches, enough to cover the ground. However, even this small snowfall is a treat this winter, when it has barely snowed at all. It hasn't been an especially dry winter, but temperatures have been above normal, and so we've been getting winter rains instead of snows. These are ugly affairs in my mind. Spring rains are soft and beckoning, as if they are seducing the soils to release the seeds hidden within. Summer rains can be dramatic, with thunderclouds and sudden shifts in light and shadow. But winter rains just add to the gloom of the short, dark days.

The brightness of snow in contrast graces our days with a cleansing whiteness and turns the night world bright with reflected moonlight and starlight. The snow gives winter evenings a shimmering light of their own. Even in the deepest part of night, snow lets me see form and shape in my woodland, and this tells me about substance: yes, the trees are still there. Without snow, I look out on winter nights and see only a black void. In my mind, winters are for snow, which we seem to be losing.

Snowy winters also give me time for appreciating shape and color, a strange thought for the season when only tree trunks and shrub stems are visible. But snowy days highlight the intricacy of the gnarled oak trunks and branches reaching upward into a muted gray-blue sky. And when I gaze at the woods for a time, I start to notice the many shades of gray and brown found in bark. They range from deep chestnut to light beige, near-black to whitish gray. The white oaks in particular delight me. White oaks over a hundred years old host a light-colored bark fungus. Thus I can gaze into the woods and easily differentiate younger trees, with rough dark bark, from centenarians with patches of smoother, white gray bark.

This morning a light snowfall is continuing. Snow flurries, states the weather report, but flurry is too active a word for today's gentle skies and muffled tones. A quiet beauty rests over the stillness when light is too dim to create shadows, and all objects are faded by wandering snowflakes, falling without aim or direction, white snow on white snow. All colors are lessened, muted, as if everything is seen through a screen. Cattle in nearby fields have faded from black to dark gray, trees from dark gray to light. The road hides under blowing streams of thin snow. The snow hushes any sounds—bird calls, branches falling, the occasional passing car—that might pierce the thin air. It's a good day for walking slowly and watching how the world can withdraw, a soft subdued day when I feel cocooned by snow and let time stop.

JANUARY 21 ∿ One might think that walking in a snow-covered woods in winter is entering a world asleep. But nothing could be further from the truth. Yes, some mammals—woodchucks, chipmunks, skunks—slumber within trees or under the ground. And I can imagine sleeping lives hidden under flaps of tree bark, insects held within decomposing trees, pupae buried in leaf litter. But walking after a fresh snowfall, as I did this morning, I can easily observe more animal signs than in the summertime. Looking up, I follow gray and fox squirrels running along leafless branches, and looking down I see trails formed by their long, thin feet. Miniature highways running from the base of one tree to that of another. Sometimes, during very cold spells, our dog, Sidney, finds a frozen squirrel and brings it home, proudly dropping it with a clunk at our front door.

Raccoons also have long feet and fingers. I don't see them often in winter because they spend weeks at a time sleeping in their dens. But when they wake up, they come to my bird feeder, using their fingers to pry sunflower seeds through the feeder's mesh. When I open the deck door to improve my view, they fearlessly look me in the eye, not running unless I take a step toward them.

Once in a while flying squirrels glide in to the bird feeders. I would not know that these small, big-eyed squirrels cohabitate the woods with me except for these occasional sightings and the scratch marks they make on tree trunks where they've come in for a landing.

We have only native mice here in the woods, the deer mice being most numerous. Their trails in the snow are linear, delicate, with a line down the middle created by their dragging tails. Deer mice build nests in our garage and woodshed as well as in our woods. Once, when walking on a snowy morning, I saw a deer mouse peeking at me from an old bird nest in a low shrub. It had added a roof of grass and twigs and taken up residence.

Sometimes I see the three-pronged tracks of a wild turkey, its feet so solidly planted that I can easily imagine its slow, proud strutting, its head nodding with each step. Sometimes the arcing, graceful trails of running white-tailed deer, their two-toed hoofs leaving crisp and distinctive tracks. Once I followed a cottontail rabbit track, the long back feet leaping in front of the short front feet. The trail disappeared abruptly in the middle of an open patch of woods. On either side of the rabbit's final footprints, gentle brushlike strokes looking like the marks of feathered wings graced the snow's surface. Walking farther, a line of blood droplets led into some shrubs, then bits of fur were dropped on the snow, then finally there were the remains of the rabbit's carcass. An owl had found its dinner.

FEBRUARY 11 ∿ This winter has been so much warmer than usual that people are starting to call it the winter that wasn't. We didn't have a hard frost until well into November of last year, a month after the norm. Then several days in December and January were as warm as springtime—60, 70 degrees. I heard that some farmers were out tilling their fields, even applying anhydrous ammonia fertilizer in preparation for getting their crops in as early as possible. Plowing in January? Temperatures as warm as springtime highs during short wintertime days? The two don't go together, at least not here in Iowa.

These incongruities provide the impetus for me to start digging seriously into my self-appointed task for the year—learning details about Earth's changing climate and how it may be reshaping our woodland and our world. I start reading about the root of the problem, human-induced increases in heat-trapping gases in the atmosphere (including carbon dioxide, methane, ozone, and nitrous oxide), focusing mostly on carbon dioxide because it's the primary greenhouse gas emitted through human activities. Thus carbon dioxide is the major climate-change culprit, a truth that can be hard to believe since it is invisible, odorless, tasteless, and a natural constituent of the atmosphere. It's also a minor atmospheric component, with concentrations measured in parts per million (ppm). But even today's minute increase of 100 carbon dioxide molecules for every million molecules of nitrogen and oxygen (the atmosphere's major components) is significantly altering the immense ocean of air that extends for miles above my head.

How can this be, I wonder? When I read that heat-trapping gases cause a greenhouse effect, the concept becomes clearer. I think of the large commercial greenhouse near my childhood home in Madison, Wisconsin, where I wandered from age six or seven well into my teens, smelling the musty earth and basking in the moist heat. Summer or winter, the sunshine warmed the stones on the greenhouse floor and the soil in the pots, then the heat re-radiated outward but was trapped by expanses of the greenhouse's glass panes. Sometimes the heat and the scents were so overpowering, they made me giddy.

Much like the glass roof of a greenhouse—although through a different process—carbon dioxide traps heat. Simply speaking, each morning, the rising sun brings light that warms whatever it strikes. I think of a summertime beach with sand too hot for bare feet. Beach sand, soils, asphalt roofs, and other objects then radiate the absorbed light energy back into the air, but as infrared (heat) radiation rather than visible light. That transformation makes all the difference: unlike visible sunlight, which can pass freely through the atmosphere, infrared radiation is absorbed by carbon dioxide. The carbon dioxide then re-radiates the absorbed heat, some of which returns to the earth to once again raise the temperature of sand, soils, asphalt roofs . . .

I'm surprised to read that this concept has been understood by scientists since the mid-1800s; indeed, climate science dates back nearly 200 years, when the greenhouse effect was first described, with major advances in precise atmospheric measurements and technology starting in the 1950s and significantly more accurate computer models having become available since the 1990s.

Greenhouse gases are crucial for life on earth. Without their heat-trapping proclivities, our planet's average temperature would be around freezing, rather than a pleasant 58 degrees. Everything on Earth—from sea ice, to plant productivity, to the strength of hurricanes, to life itself—depends on favorable temperatures, which in turn are maintained by a healthy balancing act between incoming sunlight and outgoing thermal energy.

Thus, it's not the presence of carbon dioxide that hurts, it's the steadily increasing quantity. The more carbon dioxide there is in the atmosphere, the more heat is absorbed and re-radiated, and the higher the temperature.

Carbon dioxide's long atmospheric life further compounds the problem. I'm chagrined to realize that almost half the carbon dioxide released from my car's tailpipe will go into the atmosphere and remain there for a hundred years or more, with some remaining for thousands of years. The other half will be pulled back to Earth, where it will either dissolve in ocean waters or be incorporated into growing plants. I think about my flights to visit granddaughter Ellie—and how the carbon dioxide released by the plane's jet engines will remain to reshape her grandchildren's lives and well beyond.

After a few hours of reading about distant invisible gases, I allow my mind to return to the here and now. Outside my window, today's temperature is closer to the seasonal norm, a cold 8 degrees. I've refilled the bird feeders. I have been enjoying the birds so much this winter. Of course, I say that every winter, but this year seems special because of the large flocks of goldfinches, two or three dozen at a time clinging to the feeder and flitting through nearby trees. And the mourning doves, often five or six hanging around, not constantly eating like the smaller birds, just pecking now and again and sitting there. The smaller woodpeckers, of course, downy and hairy, the red-heads and the larger red-bellied woodpeckers, and chickadees, nuthatches, titmice, many juncos, cardinals—all are staples of a winter Iowa woodland.

FEBRUARY 16 ❧ I just walked Sidney through the bright blue-skied early morning. A fresh brisk wind blew down from the north as if the air had been chilled by an iceberg. Flocks of sparrows and juncos flitted through the roadside shrubs. A red-tailed hawk rose straight up from a nearby pasture, then banked and soared fast over my head. A lovely morning, full of things on the move. I'll take this cool morning with gratitude—a day of energy and life, unlike the very warm days we've been having recently. "Temperatures will be 15 to 20 degrees above normal today." I'm getting tired of hearing that weather news.

While walking, I found a mole dead on the trail. Finding one above ground is unusual. Typically I see only the raised earthen burrows that moles create as they dig through the soils looking for earthworms to eat, using stubby front feet enlarged to the size of small shovels. Moles have no eyes to speak of and no visible ears, but they do possess large, well-developed noses. They live in a world of scent, perfectly adapted to the niche they fill in this world, as are the estimated 10 million or more other species that inhabit our planet. Humans are just one life-form among the masses.

The mole was stiff. Some creature had drilled a small hole in the back of its head to access and eat its brains—one example of the endless recycling of the nutrients and energy stored within each living cell. Without such recycling and decomposition, we'd quickly be buried in dead organisms and our own wastes. The hole in the mole's head? A shrew I suspect, a tiny carnivore with sharp teeth and a pointed muzzle. But the shrew would not have killed the mole, which was many times larger. The mole's death remains a mystery.

Despite the cooler temperatures, by the time we got home I had to wash Sidney's paws and tummy hair, both being splattered with mud. We used to have a few mud weeks every spring, when the frost was melting out of the soils from the top down, leaving slick mushy paths through the woods. Once the frost was gone, the soils would drain and the mud disappeared. But this winter the soil surface has frozen each night and melted the next day, and we've lived with mud for several months. For me, this is one of the many unacknowledged costs of the warming of our atmosphere and the disappearance of a real midwestern winter.

FEBRUARY 21 ◡ I can tell that spring is on its way. There's a certain slant to the sun's rays. And a softness in the air, the slightest bit of a beaconing warmth. Also the colors of new birth—deep peach, azure blue—are present in the sky, but only as the faintest tinges, scarcely perceptible. A promise rather than an announcement.

The woodland creatures, born with instincts incomprehensible to us, seem to know that spring is coming, even those that were hatched only last summer. The frogs and toads and turtles continue to sleep under sodden soils, but some birds are trying to attract mates, the chickadees by singing phee-bee, the cardinals with their descending whistles, the downy woodpeckers by drumming rapidly on dead trees, their hammering resounding through the woods. I hear the barred owls calling to each other in the dark. A month from now, they will be laying eggs in a secluded tree cavity in our woods, as they have done for many years. The first woodland wildflowers aren't due to appear for another six weeks, but mosses in sheltered valleys are producing new iridescent green growth. These are predictable patterns that have evolved over eons, fine-tuning each species to well-established ranges of temperature and sunshine and rainfall.

I know that once the wildflowers start to come, I'll be out wandering in the woods. I'll return home both delighted and confused. It happens every spring. During the fall and winter, I rake and burn, clip and cut, feel that I am creating order in our woods. But the thousands of plants that live here are only letting me play a game. The seeds, roots, rhizomes, tubers, bulbs, and corms are waiting in hiding. And once they start coming, I'll be awed by the profusion, overwhelmed to see such an abundance and diversity of plants exploding into life once again.

FEBRUARY 28 ◡ Another wet day—the temperatures are right around freezing so that water is falling in a slushy mixture of rain and wet snow. The roads will be icy. But I'm more concerned about the arthritis that has bothered me this winter. Sometimes it's in my toes as well as my fingers. I think it's the wet cold we've had all winter, the drizzly rain that seems to penetrate to the bone. Earlier this week we had a thin coating of snow, which came down in large drifting flakes. For a few days, the earth was coated with purity and the air held a dry bracing cold. I felt fine those days. But then the temperatures warmed a bit and the drizzle returned, along with my aching joints.

MARCH 7 ❧ I think of March as the month when the ice melts and Earth's waters flow. In a typical year, the blanket of snow first slumps, then dissolves into rivulets that trickle through the woods into creeks, the creeks into ponds, the ponds into rivers that lead to the sea, which eventually yields its moisture back to the atmosphere. On some blue-skied windy days the heaven's light, growing steadily more intense as the sun each day courses higher in the sky, seems to carry the snow directly back into the air. Once the insulating snow has melted, the frozen soils follow suit, dissolving from the top down. Then I take a trowel into the woods, dig a hole, and day by day follow the disappearance of white ice crystals as the soils reclaim their velvety black color.

In a normal year, as I trace the earth's release from frigidity, I feel something inside myself softening, becoming more open to the life around me, anticipating the green leaves and muted pink flowers that normally greet me in early April a few weeks hence. The growth of spring's plants requires time as well as warmth. Even more time is needed here in the woods because the soils, covered by a thick blanket of oak leaves, always melt days or weeks later than nearby croplands and pastures.

But this is not a normal year, and I'm missing this gradual release of earth and spirit. I'm not sure that the soils froze at all this last winter, and we barely had any snow. And now, the abnormally warm winter is suddenly reaching all-time high temperatures for so early in the year, today over 70 degrees. I took a long walk and wished I'd worn a T-shirt and shorts.

Radio announcers are gushing over how nice the weather is. Well, yes, I think. Considered in isolation, today is beautiful—warm with soft breezes and resident woodland songbirds singing their mating songs more every day. But I'm not used to Iowa being this warm so early in the spring. This month's departure from the seasonal norm has a foreboding quality. If it's in the 70s now, when it's normally in the 20s to 40s, how hot could it be in three or four months when the weather is normally in the 70s?

This question shifts me back to considering the increasing quantities of atmospheric carbon dioxide, the major greenhouse gas of concern. Today I want to learn about its sources and quantities. I open my books and start searching the web. I'm not surprised to learn that carbon dioxide naturally flows into and out of the atmosphere in a balanced manner. One example: tremendous quantities of carbon dioxide continually flow back and forth between plants and air, with plants taking up carbon dioxide through photosynthesis and releasing it when they die and decompose or when they respire. It's as if our atmosphere were a large bathtub, with water (think carbon dioxide) continually flowing in through the faucet and out through the drain. As long as the inflow and outflow remain balanced, there are no problems.

Now consider turning up the faucet's inflow, but not changing the drain's outflow. The system rapidly becomes unbalanced. Problems ensue. That's what's happened with modern human activities: they have created a larger one-way inflow of carbon dioxide into the atmosphere. Many activities have contributed, including the manufacture of cement, deforestation, agriculture, and livestock respiration. But the vast majority of excess carbon dioxide results from our burning of fossil fuels to produce electricity and heat, transport people and goods, and power industry. This fossil-fuel-produced carbon dioxide has overridden Earth's balanced atmospheric flows and created heat buildup problems.

The total global amount of excess carbon dioxide pumped into the atmosphere every single year is truly tremendous: it is measured in the tens of billions of metric tonnes. The increase has raised atmospheric concentrations of carbon dioxide from 280 ppm in 1750, at the beginning of the Industrial Revolution, to 394 ppm in 2012—a level unprecedented for 800,000 years or more. Put another way, one in four carbon dioxide molecules now in the atmosphere has been put there in the last few hundred years through human activities.

Fossil-fuel-related release of carbon dioxide varies greatly from country to country. Two nations generate far more than all others—the U.S. and China, which together in 2011 produced about 40 percent of the world's total global carbon dioxide emissions, the remaining 60 percent being emitted in far smaller percentages by the globe's 190 or so other countries. The U.S. topped the list of carbon dioxide producers until 2006, when it was surpassed by China—this shift a result of both the U.S.'s decline in fossil fuel use because of the recession, shifts to cleaner-burning natural gas, and societal changes such as more fuel-efficient cars, and China's rapid industrialization. By 2011, China was producing 26 percent of global carbon dioxide emissions, the U.S. 15 percent.

Our drop from first place unfortunately does not remove our culpability. In 2010, the U.S.'s per-person emissions remained about three times the size of China's. Also, the U.S. continues to be the leader in total historic greenhouse-gas production; we have created almost a third of the world's cumulative excess atmospheric greenhouse gases, a fact that in my mind assigns us the responsibility for leading the way in reducing these gases.

Return to the total global emissions. Despite moderate attempts at energy conservation and policy efforts to counteract climate change, every year more carbon dioxide is released into the atmosphere than the year before. Most years the global rate of carbon dioxide emissions rises by 1 or 2 percent.

If global emissions trends continue to increase at their current pace, atmospheric carbon dioxide levels are expected to approach 600 ppm by midcentury—twice the historic norm—and soar upward to over 800 ppm by the end of the century. I stop and consider what a mere 100 ppm boost of carbon dioxide is already doing to our climate. Then I try to imagine, by the year 2100, the results of adding yet another 400 ppm of carbon dioxide to the atmospheric blanket that's warming not just me but the entire planet.

MARCH 9 ∾ The singing of goldfinches, cardinals, chickadees, nuthatches, titmice, and the tat-tat-tatting of woodpeckers are engulfing the woods. Small flocks of robins have returned, as have red-winged blackbirds and scattered eastern bluebirds.

Most of these birds spend their lives on this continent but farther south, returning each spring when Iowa's weather starts to warm, migrating back and forth, north and south as weather dictates. They are harbingers of spring—short-distance migrants announcing that ducks, other water and shorebirds, and some songbirds will arrive within the next few weeks. Those birds in turn preview the explosion of hundreds of bird species in flamboyant breeding plumage, driven northward by their hormones, longer days, and warmer temperatures, anticipating abundant food and ample space for nesting and raising their young. Some of the migrants will stop and feed in our woodland, then continue north. The swarms of newly hatched bugs that smear my car windshield are, to many of them, protein packages that fuel their journey. But many birds will stay and nest here, forming streams of yellow, orange, red, blue, gray, and black feathers flitting through our woods.

The migration peaks in early May when waves of songbirds—warblers and vireos, flycatchers and thrushes and orioles and many more—arrive from southern states but also from Central and South America, sometimes flying thousands of miles to their breeding grounds, charting their course by the sun and stars, by Earth's magnetic field and topography and smell.

I am concerned about these long-distance travelers, the neotropical migrants that depend on day length for initiating migration. If the warming climate continues to advance local flower and insect production, but neotropical migrants arrive on the same schedule as in past centuries, might these birds reach the U.S. too late to sate themselves on spring's flush of hatching insects? They need abundant insect protein for their own strength as well as for raising their chicks. Could repeated mismatches between birds and insects stress and eventually shrink populations of these long-distance migrants?

MARCH 11 ∾ The warm temperatures continue. We're in the 60s today, with predictions of warming into the mid-70s in three days and for the remaining week. These are June temperatures, although we're barely into March. Some nights the temperatures still drop below freezing; other nights they don't. Last night I opened the window next to my bed and a cool delicious breeze flowed over my face. In normal years, we could be skiing across the fields through a snowstorm in March. But this year, the rule is warm, dry, and windy. I'm becoming so oblivious to this atypical weather that I don't even notice the regular announcements of "more record-breaking temperatures across the state today." The unusual is becoming commonplace. But the consequences are not. Yesterday a statewide warning was issued against burning because fires become more intense and spread faster in hot weather. This warning unfortunately was after the smoke from a burning field had clouded a nearby highway and caused a twenty-car pileup.

MARCH 19 ∾ For the last three days, the air has been hot and humid, not light, capricious, and refreshing as we expect it to be. I've been wearing short-sleeved shirts and light slacks and am still sweating. Day after day the temperatures are 30 degrees above normal. Day after day we are setting new temperature records. We're in the mid-70s this week; next week, at the official beginning of spring, we'll be into the mid-80s with no break in site. I'm having a hard time sleeping because nights are not cooling down as they should, and the air feels heavy and oppressive. Temperatures are soaring from the Rockies eastward to the Atlantic coast, although they are especially high in the Midwest and northern plains. In Chicago and New England, people are sporting shorts and swimsuits and frolicking on beaches, even though it's still officially winter.

Meanwhile the natural world has been setting records of its own as it races to return to life after a winter's sleep. Here in our neighborhood, the spring peepers and chorus frogs have been singing for a week. Insects also are responding to the heat, with honeybees and certain butterflies already emerging. And the woodland floor is rapidly changing color, with sedges and grasses greening up and wildflowers appearing literally overnight. Two weeks ago, white snow. Last week, the browns and grays of last fall's dried leaves. This week, tiny green plants that seem to grow larger in an instant, their stems and leaves inflating like balloons.

This morning the leaves of wild ginger were an inch tall, and by noon deep crimson flowers were opening at the base of the stems. The soft white blossoms of snow trillium and bloodroot, along with lavender hepatica, some of our earliest spring wildflowers, were in full bloom. Surprisingly there are also wildflowers that normally don't appear in our woods until the first weeks of April: rue anemone, spring beauty, and Dutchman's breeches, their delicate blossoms white and shades of pink. All of these are short plants that capture the springtime's sunlight, blossoming and producing seeds before they are overshadowed by the leaves of taller wildflowers, shrubs, and trees. They usually appear in close sequence, one right after the other, but this year they are blooming in clusters together, a compressed rather than sequential blooming season.

So much life appearing so fast—can it be a reflection of our changing climate? The spring's anomalies continue to fuel my curiosity about climate change, and I return to the books, today prying into the effects of rising levels of carbon dioxide. Soon my head starts buzzing with data, predictions, numbers and more numbers, the lot of them creating an image of the earth losing its ability to properly tend the intricate web of life covering its surface. The increase in carbon dioxide has already introduced enough heat energy into our atmosphere to produce diverse and profound consequences that are expected to intensify as temperatures rise further. Few of these consequences are undeniably good, and many pose serious risks. The most obvious and far-reaching effect is a rise in Earth's average surface temperature by 1.4 degrees over the last century.

A 1.4-degree temperature rise. Infinitesimal I think, until I remember that it represents a long-term global average that includes temperatures collected throughout the year, from the poles to the equator, over ocean and land, by sophisticated satellites and thousands of weather stations. Earlier this year when temperatures in the continental U.S. were unusually warm, temperatures across Eastern Europe and much of Asia were frigid and conditions were very snowy, with hundreds of people dying from the cold. Both extreme weather swings feed into the global average temperature. A 1.4-degree average global rise, which far exceeds natural variation, thus signifies that our planet's overall temperature over the past century has gone in one direction: up.

This global rise is disquieting. I realize that Earth's climate is no longer stable, nor is it fluctuating in a predictable pattern. In addition, the heating of the planet is intensifying. Most of the last century's temperature rise has occurred since 1980, and each decade since 1980 has been warmer than its predecessor, with extreme heat events becoming more and more prevalent.

What's more, today's global average rise would be far higher than 1.4 degrees if the oceans had not helped us out by absorbing atmospheric heat and buffering temperature rises. Oceans have, in fact, absorbed more than 90 percent of the extra heat energy that has been added to our atmosphere from 1971 to 2010.

If greenhouse-gas emissions continue their current upward trend, the global average temperature by midcentury is likely to rise another 4 to 6 degrees, and by the end of the century the planet could warm an average of 6 to 10 degrees or more—perhaps taking it back to temperatures last felt some 56 million years ago. A 10-degree average temperature rise, which dwarfs the current 1.4-degree rise, is indeed capable of producing profound changes: it approximates the *drop* in average temperature that initiated the last Ice Age approximately 100,000 years ago.

These numbers take on more meaning when compared to the global average rise widely considered to be the highest safe level for life on Earth: 3.6 degrees, commonly referred to as "2°C" in the media. A rise above this level, state most climate scientists, would probably constitute dangerous human interference with the climate system, interference that could lead to tipping points, for example massive ice-sheet melts. Yet with current trends of greenhouse-gas emissions, we may exceed the 3.6 degrees by 2050, forcing our planet's occupants to attempt to adjust rapidly and profoundly to new living circumstances.

Planetary adjustments. I readjust my corner of the planet by refilling the bird feeders, scooping in the black-oil sunflower seeds that these woodland birds seem to love. They flock to the feeders in droves, each bird trying to grab a seed and carry it off to a nearby tree, where it pecks off the hull and swallows the kernel inside.

MARCH 21 ꙮ The air remains hot and heavy. Temperatures in the 70s and 80s by day. Ridiculous for March. Down into the 60s at night, but not lower. I feel cheated, wanting seasons to be clearly defined. This year, however, the summer has been dumped on our doorstep like an unwelcome guest. It's as if temperatures leaped from January right into June, and the natural world is racing to catch up. Iowa's native wildflowers are well adapted to respond rapidly to spring's arrival. Most are perennials that survive winter underneath the ground. Springtime's warming air and soils, combined with gentle rains, call these dormant structures to grow once again and, using nutrition stored during the previous growing season, they send up shoots and flower buds within days. I recall our woods greening up and bursting into flower rapidly before, but never this completely or this early—a full month ahead of normal.

I'm embarrassed to admit that I am turning on the air conditioner in March. I feel guilty doing so, knowing that the climate is changing in part because of our energy-demanding luxuries. But the cool air is irresistible, and it's so easy to push the button and feel the comfort.

I know we'll be trying to escape many more heat waves in coming years. Prolonged stretches of very high temperatures are becoming more common and severe in the northern hemisphere: they are one of the most obvious expressions of our warming planet. In addition, each year we're experiencing highly unusual heat extremes relative to 1951–1980 temperatures, heat waves that are breaking previous records by increasingly large deviations from the norm. Heat waves are becoming more intense, more frequent, lasting longer, covering larger areas, and affecting a greater portion of the earth's surface. As with other manifestations of global warming, these changes are occurring rapidly, defying both humans' and nature's ability to adapt.

Some are unprecedented mega-heat waves of jaw-dropping magnitude. For example in mid-July to early August, 2010, a heat wave in Russia and Eastern Europe broke multiple regional records. Covering an area larger than Alaska, temperatures in the upper 90s to above 100 (nearly 20 degrees above Moscow's seasonal norm) dominated for weeks without a break. Smoke from hundreds of heat-driven wildfires joined smog and high temperatures to cause respiratory illness and heat stress that led to over 50,000 excess human deaths, deaths that otherwise would not have been expected at that point. Wheat crops failed, sending global grain prices soaring.

In addition to increasing health threats, death rates, crop failure, and wildfire, extreme high temperatures degrade air quality and threaten infrastructure, for example, by buckling roads and railroad tracks. Concern over the size of recent heat waves is multiplied by their rapid emergence. Extreme heat waves had been predicted for later in the twenty-first century, when greenhouse-gas levels had increased further. If greenhouse-gas emissions continue at present rates, today's high temperatures (or higher) could be the norm by the middle to end of this century, defining the permanent emergence of extreme heat, creating summers too hot to work or play outside.

The thought makes me mildly nauseous. I direct my focus to more immediate weather concerns, such as today's radio report on Iowa's apple orchards. They will be in bloom within a week if these warm temperatures continue. Apple growers are praying that there will be no frost in the next six weeks because frost would kill the year's apple crop. The radio announcer is pert in her explanation.

"If the weather turns cold, we'll be able to get out our warm clothes again. But fruit trees and other plants have no such mechanism to protect their tender buds from cold temperatures. Once they start to grow, they are vulnerable." Ironically, along with high temperatures, the news is full of concerns about rising gasoline prices.

MARCH 26 ∽ Finally, the intense heat wave of the last three weeks has broken. This morning a cold wind forced me into the basement to retrieve a warm sweater I had prematurely put away for the summer. The temperature is back in the 40s. The weather forecast predicts temperatures in the 50s today but back into the 80s tomorrow, then way back down and up again before the end of the week. "Weather whiplash," as some radio announcers say.

Although the air has cooled, it's still heavy with moisture. The humidity is over 80 percent. This morning, a thick fog surrounded my house. Taking a walk, I saw dozens of iridescent spider webs dripping with moisture, shining in the penetrating rays of the rising sun.

The very moist air, which is correlated with the atmosphere's rising temperatures, explains why my house smells musty, as if about to sport an outburst of mold. Atmospheric moisture is now increasing in many regions. Here in Iowa, it has increased 13 percent since the mid-1970s. As the atmospheric heat and moisture increase, so do mildew and mold. I'm mortified to admit that this symptom of a warming climate is now a problem here in my house. Mildew on the back sides of my dressers, on leather shoes stuffed into my closet, on old boxes in the basement—it's not something I'm proud of. I've spent an inordinate amount of time combatting these outbreaks with bleach and Lysol, but I can never completely get rid of a speckling of mildew here and there, in part because much of our furniture is family antiques without modern protective finishes. I've come to hate the mold season that now seems to extend from early spring into late fall, when warmth from the furnace again dries out the house.

The rising moisture also generates a far larger challenge: a feedback loop that magnifies the process of climate change. Warming air heats the water in lakes and oceans, which makes the water more likely to evaporate. Warmer air also can hold more moisture than cooler air. Both factors notch up atmospheric water vapor, which then traps still more atmospheric heat and further warms the air. The warmer air further warms water bodies and increases evaporation, which again raises the atmospheric water vapor and . . . around and around the cycle goes. This feedback loop is but one of many that are enhancing climate change and complicating precise predictions of climatic trends.

This spring's extreme warmth and abundant moisture are stimulating proliferation of more than mildew. Consider pollen-producing plants. I've read that allergy and asthma clinics in Atlanta, Georgia, are overrun with patients feeling miserable because pollen counts are over three times their normal limit.

I've also read that ants, bees, and mosquitoes are out in force in the Midwest because they survived the warm winter with ease and that a tick explosion is expected. Pest control companies say these insects are six weeks early and that they are also seeing other insects they haven't seen in years. In southern states, soybean farmers are concerned about the warm weather promoting the spread of the bean plataspid, an invasive insect from Asia that can devastate their crops. In Colorado, pine beetles will likely have time to mate twice this year, rather than once as is normal, which means that more trees will be killed by the beetles. This in turn can fuel the western wildfires that are becoming abundant in the Rockies; wildland fires are already eating away at Denver's suburbs, fueled by the year's very dry conditions.

Here in Iowa, some of our woodland record-breakers are more pleasant: four migrating warblers—birds normally not seen in the state until May—appeared earlier than has ever been documented before. The pine warbler, northern parula, yellow-throated warbler, and Louisiana waterthrush all have been recorded in southeastern Iowa in the last several days.

I spend time wandering in the woods whenever possible. I love doing this, especially in spring when life is returning but understory plants remain short enough for me to pass through them with ease. I use the pretext of work—monitoring invasive plants, cutting back the raspberries so they don't take over, clipping and stump-spraying the few multiflora roses that creep from the roadside in each year. But mostly I watch and listen and marvel at my discoveries. Yesterday it was a half-buried clot of sunflower seeds that a chipmunk had stolen from the bird feeder. The seeds are now sprouting. Together, they look like a yellowish green flower protruding from the chipmunk's hole.

Today I watched a pair of wood ducks circling the treetops for an hour searching for a suitable nesting cavity and listened to sporadic calls of the barred owls, who were hooting to each other even in broad daylight. Always something new, signs of the different lives supported by these woods.

MARCH 28 ❧ Now that the worst of the March heat wave has passed, I'm starting to read discussions about what happened and why. This year claimed the hottest March on record in the contiguous U.S., with average temperatures being an astounding 8.6 degrees above the twentieth-century March average, far exceeding any previous variations. The warm air helped spawn 220 reported tornadoes (a typical March averages 80), including the first billion-dollar natural disaster of the year, a tornado outbreak in the Ohio Valley and southeastern U.S. The first quarter of the year, January through March, was also the hottest in the nation's record.

In addition to setting the national record, this was the hottest March ever recorded for half of the nation's states. Here in Iowa, average temperatures were a tremendous 15.2 degrees above the March average.

The March heat that shattered high-temperature records across the U.S. peaked between March 12 and 23. Perhaps most astounding were the size and number of March warm temperature records broken at individual locations—over 15,000. The majority were daily maximum readings, afternoon highs, although nights also were extremely warm; nearly half of the records were warm minima, occurring at night. These temperatures were noteworthy for their sheer magnitude: some warm minimum temperatures were large enough to exceed previous daily highs. And a good number of temperatures broke the records not by a degree or two, but by a full 20 to 40 degrees above average values for this time of year, demonstrating the unparalleled difference between this extreme event and all temperatures in the past. Meteorologists exclaimed that they had never seen departures from the average that were this large, with some proclaiming that March was the most extreme climate event in U.S. history. "Its phenomenal character was masked by the season," remarked one meteorologist, stating that had temperatures of 20 to 40 degrees above normal been experienced in July, the nation would have burned under 110- to 120-degree heat for days on end.

Although temperatures remain above normal, last night was cool enough to open the windows, so I awoke to the sound of birds pecking at the feeders and wild turkeys gobbling: the gift of birdsong, so evident in spring when the birds are calling mates.

And so—summertime in March? How can we explain this amazing weather? Was it normal weather variation or a sign of a major climatic shift?

Today, although nearly all climate scientists accept the proven reality of human-induced climate change, they are well aware of the complexity of our climate system, and so they remain careful to differentiate between climate's long-term trends and averages over a large area and weather's local day-to-day events.

However, climate scientists are becoming increasingly concerned about the Arctic's rapid warming—currently twice as fast as the global average—and its reshaping of climate-control systems and weather far beyond the polar region.

Much of the northern hemisphere's weather is shaped by the polar jet stream, a high-altitude river of fast-moving air that circles the globe, separating cold Arctic air masses from warm subtropical air masses to the south. This jet stream is energized both by the temperature differential between the Arctic and the U.S.'s temperate zones and by the spinning of Earth.

But this temperature differential is shrinking due to Arctic warming and the rapid melting of the Arctic ice cap, which in turn is weakening the jet stream's flow. Normally the eastward-spinning polar jet stream moves weather fronts from west to east across North America at a good clip. Research is starting to show that as the Arctic warms, the jet stream is slowing and changing course, becoming lazy and wavier. The result is large U-shaped troughs and waves in the jet stream that pull unseasonably warm air north or push unseasonably cold air south, creating uncommon but persistent weather patterns: cold or heat, floods or drought, rain or snowstorms.

These troughs and waves may stall long enough to block the usual movement of weather systems across the continent. Such blocking patterns have been tied to other prolonged, stagnant, extreme-weather events such as the 2010 deadly Russian heat wave and the massive Pakistani flooding that same summer that comprised the country's worst natural disaster ever.

This March, the jet stream formed a gigantic northward-pointing loop over the central U.S., which was occupied by warm Gulf air and held in place by an upper-level circulation pattern. Was this pattern related to climate change? More research is needed, but a number of climate scientists are concluding that these types of extreme-weather events are consistent with global warming trends and that such events are likely to increase in coming years.

THREE

Memoir
Awakening, 1947–1965

SUMMERTIME IN MADISON, WISCONSIN, DURING THE 1950S.
I am a young child lying on the sofa, listening to the cicadas dron-
ing incessantly, their buzzes throbbing through the treetops and
through the open window, its curtains lifting slightly in the breeze.
The days are hot, but it's a pleasant enveloping heat, like the comforting wrap of a soft blanket. Looking out the window I see mon-
archs flitting about, seeking milkweeds for laying their eggs. Above
them hundred-foot-tall elms vault skyward, providing a canopy
over the road and adjacent houses. The trees' branches form a leafy
sanctuary, a living cathedral that day after day welcomes me back
home to my mother's arms. Those branches are so large, so solid,
their light gray trunks so broad, I am sure they will be there forever.

Fast forward to the late summer of 1965. Our country is con-
vulsing, but I am immune to everything outside the hospital room
where I, a teenager, stand holding my mother's hand, waiting for
her to open her eyes, something she does less frequently and for
shorter periods each day. With every passing day her flesh shrinks
and her body turns more skeletal; her color fades, her hair thins and
becomes duller (those rich chestnut curls that I twirled through my
fingers as a youngster—where did they go?). Her raspy breathing
grows less regular.

Looking back now, I remember how those August hospital afternoons seemed to stretch on forever, the hands of the wall clock
barely turning. The sun poured in through the west-facing window,
creating a heat-laden August whiteness devoid of motion or color. I
had plenty of time to consider events of the past year. Mom's cancer

had been diagnosed only four months before, in springtime, but now I realize that she'd had symptoms since the past fall—complaints of fatigue and not feeling good, declining weight and appetite. She brushed them aside and we did too, my dad and sister and I. We believed that Mom, like the earth itself, would be here forever. She was always robust, the healthy one in the family, the resilient one who never caught our colds or flus. Meanwhile the functions of her body were silently shifting. Deep within her, the cells that comprised her body were going wild, dividing way too rapidly and claiming control, seeding tumors in her liver, lungs, stomach, bones, eventually in her brain, cutting off her body's ability to operate as intended. Continuing without notice until her doctor felt her enlarged liver during a routine checkup. By then, she had passed the tipping point. There was nothing more anyone could do. Despite medical treatments, she declined rapidly.

If only we had been attentive to her early symptoms, I would think; if only we had read and believed the warning signs. Could things have been different if we had found and treated her cancer earlier? Would she still be working in the garden and designing her stitcheries? Would our home still be a safe refuge?

The doctors acted as if she would be leaving the hospital soon. They never mentioned the word "death." But I knew that this was the last of her several hospital stays. She would not be returning to the warm, embracing home she had spent her life making, the house where our family had lived for the past twenty-three years. She was on her way to another world.

Two years after Mom died, the sheltering elms that had formed my leafy sanctuary dropped their leaves and perished, victims of the Dutch elm disease caused by an invasive fungus. The fungal cells multiplied rapidly, silently, and without control, then spread throughout the trees, killing them by plugging their vascular tissues. Buzzing chainsaws excised our once-leafy canopy, exposing houses and yards to the scorching heat of the sun. The city replaced the dead giants with trees the size of broomsticks.

Perhaps it didn't matter. I was away at college by then. I didn't live in Madison anymore. My permanent home was gone. But when I came back to visit friends during college breaks, I often walked in the cemetery where Mom was buried and put flowers on her grave. Then I wandered the few blocks back to my old neighborhood, now alien ground, wondering how everything I had counted upon had vanished.

Rewind to 1951. I am four, a member of the post–World War II baby boom. I wake to the sun's low rays slanting through my bedroom window and my parents' quiet talk in the kitchen. I throw on shorts and a T-shirt and race downstairs in time to hug my dad goodbye before he leaves for his research laboratory on the university campus.

Soon after he goes, my friend Davey Myer sings a two-tone chant through the mail chute: "Connie, Connie." I tug open the heavy oak door. Davey, his knees already smeared with mud, clutches a paper bag of Cheerios—his breakfast. He follows me to the kitchen, where he perches on the edge of a chair and stuffs Cheerios into his mouth with his fingers. I pour my Cheerios from a box into a bowl, flood them with milk, and consume them with a spoon. Before we've finished eating, we hear the bell of the milk truck as it crawls down the street. We race outside and jump onto its running board, riding around the block and pretending we're helping the milkman, a congenial fellow, with his deliveries.

In the heat of the day, Davey and I come inside for some lunch and a game of Chutes and Ladders. Mom feeds us grilled cheese sandwiches. Then back outside for the day's final hours, roaming the vacant lot next door, searching for caterpillars or maybe the stiff brown cocoon of a cecropia moth, which we want to place in a canning jar with holes in the top, hoping to see it hatch. We soak in the summer sounds of cicadas and crickets, the summer smells of moist earth and heat, the summer sights of laundry drying on the neighbors' clotheslines and tomatoes ripening on the vine. Finally, Davey goes home, I go inside for supper and a quick bath, and then I pop into bed where Dad reads my sister and me stories while Mom plays the piano in the living room, usually Bach, sometimes hymns. Comforting music, orderly predictable patterns that lull us to sleep and paint dreams of permanence and peace in our deepening subconscious.

I was given all this at birth, this and a secure home without fear of shortages. No lack of love, of food, of birdsong or fields to roam or walks to take. No shortage of dreams and plenty of space to follow my own inclinations, which inevitably led outside to the trails I wandered and to observations of plants that magically appeared and increased with exuberance. I was a privileged child. From my birth, I was fed a knowledge of the heart's magnitude and nature's abundance.

Although I didn't realize it at the time, my parents' simple living patterns were establishing ground rules for my life. Our family functioned well in part because we knew what we could count on and what to expect. I knew my boundaries and assumed that my needs would be met: play hard, don't cross the road, then come home to a warm meal and a soft bed. Assume stability and security. Expect it to continue.

My early life was also educating me in nature's patterns, teaching me that our planet moves and operates in circles and cycles. Everything I watched, everything I did taught me that events repeat themselves, the days yielding to darkness and darkness to light, creating an orderly repetition that was bigger than my own life. The new day's sunlight streaming through windows on one side of our house and then, as the sun set, streaming through windows on the other side. The cold of winter giving way to spring's seducing warmth, pulling me outside to race through streets and fields. The seasons singing in orderly rhythm, with plants and animals following suit. Springtime's fat buds on the salmon-blossomed flowering quince opening first, before trees grew leaves that shaded our home in summer. Trees in autumn dropping leaves that would be raked into piles for jumping into and throwing up in the air, leaves for burning in smoky gutters, emitting the odor of fall. The geese in large vees migrating south. Predictable cycles and patterns that never failed my expectations.

I was a child. Without imagining any alternative, I trusted the planet's stability and permanence. I assumed that regardless of what we did, human life and my family would go on forever; it could not in its most fundamental manner ever change. I also believed that my life-sustaining mother was solid and good and would always be there to welcome me home at the end of the day—or at least as long as I needed her.

It's 1955 and I am eight. The house is quiet when I wake. Dad must be at work. My sister, who is four years older than me, is still sleeping. But where is Mom? Probably in the garden. I pull on shorts and a T-shirt, clump down the stairs, and walk onto the screen porch. Sure enough, Mom is in the backyard pulling weeds from her patches of cat's whiskers and dahlias. I know them and many other plants in our yard: barberries with their oblong red-orange berries, hosta buds that pop when I squeeze them, blue spruce with needles stiff enough to be used as a comb for my doll's hair. I think I was born with a love of plants.

I also love the feel and smell of the garden's soft soils filtering through my fingers. I already have my own vegetable garden that I tend faithfully, a small plot dedicated to carrots and beans and tomatoes, plants that are easy to grow, plants that feed me but also nourish my rabbits who occupy a cage on the garden's edge. But I have learned to tend other kinds of plants as well. I know that raspberry canes need to be pruned back after they bear fruit and that strawberry beds need thinning, but the ferns alongside the entrance drive need encouragement to grow more. I talk to plants, make up names for them, study their shapes and smells. I know that each plant in our small yard has its own place, its own way of behaving and functioning.

Mom looks up and smiles at me but keeps pulling. She is an earthy woman, simple in desires and rooted in traditions and nature. I enter the garden and snuggle with her for a few minutes, then notice a cecropia moth cocoon on the overhanging branch of a small maple. I consider putting it into a canning jar but decide against it, knowing that the moth's large brown-and-orange wings would be injured when it emerged.

Soon Mom quits her morning gardening and goes inside to fix breakfast, signaling me to follow along. We sit together at the kitchen table, talking about the day's activities. Mom asks, should we go to a nearby U-Pick strawberry patch and bring home enough for both shortcake and jam-making? I smile a yes, hoping my sister will come along.

The jam-making was nothing unusual. Our home was a toolbox for living. My mother used the kitchen to cook and can our food, the sewing machine to make our dresses, and her knitting needles to spin out multicolored sweaters and hats. She braided and hooked rugs, filled pottery jars with oatmeal cookies, baked bread, covered worn furniture with slipcovers, and embroidered wall hangings to add color to our rooms, stitching pictures of flying birds and falling leaves, snow caught in midair, water flowing over seashells. She also made our house—which was minuscule compared to those of today—into a home. Although it was small, it held all that was necessary: a fireplace where Mom popped popcorn on winter nights, wing-back chairs for curling up with a book, angular dormered bedrooms that invited active imaginations and good dreams.

Dad's creativity spilled from his basement woodworking shop, where he turned out simple furniture and fixed a constant flow of broken objects. When I needed a new cage for my rabbits, Dad whipped one together. His creations sometimes met unusual ends. I remember my parents laughing about a small but very nice mouse cage he'd once made for me. When my pet mouse grew old and died, Dad put the cage out on the curb, where it was promptly picked up and used by another child. A few years later, Dad and Mom saw a neighbor walking down the street using the very same mouse cage, repainted and with a handle added, as a lunchbox.

I was now old enough to wander through the neighborhood freely. I investigated clumps of shrubs behind garages, woody islands of small trees that separated one house from another, the bark of elms that arched over our quiet street. As I did so, moving from yard to yard, waving to neighbors out working in their gardens, I was easily immersing myself in the community—our compact neighborhood with its postage-stamp-sized yards. We knew when our neighbors were yelling at their kids or walking around the block. We smelled what they were cooking for dinner and giggled at underwear hanging on their clotheslines. We naturally became a part of each other's life. One of my first jobs, assumed as a preschooler, was to carry warm food three houses downhill to an elderly couple who found cooking difficult.

Life was so much simpler then, or so it seemed. Considering our consumption patterns, that surely was true. There wasn't much to consume in the small shops that we frequented, and anyway our houses didn't have room for much. As for locally grown food, almost everyone in the neighborhood had a vegetable garden—that was the norm. A local farmer delivered eggs and freshly plucked chickens to the door each Friday afternoon. There was little need to search for organic food: the massive application of agricultural chemicals was in its infancy.

Now, looking back, I can also see distinct environmental advantages of living at a time when houses were small, neighborhoods were compact, and much food was locally grown: not only was there a distinct and close community, we also required fewer resources and emitted less problematic carbon dioxide into the atmosphere. My father walked a mile to work, my mother walked to the corner grocery, and my sister and I took the public bus to school. Yes, we had a car, but our single vehicle seldom left the driveway. Also, in my family, the time and creativity that my parents invested in making many household objects gave them a worth that can't be claimed by a factory product. That meant that we repaired things and made them last. Disposal was the end of a very long chain of use, not a routine assumption.

It's 1959 and I am twelve. I've given up cowboy boots for saddle shoes, but I still spend as much time outside as I can. At night, when the weather is favorable, I drag an old bed pad and sleeping bag onto the upstairs airing porch, willing the large silver maple in the neighbor's yard to put me to sleep as it waves overhead in the breeze. On Saturday mornings, I explore the wooded city park half a mile from home, with its abandoned quarry and shrub-covered rocky outcrops.

Throughout my youth, the natural world never failed to entertain me, and my experiences outside flowed easily into studying the natural world. Sometimes I penetrated the nearby hilly cemetery, peering into a newly dug casket-sized hole and noting the different-colored layers of soils. I knew how to read the coming weather by watching the skies. Dad taught me to identify trees by their shape and bark. I pictured myself as a keen observer of the natural world. Without realizing it, I was absorbing details about how nature, like an all-providing mother, supplied the needs of its creatures.

Usually during my sojourns, I took notes on a pad that I kept in my pocket. But sometimes I wandered without thought, letting the natural world carry me away, the brightly colored swards of autumn leaves transforming sidewalks into rainbows. Springtime's gray days and steady rains called me outside for slow, solitary saunters as I listened to the raindrops playing music on newly opened tree leaves. On those days, my struggle to stay warm and dry was eased by the expectation that Mom would offer me soup or hot cocoa when I returned home. My home and parents still held me safe and secure within their embrace.

Although I didn't yet understand details, I was starting to form a sense of nature's larger miracles—for example, the fact that nutrients circle around the globe as well as within my body. That the silent magical decomposition executed by trillions of bacteria and fungi allows life to prevail. That somehow all life depends on energy pouring down from the sun. That rain falling on my face ends up in the oceans, from there rising again to the skies. That all this complexity is both gift and responsibility.

Am I idealizing the environmental virtues of my earliest years? Perhaps. I was largely unaware of incipient problems that were multiplying along the sidelines. Before World War II, industrial development had been too limited to noticeably affect global climate.

And when I was born in 1947, our planet held only about a third of the 7 billion people living on Earth in 2012. But following the war, U.S. industry started growing exponentially, and the postwar baby boom made large American families the norm. Consumption also was ramping up. It sat in our driveway in the form of a metallic-gold Pontiac that swayed down the road, a gas-guzzling tub that my dad called Goldie. Use of pesticides and other synthetic chemicals with unknown side effects was increasing. Problems with air and water pollution were growing. They didn't prevent us from biking to Lake Mendota for a swim, although rising nutrient runoff would soon lead to toxic algal blooms. Suburbs were coming into being, setting the stage for unsustainable land use and dependence on automobiles. Habitat for native species was declining.

Although these problems were rising, they were largely overlooked. Dirty skies were the sight and smell of progress and of plentiful jobs; environmental degradation was seen as an inevitable byproduct of a healthy economy. Rachel Carson was writing her book *Silent Spring*, which, in 1962, jumpstarted public awareness of the multiple dangers of pesticides. But on the whole, at least in my limited world, environmental problems were uncommon, and those that were starting to manifest elsewhere were easily ignored. I remember an idyllic world, one in which I was embraced by a family and neighborhood that cherished, nurtured, and encouraged me. I assumed that life was an open field full of secrets to be uncovered, wisdom to be discovered. I believed that all problems could be solved. Details of my life might change, but on the whole the earth would survive and continue to function in a manner that I understood. I believed nature's eternal promises. Beyond that, I knew that the door to my childhood home would always remain open, providing me a refuge where my mind could explore and my body could rest.

Return to the early summer of 1965, when I was eighteen. I had graduated from high school a month earlier with the usual good-student honors and accolades, but somehow my successes do not seem important. Mom is home recovering from surgery, an unsuccessful attempt to excise her malignant liver tumor. My sister is married and awaiting the birth of her first child in Texas. For the past several months, my dad has been commuting to a new U.S. Forest Service job in Washington, D.C. He is frequently on the road. And so I become my mother's caretaker. I shop and do laundry and clean. I search for mild foods that Mom can tolerate. Simple egg dishes. Custards. Milk shakes. I greet visitors, talking to them myself when she is too weak to leave her bedroom. After the visits, I summarize the details for her. "Marian said she was praying for you. Joan brought you flowers. Dora, a few strawberries from her garden, she wishes they were bearing better, she wanted to bring more." Mom listens with her eyes closed. I never know if she hears me.

My parents still seem to think of this cancer as a problem that can be reversed. The doctors talk optimistically of cures from a new technology, a chemotherapy drug in the development phase. And so every day this week I take Mom to the hospital, where we sit in the cancer ward: a row of heavy wooden chairs lining either side of a long hallway, each seat occupied by a patient or the patient's caretaker. Those sitting on one side of the hallway stare at the misery of those on the other: the sallow bodies, shrinking limbs, deformed faces lacking jaws or throats pierced with holes, heads bandaged, arms trailing IVs, bodies sprouting plastic tubes. No one smiles. Doors open, names are called, patients disappear into white cubicles with cots where injections are given. Sometimes I hear crying, sometimes whimpers.

Finally Mom's name is called. The veins in her hands and arms have collapsed, and so today the doctors pry her feet, searching for a point of entry. I hold her hand as she winces and tears roll down her face. When the injection is done, I help her into a wheelchair and bring her home, where she collapses into bed, exhausted from the medication and effort. She gets up only to vomit. I clean up after her and tuck her back into bed. When I'm back in the kitchen, I hear her crying in pain.

It takes Mom a long time to fall asleep tonight. The pain is getting worse, but there is little talk about painkillers—or about what's killing my mother. Now, finally, she is resting calmly. I tiptoe around the kitchen washing the few dishes and gulping down some leftovers—my dinner—then slip out the door and wander around our block. Again, and again, and again, stopping at our house whenever I pass by: Does she still slumber? OK, walk around the block again. During those circles, I gaze into the lighted living rooms of first one home, then the next. Here a family is watching TV. In the next house, the father reads the paper and the mom sits at the table with her children. Checking homework, I surmise. In the next, I think the kids are doing a jigsaw puzzle, but I can't be sure. We used to do jigsaw puzzles. We used to sit and talk around the table. Where did those times go? That family? Where am I now? Who am I?

The summer months pass. Mom's strength declines. Her breathing slows, her body shrivels even more, her limbs become more skeletal. Malignant cells continue to spread, stealing any semblance of normalcy, conquering the farthest reaches of her body. I sit in her bedroom and hold her still hands, whispering my love to a body incapable of responding. There is no turning back now. In a few weeks, she will enter the hospital for the last time, and there she will quietly slip into a coma. I will sit with her through the long, hot, white August afternoons.

We all assume that I will leave for college that fall, just as if I were a normal eighteen-year-old heading out for a new life. So a few days before classes start we load my trunk of clothes and boxes of books into the car and Dad drives me away, passing the hospital on the way out of town. "Would you like to stop and say goodbye?" he asks softly, not looking at me.

I had learned to bite my cheeks and stopper my tears, but that day, glancing at the white cement building where she lies, picking out the exact window she would be looking through if her eyes could see, unable to reply to my father, I weep. The tears flow down my face for the next hour as we speed through town and beyond into the countryside with its fields of grazing milk cows and rolling pastures spotted with silos. We race toward an ivy-covered college campus hundreds of miles to the east but far away from the dwelling place of my heart, the home I had assumed would last forever. Mom stops breathing three days later. I fly home to her funeral, then two short days later return to my college classes. My dad quickly sells our Madison house and moves to a high-rise apartment in Washington, D.C.

Only then did I realize how life-sustaining my home had been—how everything I had needed had suffused that small structure. Losing my mother, my home, the entire landscape that defined my childhood, everything I held dear, was a harsh way to learn a fundamental truth: the basic elements of one's life can change in an instant. The unthinkable—the unimaginable—is indeed possible. Once you pass the tipping point, you can never go back again. Then the best you can hope for is survival and memories. It has happened to me once. Could it happen again?

PART II

Spring

FOUR

Weather & Climate Journal
April–June, 2012

APRIL 2 ∾ Sometimes, in the darkness of winter, I forget all the life that's hiding just under the ground's surface. I forget the ability of roots to send shoots upward that then form leaves and flowers of all shapes and colors, wonders of diversity. And the wealth of insects and birdsong. That's why each spring is a discovery rather than a repetition. Nothing is ever the same, neither in the woods around me nor in my heart.

The days are once again moderate, with temperatures in the 70s, warmer than normal but at least not unbearably hot and muggy like March was. I spend as much time as I can in the woods, listening, walking slowly, stooping to feel the softness of new-grown moss, connecting to the lives appearing around me, sensing those that remain unseen as well. I hear the barred owls calling every so often and know that their chicks are newly hatched, tiny unseeing fluffballs in one of the hollowed trees that dot our forest. Their exact location remains a mystery.

Last night I was out wandering as the sun dropped in the west, the sky around it a glistening saffron-tinged yellow reminiscent more of the day's beginning than its end. The wind rose as the earth darkened, so that fading chatters of woodland animals were countered by the strengthening sounds of waving trees, the animal and tree and wind sounds mingling as sunlight shimmered on the distant horizon.

APRIL 4 ∾ I'm spending a lot of time trying to rid our woods of garlic mustard, an aggressive invasive plant brought to this continent from Europe in the 1860s. Like the native wildflowers, garlic mustard is a month or more ahead of time this year and is now starting to flower. Garlic mustard plants are more abundant than ever, possibly because there wasn't much dieback during the abnormally warm winter. I call it the Plant from Hell, but the plant isn't bad in itself. It just came to the U.S. without its usual population controls: tiny beetles that feed on its leaves, flowers, and roots. Lacking those controls, garlic mustard is free to grow larger, reproduce without check, and invade woodlands, where it smothers the smaller native wildflowers. Here it's a species out of place, outside of its natural web of life. I am weary of dedicating every spring to patrolling and eradicating garlic mustard.

Nearly all the hundred-plus plant species in our woodland are natives, which means they have lived in the oak woodland community for thousands of years, adapting to each other and to the midwestern environment. They grow in an orderly fashion. But a small number of plants imported from other continents are aggressive species that thrive here, are extremely adaptable, and spread with ease. These aggressive nonnatives, for example, bush honeysuckle, multiflora rose, European buckthorn, and garlic mustard, have a long growing season and easily transported seeds—traits that give them a competitive advantage. I have to keep them in check constantly or, slowly but steadily, the woods would become a thicket of these few invaders.

In the past, very cold winters in the north have restricted many nonnative invading plants and insects to southern states. But now warming winters are coaxing a number of aggressive invasives to move northward—kudzu, for one, a woody vine that rapidly overgrows and smothers anything in its path. And fire ants, with their burning stings, that attack and can kill small animals. And termites, which in addition to tunneling through our homes, can change the energy flow of woodlands by decomposing large stores of downed wood within a few years.

As our world warms further, new species will join the ranks of invasives moving up from the south or in from other parts of the world, mixing with and displacing the unique plants and animals that rely on this particular environment. Displacement of native plants and animals by new invasive species is one of several ways that our changing climate could unravel the tightly knit interrelationships that have held plant and animal communities together for millennia.

APRIL 5 ∾ Now that the extreme heat wave has passed, cooler days are slowing down the wildflowers. Even so, flowers I normally see weeks hence—Jacob's ladder, wild blue phlox, early buttercups, Canada anemone, and jack-in-the-pulpit—are coming into their own, adding soft blues and golden yellows to our woodland floor. Last night, the weather report warned of a possible frost that could have been disastrous for fruit trees, which along with many garden flowers also are blooming a month ahead of schedule. Fortunately temperatures remained above freezing.

I walk in our woods whenever I can. Once surrounded by plants, I might hear an occasional car on the road or the talking of bicyclists as they spin past, but I'm mostly oblivious to such sounds. My focus shifts to the dozens of native plants growing here. And to the animals: the toads and frogs, salamanders and snakes, the multiple birds. The flying and fox squirrels, chipmunks, voles and moles, foxes, raccoons (one is taking up residence in the garage), on and on. But I know little of the "simpler" life-forms. The yellow moths that rise in a cloud as I brush through the leaves, the many insects and spiders, the sprouting mushrooms and mosses. If I include soil fungi, insects, nematodes, and bacteria, I realize that I am surrounded by thousands of kinds of organisms, each with its own purpose and perceptions, each with its own set of operating instructions carried in a complex genetic code: when to mate, what to feed its young, how to build a shelter, where to find refuge when storms threaten.

This diversity of species—most of which I can't even see—helps tend the planet and keep it functioning. I contemplate the natural world's integrity of purpose and form and am filled with reverie. At such times, I can lose myself in this small woodland, as much as if I were in a vast desert or mountain range. It's not a sense of alternative reality; this *is* reality. This is the way our planet has operated for millions of years, species adapting to one another, evolving and learning so they could better fit their niche, perfecting a sustainable world for all life, humans included.

I think that in past times, people were more aware of this larger whole and its importance. Until the last few hundred years, nearly all of us were immersed in prime natural areas like those that our conservation organizations now struggle to save. Natural lands controlled our existence, not vice versa. It's only been in my lifetime that humans have so overwhelmed the natural world that many of us are now more accustomed to the feel of concrete under our feet than the soft soils of forest and grassland. That our ears are more attuned to the beeping of car horns than the song of birds. That our children can identify the make of a vehicle better than common plants or animals. A few days ago a friend brought her young grand-daughter out to our woods. She was fascinated by the mushrooms sprouting from a tree stump near the trail. "This is the first time she's seen one of these," my friend commented.

In 2009, for the first time, more of the world's people lived in large cities than in rural or nature-dominated lands. Maybe it's inevitable that we lose our sense of nature's presence and importance. With each passing year, there are more and more people on the planet, living more and more crowded together, cities spreading into the surrounding countryside, leaving less and less room for other life-forms.

APRIL 9 ∾ I slept out on the screened porch last night, where the air is moving and alive. I can't resist being outside at this time of the year, especially in the day's earliest light, when wild turkeys call mates and phoebes sing their dawn song. Then I watch the gradual unfolding of a perfect day. The white-gray sky brightens to blue. A stillness holds the woods as insects and birds start to carry out their assigned tasks—pollinating flowers, building nests, calling to mates. The sun rises rapidly, and by the time its light is arching through the trees, spreading warmth across the land, the birds have quieted except for the calls of chickadees and cardinals. This is a time of peaceful enchantment, when all is right with the world.

APRIL II ∿ Last night frost shrouded the land, the frost that fruit growers have been fearing. Temperatures dropped into the twenties for several hours across most of the state. I walked in the woods early this morning, searching for results. The damage was patchy. Some of the tree buds and young leaves were frozen solid. The forest floor mostly escaped, except in the valley bottom where cold dense air had settled. There frozen leaves were already withering even as the sun was rising, especially the thinnest, most fragile leaves. My lone apple tree, perched on a small mound near the road, seems to have escaped, but I'm sure many others in the neighborhood were damaged.

APRIL 16 ∿ I greeted yesterday's forecast of rain with enthusiasm. We could use what's called a soaking rain—a long, gentle rain that sinks into the ground. Instead we got a nighttime gully-washer. The windows streamed with water as if they were being sprayed with a hose, three inches of rainfall pummeling the roof in as many hours. For that entire time, nearly continuous lightning lit the woods with a mysterious white-gray light. Robert and I, unable to sleep, snuggled into bed and gazed out the window, but Sidney, terrified by the booming thunder, went to hide in the basement.

This morning, I went outside to survey the downpour's results. The path to the house had a gully eroded down the middle, six inches deep in places. We'll have to get a load of gravel to fill it up. Alongside the house, where I'm doing some gardening and landscaping, soft soils were washed downhill and deposited twenty feet away. I'll be doing some heavy shoveling to get the mud back in place—not easy with my aging knees and hips. Driving into town, I noted freshly plowed farm fields with foot-deep channels and low fields with standing water. In the city, streets were flooded, the water backing up from drains that were blocked by eroded soils and debris. Across the county streams were running full. Flash flood warnings abounded.

This intense rainfall brings home the fact that climate change produces far more than higher temperatures. I could cope with a bit more heat, although it wouldn't be pleasant. But Earth's insidious temperature rise is intimately tethered to the planet's basic functions, such as the way water cycles over and through Earth's surface. Water evaporates more readily at higher temperatures. Today, because of significantly greater evaporation from the planet's surface, and because warmer air holds more moisture than cooler air, the global amount of atmospheric water vapor has increased. That means there's more moisture available for rainfall and for flooding. In the U.S., annual precipitation on average has increased 5 percent in the last century.

However, our planet's water regime is not changing uniformly. Here in the Midwest, the average annual precipitation has increased 9 percent since 1991, and some higher-latitude locations have 20 percent more precipitation than a century ago. But climate change pushes the extremes: areas in the southern U.S. have lost annual precipitation in the last few decades. In coming years, a general pattern of even wetter conditions in the north and drier conditions in the south is expected to emerge, with droughts intensifying and covering larger areas of the southwestern U.S.

Perhaps more importantly, gentle rainfalls are clearly ceding to heavier precipitation that amplifies runoff and erosion, like last night's assault. Since 1970, small rainfalls have decreased while large rainstorms have become more frequent and intense, dropping increasing amounts of water. And total annual precipitation is increasingly concentrated into these heavy downpours. Since the mid-1900s, here in the Midwest, the fraction of total precipitation that falls in very heavy events has increased an amazing 37 percent; in New England, that amount has risen 71 percent, although it's only grown 5 percent in the southwestern U.S. These shifts have been strongly linked to climate change.

Here's another shift: across much of the country, rainfall has adopted a different calendar. More of each year's precipitation is falling in winter and spring, while summer and fall are becoming drier.

All these trends—more extreme precipitation events, a greater proportion of total rainfall coming in heavy downpours, fewer gentle showers, and changes in the seasonality of rainfall—are expected to intensify across many parts of the globe as the planet warms further.

I wonder about these trends accelerating in the sky above me. I have always loved gazing into Iowa's huge skies. I walk to the hilltop at the top of our lane, tilt my face upward, and slowly turn in a circle, imagining that an entire new world is opening to me, its mountains and seas, plains and ridges, all the globe's shapes and colors written on the sky by water's pen. So many clouds, I think.

But last night, as I lay in bed, thunder rolling through the forest around me, I saw the skies in a new and different way. I watched clouds climbing and towering and collapsing upon one another, shimmering clouds doubling in size time and then time again, clouds in sheets and spirals, white and lobed, chuting out funnels of rain that were turning creekbeds into torrents of mud.

Seized by this vision, I grasped the power that was being generated as our skies warmed, the growing heat translating to unmitigated airborne thermal energy pursuing release in storms such as this one. And I had a premonition of how these forces increasingly will feel: hot skies soaking moisture from the earth, their rising temperatures releasing raw energy that is discharged in downpours and winds that continue to grow in intensity, duration, and extent. Climate change reshaping not only our land and daily actions, but also our relationship with the earth, as well as our very thoughts, fears, actions, and dreams.

The springtime's increasingly unpredictable and extreme weather seems to be changing the way people think. A new poll, the most detailed to date, states that for many Americans, the changing climate is no longer a distant threat. "It just seems to be one disaster after another after another," stated the Yale researcher commissioning the survey. "People are starting to connect the dots." The concern and awareness expressed by nearly 70 percent of those surveyed definitely mark an intensification of public opinion, and it's backed up by other recent polls. Interestingly, over a third of

Americans surveyed also reported being directly affected by the remarkable string of weather-related disasters of this year, which included droughts, floods, tornadoes, and heat waves. People must be feeling more vulnerable. The story is no longer one of distant islanders watching the rising tides—it's coming closer to home.

Here in Iowa, in advance of Earth Day this coming weekend, fifty-six religious leaders have issued a statement defining climate change as one of today's most pressing challenges and asking individuals, families, congregations, businesses, local communities, and the state to take responsible precautionary actions to limit climate change and adapt to unavoidable climate impacts. They called for leadership in addressing responsible energy use in order to protect the earth and its most vulnerable populations, pointing out that while we will all be affected, the people and nations who have contributed least to climate problems will tend to suffer the most.

Climate change is at its heart a social justice issue. It will affect all of us, but not equally. The poorest nations, the poorest people are the least able to prepare for increasingly severe storms or rises in sea level, and they have fewer resources for recovery efforts once such problems occur. Magnifying this problem, many developing nations are located in the tropics, where even a small temperature increase would take the climate beyond the narrow range that's existed for many years. This region is expected to feel climate change rapidly and profoundly, with heat waves of unprecedented extremes and duration and little recourse for escape. Hardest hit will be Africa, already one of the hottest and driest places on Earth and also the poorest continent. The Maldives and other small-island nations with little political clout will literally be covered by the seas—which are rising in part because glaciers around the world are shrinking. Glacial melt in turn causes problems of its own. The rapid melt of Himalayan glaciers north of India could pose a substantial flood risk to lowland villages in the next few decades. With fewer social consequences, Glacier National Park will be glacier-free within a few decades.

In the U.S., people with fewer resources and limited choices will become even more vulnerable. They will be exposed to the weather and its extremes, while the richest people may be able to move away from climate-stressed regions or retreat to air-conditioned homes and cars, at least at first.

Looking out the window at the woodland that I love, I take that truth one step further. I consider the woodpeckers at the feeder, the chipmunks scurrying through the woodpile, the frogs and toads recently wakened from their winter of sleep. Will they be able to escape the heat or hide from the storms? The trees cannot relocate; most animals cannot move to a cooler locale. And so, I fear that many residents of our woodland, like the poor of the earth, may become early victims of the planet's rapidly changing climate patterns.

APRIL 20 ∾ There's a chill in the early morning air. I walk Sidney down the usual trail, and a male wood duck flies overhead, absurdly beautiful with his iridescent green crest, red eye, and intricate white head markings. I have seen him often in the past few weeks, sometimes perched high in a tree with his mate. I'm convinced that they are nesting nearby, I suspect in a cavity in a large dead tree not fifty feet from the house. I imagine the baby wood ducks plump and filling their eggs, readying for their grand entrance into the world. I would love to see them leap from their nest down to the ground and waddle off after Mom to the pond, a task they will complete soon after hatching.

The barred owls are also nesting nearby. I hear and see them often. Last year their nest was within easy sight of the kitchen window. At dusk I would watch the parents take turns bringing mice, chipmunks, and other small animals into the nest like timed feeding machines, one arriving about every five minutes. One parent left the nest as the other flew in with a twitching rodent in its bill.

And I know pileated woodpeckers are nesting someplace in the woods. Their strong bills resound like jackhammers on dead trees.

The smaller animals are no less delightful, just less obvious. I roam the woods daily in search of them, my head bent to the ground, a slow meditative sojourn during which I smell, listen, watch for movement. I get so I can barely tolerate being inside the house. I must respond to the call to come outside where there is so much movement, so much life. These wanderings have become addictive, these daily searches for small violet-colored showy orchis blossoms tucked between egg-shaped leaves, droops of black-cherry flowers blown to the ground, minute fern fronds piercing the duff. Always something new. I lose track of time and place—sometimes lifting my head and wondering where I am, what I am doing. I stand dazed for a minute. Then I relocate myself, drop my head, and proceed slowly until darkness brings me back toward the light shining from our kitchen window.

APRIL 22 ❧ The sky is an azure blue today, without a hint of rain. This is the first clear day we've had in a while. With a crispness in the air and new plant growth everywhere, this feels to me just the way spring should feel.

When I was a child, I used to color pictures in combinations of greens and blues, trying to replicate the union of earth and sky in all its variations. Today, those variations are playing out in spades. Trees in mature woodlands, seen from a distance, range from the fresh lime of newly opened leaves to the deeper green of larger leaves that opened a few weeks ago. What amazes me is that all these leaves, already formed last fall, have lain dormant in the bud through the winter, waiting like minuscule balloons for the first rush of water to move upward from wakening roots and expand them.

Oak leaves are the last to open. The white oaks now have tiny leaves as large as squirrel ears—a size marking the proverbial time to plant corn and hunt for morel mushrooms. These leaves are tinged a peachy copper color, so that from a distance, our woodland consists of mounds of treetops ranging from coppery red through all tones of green. Some oaks are still producing pollen, which is transported by the wind to fertilize tiny oak flowers that through the summer will ripen into acorns, which in autumn will fall with a ping on the roof, then roll to the ground to start the cycle of growth once again.

The sporadically cooler weather has slowed the drop of

wildflower petals, so that we've had an ongoing cloud of knee-high wild geraniums coloring acres of the forest a soft lavender, interrupted by patches of shorter plants—white, lemon-yellow, and deep purple violets and delicate cream- and butter-shaded lily blossoms (trout lily, bellwort) nodding in the breeze. Today nectaring red admiral butterflies flit through the flowers, their black wings patterned by deep orange stripes and white specks. This butterfly periodically flaunts large population surges, and this is the year. I can locate dozens in one glance. Their quiet flight is joined by the buzz of large bumblebees feeding on the geraniums and the raucous pecking of the pileated woodpeckers deeper in the valley.

I can still find a few rue anemone and spring beauty wildflowers if I look in the most sheltered, coolest sites. But through most of the woods, the early flowers that usually signal springtime have gone to seed. Taking their place are those that normally bloom in May and beyond. Mayapples, with their umbrella-like leaves and plum-sized fruits, have become April apples this year, and wild licorice, false Solomon's seal, tinker's weed, and Virginia waterleaf are now prematurely entering their prime. Even some of the summer mushrooms are already in fruit, at least a month ahead of their normal appearance.

APRIL 23 ॐ I heard it again today from a friend. The climate is always changing. Today's weather is weird, but it's part of a natural cycle—it's nothing to worry about.

My friend is partially correct. We live on a restless planet with drifting continents and constantly evolving life-forms. Earth's climate, just like its landforms and living creatures, is always on the move. Sometimes in the distant past, natural climatic changes have inched forward; at other times they have exploded with unbelievable intensity and rapidity. However, today's carbon-dioxide-driven push toward a new global climate is far stronger and more rapid than anything we've seen before in the history of human civilization.

Considering changing climates of the past, we can identify earlier periods that have been both colder and hotter than today. Hundreds of millions of years ago the planet may have been completely frozen or nearly so, a "snowball earth." But for much of Earth's history, our planet has been warm enough to be mostly ice-free. During some ancient times, atmospheric carbon dioxide has soared as high as 2,000 ppm, with global temperatures rising in tandem.

One extreme example of a hot, iceless planet occurred about 56 million years ago, when global surface temperatures rapidly rose 9 to 15 degrees following a tremendous increase in greenhouse gases due in part to a massive volcanic eruption. Temperatures were high around the globe, polar regions hosted crocodiles and leafy trees, and oceans were as much as 660 feet higher than now. This Paleocene-Eocene Thermal Maximum is viewed as the best analogue for modern climate change.

Even here in Iowa, we have evidence of other ancient warm climates. Walking along the reservoir near my home, I find abundant corals and other fossils that speak of the tepid, shallow, shimmering seas covering this land hundreds of millions of years ago. About 300 million years ago, portions of the seas ceded to jungle-like tropical vegetation growing in steaming swamps and coastal floodplains; the coal deposits of southwestern Iowa are their legacy.

Approximately 2.7 million years ago, at the commencement of the Ice Age, the planet's temperatures started dropping sufficiently to cover the poles with ice and, in the northern hemisphere, send waves of massive glaciers periodically flowing southward. Global average temperatures varied over tens of thousands of years by as many as 18 degrees. Carbon dioxide levels, however, at least until the Industrial Revolution, remained fairly stable, cycling slowly between 180 and 280 ppm. Throughout this period, atmospheric carbon dioxide concentrations and average temperatures rose and fell in lockstep. The tempo of warm and cold periods was driven by cyclic changes in Earth's orbit, and the related growth and dieback of vegetation helped produce spikes and dips in carbon dioxide that reinforced the global temperature changes.

A hundred thousand years ago, during a warm interglacial period, sea levels were roughly 15 to 30 feet higher than those of today. Fast forward to the deep glacial cold of 21,000 years ago, when average temperatures were about seven degrees lower than now, and huge glaciers extending south into the Midwest locked up much of the planet's water; sea levels were more than 330 feet lower than now.

So yes, the planet's climate has changed through the ages. But here's the rub: none of the above planetary changes happened while modern humans walked the earth, at least not by the billions. Large climate changes like those described above are normal for our planet, but not for modern people—because modern human societies were not around then.

Our species—*Homo sapiens*—has roamed this planet for a mere 200,000 years. For nearly all of that period, we existed in small transient bands of hunter-gatherers, our total global number less than a million. We skirted the edges of glaciers, ate what we gathered by hand and killed with spears, and protected our bodies from glacial winds with animal skins and small campfires. Temperatures varied and glaciers advanced and retreated, nudged southward by shifts in the tilt of the planet. But because we lived as wanderers and there were so few of us, when freezing temperatures advanced, we could readily walk south to warmer climates.

In contrast, for about the last 10,000 years, after the melting of the last glaciers, Earth's climate has remained astonishingly stable. During this period, global average temperatures have never varied more than 1.8 degrees, and sea levels have not changed dramatically. This is the period when modern prairies established themselves in the Midwest, the prairies that gave Iowa a quarter of the world's richest topsoils. And this is the period when modern oak woodlands first intermingled with the prairies and established themselves on the landscape where I now live.

During this period of remarkable climatic, oceanic, and environmental stability, we humans developed what today defines our species—sedentary agriculture, domesticated animals, written language, musical notation, metalworking, and civilizations with all their social, economic, and political structures. Indeed, this last episode of environmental stability has allowed us to settle in one

place and depend on cooperative, predictable weather. The beneficent climate has permitted us to build large cities near oceans, where
food sources are readily available. All these amenities have enabled
the human population to soar from under a million to a few hundred
million 2,000 years ago, to a billion around 1800, to 7 billion this year,
2012. All that we today claim as normal, everything that we rely upon
for living our modern lives, is in reality a gift of the climatic stability
of the last 10,000 years, during the epoch we call the Holocene. Even
the variability I savor in Iowa's climate usually plays out in a fairly
predictable way, or at least it has until very recently.

Today's climate change not only threatens to take us beyond the
temperature boundaries that we find most conducive to health,
comfort, and productivity. It also is occurring in decades, at a speed
that allows little time either for human or for nature's adaptation,
rather than over thousands of years as in the past.

APRIL 25 ∞ A few days ago, Mexico passed some of the planet's
strongest national climate-change legislation. Now our southern
neighbor, with the eleventh largest economy in the world, has legally
binding emissions goals: Mexico must reduce carbon dioxide emissions by 50 percent below 2000 levels by 2050. A third of the nation's
electricity must come from renewable sources by 2024. Although
the bill was initially resisted by Mexico's steel and cement industries,
it passed with bipartisan support and with a unanimous vote in the
Senate. Passage of this strong national legislation was attributed to
the increasing frustration with unsuccessful international efforts to
curb greenhouse-gas levels.

Mexico's legislation is a sign of hope. It is the sane thing for any
nation to be doing, and very different from our own national approach: the U.S. has no set climate policy and has never ratified a
binding international agreement concerning greenhouse-gas emissions, as most other nations have done.

Meanwhile, back in our woods, the early morning air feels cool
and crisp even though the forecast is for a high temperature 10 to
20 degrees above normal. The disjointed mixture of temperatures

and natural events leaves me struggling to define annual cycles. It looks and feels like June now, with trees fully leafed out and assuming the deeper shades of green usually typical weeks and months hence. But the trees are not yet hosting an abundance of May bird migrants from South America. The first few warblers, rose-breasted grosbeaks, Baltimore orioles, and ruby-throated hummingbirds have just arrived, but most warblers and flycatchers are still on their northward journey.

I can't help but wonder if woodland plants and animals are sensing the shifting of their seasonal timeframe. They time their life processes—migration or emergence, reproduction, budburst, and the like—according to environmental cues such as temperature and day length. The many species living in our woods have adapted to a relatively stable climate, developing interlocked activities that have sustained life for all. Normally, frogs and toads emerge when open water promises food for their future tadpoles. Bird eggs hatch when certain insects are available to feed the young. Flowering plants bloom in rhythm with their pollinators' emergence. This year, I question whether the proper flowers are open to feed emerging insects, and whether the proper insects are available to feed hatching birds and pollinate our early flowers. And what about insect-eating migrant birds? What will happen to them if the springtime burst of insects is over before they arrive?

A few years ago, for a month of Sundays, I splayed out on dried oak leaves, my face near the ground, observing the delicate pink-striped wildflower spring beauty wave its bright pink pollen-producing anthers in the breeze, attracting visits of cuckoo bees, green bees, and bee flies. The flowers, which constantly turn their faces to the sun, would close when a cloud passed over and reopen when the sun (along with the small bees) reappeared. What might seem like a mundane event—a minute insect carrying pollen from one flower to another while feeding on nectar—quickly became magical. How many similar interdependencies among species exist in our woods?

Studies are showing that yes indeed, as average temperatures rise, many of nature's synchronies are being disrupted. Crucial life processes, from the singing of frogs to the emergence of insects, leafing of trees, and arrival of migrating birds, are now routinely happening earlier. In Wisconsin where I grew up, for example, spring temperatures arrived about a week earlier in the 1990s than in the 1930s. Correlated with the warming temperatures, by the end of the 1900s, is the fact that birds such as Canada geese, red-winged blackbirds, house wrens, and robins were arriving earlier, and a third of the spring wildflowers were blooming earlier. This year, in Iowa, the extreme March heat prematurely attracted an amazing thirty-five bird species, including shorebirds, vireos, wrens, warblers, sparrows, and more, with many species setting all-time records for their earliest spring arrival.

The well-tuned clockwork of nature is being disrupted in many other ways. Butterflies are emerging earlier, when they may die from lack of proper food plants. High-altitude hummingbirds are returning to breeding territories after their favored nectar plants have bloomed. The sex of hatchling painted turtles, like the ones I find down by the pond, is determined by the incubation temperature of the turtle egg, with higher temperatures producing more females. As temperatures rise, a badly disrupted sex ratio could lead to local declines and eventually extinction.

How many other crucial natural processes are now mismatched because of shifting temperatures or rainfalls? Are the disruptions fatal, or will interlocked species develop new interrelationships? So many questions remain unanswered. Surely, oftentimes, such disrupted synchronicities will affect species without human notice, becoming unacknowledged costs of climate change.

MAY 1 ∿ Fog floats through the forest, bringing with it a chilly wet cold. Droplets of moisture wet the deck, although it's not raining. Increasingly the air seems to be saturated, as if lakes are now airborne.

So much more moisture and more intense rainfall. Climate change. More damp, damp days like today, along with the higher temperatures. The rate of temperature rise is accelerating markedly here in the Midwest: using the average temperature rise from 1900 to 2010 as a baseline, I see that the average temperature rose twice as fast between 1950 and 2010, and three times as fast between 1980 and 2010. What surprises me are the details of the rise. Average temperatures are rising more at night than during the day—rising atmospheric moisture tends to increase cloud cover, which prevents nighttime's usual heat dissipation—and winter temperatures are rising more than those of summers. In Iowa, winter temperatures have increased six times faster than summer temperatures. My home state now has an average of five more frost-free days per year than in the mid-1900s when I was born. I wonder how my mother's gardening would have been altered by this evolving climate.

MAY 2 ꩜ I continue to hear news shorts about Iowa's unusual warmth this spring. Yesterday, the state climatologist's office announced that this April, Iowa had only two isolated reports of snow or sleet, the fewest such events since 1890. Although April's temperatures were cooler than those of March, the April average remained several degrees above normal. Also, National Weather Service records show that the first four months of 2012 have been the warmest on record for Iowa, with this year's average temperature exceeding the previous record by a whopping 3.5 degrees. The past month, which felt cool to me after March's heat wave, was still the nation's eighth-warmest April on record. Another new record: this is the first year that April's average temperatures were lower than those of March. Planting of the corn crop is ahead of schedule, but farmers are concerned about the dry soils.

My concerns focus less on temperature extremes than on temperature unpredictability, its divergence from the long-term seasonal norms. The weather seems to be all over the place, with ups and downs that make me feel like I'm sailing on mammoth waves. More weather whiplash. Last night we turned on the furnace to rid the house of a biting chill; this morning, with temperatures in the 80s and high humidity, we'll probably be turning on the air conditioning. Yesterday I wore mittens to work; today, a summer T-shirt.

MAY 3 ∿ I'm sitting on the back deck. On nights like tonight, I can't force myself to go inside. The air is warm and humid, and dozens of American toads are calling down at the pond, each one singing a continuous long note but each one a bit different in pitch. Their songs are punctuated by a repeated solitary note—pip pip pip pip. What could it be, a bird or frog? An insect? Clouds race across the sky, west to east, voluminous gray puffs with shining white edges from the light of the full moon, which is steadily floating in the opposite direction. I've been watching it arc overhead. It's passed from the crown of the hickory to the tip of the red oak, where it now hangs, nearly full, shimmering through the delicate lacework of half-opened leaves.

About every 30 seconds, the heavens dip earthward and a gust of wind passes through the woods, shaking leaves and sounding like a wave, but a gentle inviting one, a summertime beach wave that laps around my ankles. Tree frogs interrupt the steady churring of the toads—a buzz to the right, then one to the left. I'm sure that all the trees surrounding me have their resident tree frogs. And what else, I wonder? What bats nest under flaps of bark, what stick bugs munch on oak leaves? What fungi encircle the oaks' roots? How many lives surround me, how many ways of seeing colors and forms, of hearing calls? All around me is alive, one united life.

MAY 4 ∿ More of the same. Hot and humid. Big storms. Flash flood warnings. This time of year is supposed to produce mostly calm blue skies, sometimes stiff breezes, temperatures moderate and inviting, and the earth glittering in newness and resurrection. Halcyon days, when I open all the windows in our house and the world blows through. Good clothes-drying days, I call them, days when I wash the laundry just so I can watch it wave in the wind as it dries. There are never enough of these days. They could fill a lifetime without my tiring of them.

Instead, this year we seem to swing between very hot gray days with storms and chilly gray days with storms. I have been forced to use the clothes drier because I can't dry the laundry outside. Using electricity instead of sunlight to dry our clothes of course releases one more bit of carbon dioxide into the atmosphere, as do the air conditioners we are all using now. I feel like it's a gigantic conspiracy, this circle of being pushed by inclement weather into doing things that make climate change worse.

Then again, "being pushed" is my own evaluation of the situation. I grew up without a clothes drier or air conditioning. Today I assume that both are necessities.

I guess every cloud, including those that seem so overly abundant this spring, has its silver lining. Here is mine: Sidney, who used to tremble and flee to the basement whenever distant thunder rumbled, is adapting to intense weather. Last evening, when we were walking into what seemed to be a tightening circle of wind and lightning, I was the one who fearfully turned for home; she would have kept going.

MAY 7 ∾ Another gray, wet, warm morning. Ninety percent relative humidity—how can the air hold so much water? Rain fell last night, but for once it was a comforting gentle rain, a nourishing rain that coaxes nature forward, not one that washes away soils and emerging seedlings. People are starting to comment on the gray, the wet, the violence of the storms we've been having, the localized flash floods larger than any seen before.

Yesterday, weather predictions called for rain, but nature surprised us and the morning storms veered to the north. We had sunshine and a rare dry afternoon. I spent it in the woods, which are now knee-high with wild geraniums and American bellflowers and the fresh green stems of various ferns, tick trefoil, tinker's weed, and dozens of other plants. It happens to me every year: one day orderly clumps of small spring wildflowers dot the woodland floor, and I kid myself into thinking that the woods are a neat, controllable garden. Then, in a few days, the taller summer plants take off and shrubs come into leaf. Multiple shades of green explode everywhere. I pull on my rubber knee-highs and wade out into the lush profusion.

I've been leading nature walks in our woods this spring. I point out the sedges and the spring wildflowers, talking about how to differentiate the several small-flowered anemone species. I explain that early settlers thought hepatica would treat liver ailments because the plant's leaves are liver-shaped. I show the deep red juice that drips from the roots of bloodroot and the small white spurs—elaiosomes—protruding from bloodroot seeds, spurs that are high in fat and protein and are eaten by ants who then disperse the seeds.

I try to explain the sanctity of this special place to my visitors, that these woods feed the spirit even as they create habitat for thousands of species. But their benefits extend far beyond the woodland borders because of the young birds raised here that fly off elsewhere, the water-holding capacities of the soils, the pollinators and pest controllers that breed here and radiate outward, the soaking up of atmospheric carbon by leaves and shoots, the numerous benefits we collectively call ecosystem services, many of which we don't even recognize. The way such sites are the glue that holds the human-modified world together.

I also try to explain how these special natural areas need us to preserve them but how we need them and their benefits even more. Our health and well-being depend on the planet's health and well-being. However, I don't think I explain this well enough. My visitors, as perceptive as they are, may not understand that when I talk about the survival of unique woodland species, I am talking about the survival of the human species as well.

MAY 10 ᴄᴡ Yesterday was a normal Iowa spring day, at last! Daytime temperatures in the low 70s, nighttime in the 40s, low humidity, clear blue skies, the faintest breeze wafting sweet scents from distant wild plums. Sunshine sparkling off the new growth and white oak trunks, which became shimmering blades in the forest. A heavenly day, the kind of day I grew up to expect but which now seems to be increasingly rare. A reprieve. Looks like today will be similar, and the next day after. I'll plant my flower boxes and finish some landscaping outside, living as if this weather will last forever, forgetting the way-too-hot world of the last two months.

On days like today, I open all the windows in the house so that the sounds and scents of the forest can enter. Our home becomes a world of beauty and abundance, something so solid and whole that I assume nothing could ever disrupt it. Today is the way life should be, I think, as I take my tea out onto the porch, immerse myself in a good book, and live totally in the present.

Then a snag rips my emotional fabric. I realize once again our desire to forget weather problems of the recent past. This tendency was obvious after the major Iowa floods of 1993 and 2008. At first, many people across the state worked to reduce the impacts of future floods, but soon most had shoved aside the memory of their devastation. They incorrectly assumed that if we'd just had one very large flood, the probability of another was greatly reduced. It doesn't take long for us to push bad weather into the distant past. But doing so, I now know, decreases our ability to work for change and thus to address those problems that are bound to come.

MAY 18 ∽ Andy paid us a surprise visit last week, showing up on our doorstep on Mother's Day. This was the boy who always had a frog in his hand and sometimes one in his pocket. The boy who brought home a box of baby chicks the day before we were leaving for an extended vacation. The boy who used to rescue baby raccoons when their mothers were killed and feed them with a bottle.

The first night home, he slept with his windows closed; it had been a long time since he wanted to open up to the outside world. After that, he opened windows wide and started tracking the locations of calling owls, the frequency of bats swooping past the porch light, the howling of coyotes. He listened late into the night, linking animals to the clock on his bed stand. During the day, he buzzed down the trail to fish in the pond, just as he used to do as a boy. He returned with stories. "Remember when I'd go fishing near the reservoir, how once I saw a *huge* monster fish that I never could identify?" I sensed him relax as the images of his boyhood came to the surface, making us all laugh.

During the day, we sat on the deck and played cribbage, taking time out to watch the red-breasted grosbeaks peck at sunflower seeds and the silly downy woodpecker who's fixated on our hummingbird feeder. We watched the squirrels and chipmunks clean up seeds spilled from the feeding platform and listened for tree frogs in nearby oaks.

How different these woods are from the big city where he now lives. It's not just the quiet and lack of traffic and the open and friendly people. Not just his sense of safety, the deep relaxation that penetrates his body when he's here. Not just the constant movement of air, the sounds of animals, the sense that the world is alive. It's all of these, plus the draw Andy still feels toward the woodland lives all around him, to the peaceable kingdom where he spent his youth.

MAY 21 ❧ In just a few weeks, we've gone from a very wet early May to bone-dry weather, with frequent strong winds, high temperatures, and low humidity sucking the topsoils dry. In croplands, Iowa's black, friable, loamy soils are becoming a gray-brown deadpan fraught with fissures—cracks that speak of the lack of water. Rain was predicted several times in the last week, but each time either the skies remained clear or the storms took a circuitous route and avoided us. Normally May rains fall every few days in Iowa. This May, some nearby locations have not received rain for nearly three weeks. Newly planted soybean seeds lie dormant in the hot earth, unable to sprout and color the fields green. Usually I can depend on spring rains to water the flower boxes on the deck, which I planted a week ago. This year, I need to water them myself.

Fortunately, here in the woods I don't see much drying of soils because the ground is richly covered by lush perennial plants, a sea of green that I wade into daily, always sure to find one treasure or another. A late-blooming anemone, a mushroom or two, an iridescent beetle. This week, I've noted a number of fruiting stalks of milky-white baneberries, one stalk per plant. And poke milkweed is starting to bloom, each small pink-white flower part of a larger ball of flowers that seems to radiate light in the woodland green. These globes of flowers extend a foot above the surrounding vegetation, the result being quite startling. Sometimes other surprises await me. I remember once last fall when gazing at the base of a hickory, I noticed a deer mouse curled into a ball in a crevice of loose bark, its beady black eyes watching me. We held the gaze until I took one step forward, my movement causing the mouse to uncurl and scurry up the tree trunk.

Later in the day, driving into town, I saw a good-sized painted turtle crossing the road. I stopped to shepherd it to safety, then realized that it was migrating to a nearby pond. I thought I'd help it along, and so I picked it up and carried it toward the pond. When we got close, the turtle craned its neck and started waving its four legs in the air with vigor, as if expecting that doing so would speed its arrival. It obviously smelled the water. Placed on the grass, the turtle took off at a run and dive-bombed into the pond, going straight to the bottom where it was safe.

MAY 28 ❧ The dry weather continues. Each day there's a significant probability of rain—40 percent chance, 50 percent, 60 percent. Each day the western skies darken, the winds blow. I bustle about, getting laundry inside. But then the dark clouds pass overhead and keep going—dropping at most a 30-second shower, barely enough to wash the dust off the tree leaves. I watch the clouds blow eastward as the western sky shines bright and blue once again.

With Iowa's dry weather becoming more extreme each day, I wasn't surprised to hear discussions of possible drought on the evening news. Climatologists are using the term "flash drought," envisioning the quick burst of dry heat as parallel to the flash floods that are becoming more common in the Midwest. High temperatures and cloudless skies are interacting with lack of rain to scorch plants in a matter of days. Drought concerns are focused mostly on states to the south of Iowa, although dry conditions are moving north and most of Iowa is already abnormally parched. "The faucet's been turned off across the Midwest," the weather report summarized.

Iowa has been plagued with severe floods the past four years; areas that were under water last year are drought-threatened this year. Climate variability—it seems to be the name of the game, the land swinging from one end of the water pendulum to the other. Where is the moderate climate, the predictable weather that has defined the human condition and our cultural development for thousands of years?

I once knew a woman from Nepal, the wife of a senior distinguished scientist and administrator, who lived in relative luxury. She visited our home many years ago and raved about our houseplants, moving slowly from one to another, feeling their leaves, asking about their growth habits, pronouncing their English names as if she was being reunited with long-lost friends. After a bit, she told me that she loved houseplants and wanted to have some in her home in Kathmandu, but didn't have the water to keep them alive. She had pots, she had soil, but she didn't have sufficient water, which was pumped to her rooftop holding tank and used with extreme discretion for drinking, cooking, and washing. I cannot imagine not having enough water to keep a violet on my kitchen windowsill, a pot of Boston ferns or philodendrons in the living room. In this land of floods and violent streamflows, I, who have never lacked anything in my life, certainly have not lacked water.

MAY 30 ᴄ᷈ᴡ Robert and I married after he had spent a year working at Byrd Station, Antarctica. When he returned, we talked about repeating his South Pole adventures together by trekking in Greenland, then an unyielding mass of ice. I thought about that daydream yesterday, when I read that a small town in southern Greenland, Narsarsuaq, had reached a temperature of 76.6 degrees, shattering the record high for the month by more than four degrees.

With all the weather extremes this year, Narsarsuaq's report—the second highest temperature ever recorded in Greenland—could be easily overlooked. But Greenland lies mostly above the Arctic Circle, where climate change is being felt first, fastest, and most feverishly. And, as with other Arctic changes, Greenland's warming air has far-ranging implications that could, through producing enormous rises in sea level, reshape the globe's geography.

Greenland has been draped in ice for over 18 million years. But in recent decades the ice sheet, sweeping over 85 percent of the world's largest island, has succumbed to poor health, its mass shrinking, melting away in a cascading process, with more ice dissolving into the sea each year. Ice loss is propagated in two manners. First, the oceanic "toes" of Greenland's outlet glaciers, ice extensions from the land into the ocean that prop glaciers firmly in place, are being nibbled away by warming waters. Once these glacial extensions dissolve, the glaciers are free to speedily slide downward into the sea. Second, massive holes and cracks are increasingly riddling Greenland's ice sheet and carrying rivers of surface meltwater down underneath the ice sheet. There the water lubricates the contact plane between land and ice, again speeding the ice's downward flow of land into the ocean. Both Greenland's melting of ice and its flow into the sea are accelerating. The rate of ice loss has multiplied almost five times since the mid-1990s.

Our youth-inspired Greenland trip never materialized. No time, not enough money. But I think about it sometimes, wishing I had walked that barren ice mass before it was diminished by today's meltwater lakes, icy streams, and terrifying waterfalls speeding down seemingly bottomless chutes into canyons underneath the ice sheets.

JUNE 3 ❧ A week ago our local landfill caught on fire when a discarded grill with live embers was pitched there. Since then, the fire has been pouring out a steady black plume, its dense smoke drifting upward from smoldering tire chips that are part of the landfill's lining. These 1.3 million shredded tires are also releasing a potent mix of air pollutants, possibly including carbon monoxide, dioxins, benzene, and metals such as arsenic, cadmium, and mercury. State health officials are assuring downwind residents that the smoke does not threaten health, even as they are warning people to avoid exposure to the visible smoke plume.

I don't fear the fire or its smoke plume. I am several miles to the north, and I don't see any smoke coming our way. The atmosphere is huge; surely the smoke will disperse and disappear, I naïvely think, before remembering that we humans have already altered two of our globe's largest entities by changing the atmosphere's elementary composition, temperature, and thermal energy content and by warming the oceans and increasing their acidity.

JUNE 12 ∞ Today I touched the raw fecundity of our woodland. Twice. First, when taking an early morning stroll through ferns. A newborn fawn—a dappled chestnut circle of fur—lay between fronds, its erect ears failing to twitch, its black eyes refusing to look. It was no larger than a good-sized rabbit, no older than a few hours, so fragile. Creeping forward, I was flooded with feelings of tenderness, warmth, and admiration for all it understood already about its world: how to lie still, how to avoid danger, how to wait for its mother's return. I wanted to lean over and touch it, to pick it up and cuddle it. Looking at the fawn in its frailty, I remembered the feel of my own babies snuggling into my arms, assuming that the world was a good place worthy of their trust, their smiles, their observations and acceptance. Just as I could not have refused my infants' needs, so I could not have denied the fawn its safe repose. I could no more have threatened that small creature than I could have cut off my own hand. And so I whistled to Sidney, grabbed her collar, and pulled her back with me to the trail.

That afternoon, I was far less solicitous to the large snapping turtle crawling up the trail toward our front door. Her legs and neck bulged out three or four inches beyond her foot-wide dun-colored shell. Her eyes followed me and caught my gaze, looking without fear as if she knew she was invincible. She could remove a chunk from my leg in a fraction of a second, and she could populate our woods with fellow snappers by laying a single clutch of eggs, which was what she was attempting to do. I viewed her with curiosity, but she seemed to look at me with malevolence, scratching her thick-clawed feet in the gravel near the front door, pushing away the stones to form a hole a few inches deep where she could drop her eggs. An hour later, she remained absorbed in her task, and I was absorbed in mine.

I did not crave a dozen baby snappers rustling through the greens near our door, nor did I desire growing snappers crossing our trail at night—their claws rustling in the gravel, their bodies forming uneven terrain under my feet, their mouths opening wide and honing in on my flesh. I stepped carefully around the turtle. Fetching a hoe and placing a sturdy box in front of her, I heaved the mother snapper into the box, pushing with all my strength as she snapped repeatedly, her mouth opening a full three inches, her head moving so fast that I could barely follow her thrusts. Driving to a remote location in a nearby park, I freed her and simultaneously released my fear.

JUNE 21 ॐ When Matt was three, we started our annual family drives to northern Minnesota to canoe in the Boundary Waters, near the Canadian border. That's why today's radio report of rainfall and flooding in Duluth and more broadly along Lake Superior's north shore, our regular route to the northern wilderness, caught my ear. In the past two days, torrential thunderstorms brought over ten inches of rain that cascaded down Duluth's steep slopes, an amount that caused extensive flash flooding, created sinkholes, crumbled roads, converted manholes into geysers, and drowned animals in the zoo. Rivers in the area reached their highest levels on record. Multiple precipitation and flood records were broken, some by several inches. Highways were flooded and destroyed, leaving travelers stranded at restaurants and rest stops. It was yet another example of the warming atmosphere releasing heretofore unheard-of amounts of moisture—but this time in a place where we could have been, a place that I love. I couldn't help but think what we'd have done if we had been there, our crew eager to launch our canoes but instead hunkering down in our car as the waters rose around us.

Precipitation is becoming ever more dramatic as the atmosphere warms. And as with temperatures, it's the extremes that produce the largest havoc. Consider Pakistan in 2010, when record-breaking monsoon rains fed floods that at their peak covered a fifth of the country, significantly affecting nearly 20 million people and causing billions of dollars in lost infrastructure, crops, and livestock.

Record floods have been increasing here in Iowa as well, and while they pale when compared to Pakistan, still the costs are high. In 1993, for the first time ever, ongoing heavy rains sent water gushing over the spillway of the large reservoir half a mile west of our home, causing major flooding downstream in Iowa City. Many people thought we'd had our big flood of the century, until the waters rose even higher in the summer of 2008, when I worked at home for ten weeks because my university offices were closed by floodwaters. The 2008 midwestern flooding was among the worst in U.S. history, with damages of $15 billion, making it the third most costly flooding ever in the nation. Today, recovery is ongoing. The university's art and music departments are still in temporary quarters, their buildings empty shells along the now-peaceful river.

Floods are complex responses to multiple factors including land use. Here in Iowa, floods are fed by agricultural lands that no longer absorb or hold rainfall like the prairies once did. But climate change, expressed as heavier and more extended rainfall, also may be amplifying floods. The predicted ongoing increase in heavy rainfall through this century implies a still greater potential for localized flooding and increased flood intensity in coming years, just as coastal flooding is predicted to increase as ocean levels rise further.

JUNE 24 ∾ Summer has officially arrived, and with a bang. During the weekend following June 21, the summer solstice, we've had record daily high maximum temperatures across most of the country (92 degrees in Connecticut, 96 in Maryland, 101 in Salt Lake City, a whopping 110 near Phoenix) except along the far west coast, where temperatures were in the 50s and 60s, record June lows. I wonder what Californians are thinking. Are they giving thanks for a changing climate that brings cool temperatures in the normally hot summer?

Here's the thing: there always have been and always will be both cool and hot weather extremes. A single event of either type neither proves nor disproves climate change. Instead, one needs to consider the proportion of cold to hot extremes throughout the year. If the climate were stable, one would expect an equal number of record-high temperatures and record-lows: a 1-to-1 ratio of record heat waves to cold spells.

When I was a young child in 1950, weather happened in this predictable ratio. For every record-breaking heat wave, there was a record-breaking cold spell somewhere else. But since the 1980s, the number of unusually hot days and nights has steadily increased in the U.S., while the number of exceptionally cold days and nights has decreased and is now the lowest on record.

By 2010, this shift resulted in a ratio of U.S. record highs to lows of 2:1—two sweltering heat waves for every bracing cold spell. The 2:1 ratio becomes more skewed if you select a shorter time period. Take this very hot year, for example, from January through March: the ratio of record-daily-high temperatures to record-lows was 17:1. All this goes to say that we now have a much greater chance of experiencing warmth than cold.

If greenhouse-gas emissions continue at current levels, the national ratio of hot to cold extremes is predicted to increase to 20:1 by midcentury and to 50:1 by the century's end. That is, by 2100, we'd have 50 record-high daily temperatures for every single record-low. We will still have cold snaps, but they will have become rare. High temperatures will have become the norm.

Often when thoughts of changing climate upset me, as does the prediction of overwhelming future heat, our woodland sends me comforting affirmation of life's endurance. This morning it came in the form of a dust ball I noticed on the bathroom floor. The dust ball wiggled. Looking closer, I recognized a tree frog caught inside the dirt, the sad result of its living near a screen door that doesn't quite close, which leads into a house that is less than immaculate. The tree frog was miserably shriveled. How long had it been hiding in a corner, I wondered. I removed the threads of dust that had been hampering the frog's movement. Then I took it outside and put it in a shallow basin of water underneath the front deck, where insects were sure to abound. Just a few minutes in the water renewed a look of health to the small frog, which took a giant leap and was gone.

JUNE 26 ⌒ A heat wave that's been broiling in the Rocky Mountains and Great Plains is intensifying and spreading. Denver hit 105 degrees yesterday, its highest temperature in more than 140 years of record keeping; today, the city reached 100 degrees or more for the fifth straight day, another record. Several towns in Kansas reached 109 to 114 degrees in the last few days, temperatures that either equaled or exceeded 1930s Dust Bowl records. Little Rock, Arkansas, spiked at 105, one of the many 100-plus high-temperature records set yesterday. Newspapers are calling this a historic heat wave that is heading toward the Atlantic coast, where it's predicted to bake, sizzle, and fry much of the eastern third of the nation for the next several days.

The widespread intense heat has contributed to wildfires raging across the western U.S. by drying out vegetation and decreasing relative humidity, making it easier for fires to ignite and spread—this in a region already fire-primed by drought, lack of winter snow cover, and abundant dead pines. Parts of Colorado are breaking records for having the hottest, driest span ever documented for a spring and summer, weather that is fueling one of the state's worst fire seasons. Major wildfires are also spreading in Utah, Montana, Wyoming, New Mexico, Arizona, and Idaho, with fires in these states covering hundreds of square miles and being fought by thousands of firefighters. The June wildfires are occurring unusually early in the summer season.

Northern Florida is suffering from another type of extreme weather: heavy rains and sustained winds reaching up to 40 miles per hour. The weak tropical storm causing this havoc dropped over 20 inches of water in one location in one day. Numerous floods are destroying roads and infrastructure inland, and ocean storm surges are expected to amplify dangerous flooding along the coast.

JUNE 28 ⌒ The western heat wave has arrived. Temperatures yesterday reached 101 degrees to my west (in Des Moines) and today they reached 104 to my east (in Keokuk). The heat is paired with increasing worries about very dry weather. Only a quarter of Iowa's soils have adequate moisture for crops. I'm learning to read the drought maps that are commonly displayed on the news. They show the relative intensity of drought, with the least intense category being "moderate," the most intense being "exceptional," and "severe" and "extreme" categories in between. Flipping through a sequence of recent national maps, one for each week, I watch the orange (severe drought) and red (extreme drought) blobs expanding and creeping northward.

JUNE 29 ∾ It's still June, but it feels like deep summer to me. Like hot July summer, when I rock on the porch swing, drink iced lemonade, and talk slowly with gaps between words and thoughts. A lazy time of year, maybe the very laziest. I trace this midsummer impression to the heavy feeling of the air and the late-afternoon singing of cicadas, which this year started their drone in June rather than July, a full month early. And to one more thing—the arrival of local sweet corn at the farmers' market.

This year some of the field corn used primarily for livestock feed, biofuels, and processed food products won't make it. The dry soils are taking their toll, with many fields showing scruffy growth, curling and brown leaves, and bare patches of soil. But farmers who planted sweet corn during the abnormally warm March weather and then watered it through spring are now reaping the benefits: a crop nearly a month ahead of time, enough to charge a premium for each ear.

I bought the early sweet corn. Who can resist it? My sons say that Iowa's sweet corn is better than any they can buy anywhere else. But eating Iowa sweet corn in June feels strange, somehow disjunct and wrong. My gardening neighbor, an ex-farmer, explains it this way: We grow up linking events with seasons. The seasons help us order our lives. They become part of our self-identity. She expects to plant her gardens at certain times of the year, to weed and water them at other times. When those times are mixed up, when there's dissonance between what we experience and what we expect, it's very uncomfortable. "The midwestern seasons that I love are no longer predictable, they are out of synch, and that frightens me at a deep level," she says, adding the question, "I wonder which of my flower gardens will still be blossoming by late summer and fall?"

This year, the seasonal dissonance is traceable to the record-breaking March heat wave followed by an April hard frost. The heat pushed the plants forward, the cold pulled them back. The heat wave is still affecting life here in the woods, where summertime's tall wildflowers—woodland sunflower, joe-pye weed, cup plant—were blossoming in mid-June or earlier, instead of mid- to late summer as is the norm. But I have also observed results of the April freeze. The leaves of baby oaks were killed back and replaced by a second spurt of growth. They looked strange during the transition, minty-green new leaves under umbrellas of dead brown ones. Leaves of a few other trees also froze and withered, and a few soft-tissued plants simply disappeared. But on the whole, the woods seem to have suffered little permanent damage. Not so for the acres of frost-killed blossoms of apple trees in our local orchard, which surely will face major financial losses for the year.

Extreme heat, rain, wind, fire. Thoughts of being in the whirlwind rapidly overwhelm me, and my mind retreats to the woodlands around me, which have actually been quite pleasant these last several weeks. At night, cool, dry breezes blow through the bedroom windows in spurts, filling the room and then retreating, as if the woods were inhaling and exhaling with a whoosh. The healthy pulsing of the planet, flowing in time with the rhythmic sucking of my lungs and the pumping of my heart. The wash of ocean waves and tides, the circling of the sun, the passing of the seasons. The great ebbs and flows of our world, things that we think can never change. When inclement weather forces me to close up the house, I forget these basic realities. But with the house open, when I continuously feel and hear the air move and the animals rustle and sing, I remember how closely my life is tied to everything and how profoundly my actions affect all, as if the many parts of our planet comprise a single living whole.

It comes down to love, I guess, and to the acceptance of cause and effect and my caretaking of the multiple lives that surround me. I remember when our boys were young enough to tuck into bed. I'd feed them, bathe them, rock them, read and sing to them, pray with them, and then watch them nestle under clean sheets and blankets, their eyes heavy with sleep, closing, opening, one last kiss, then closing again and they were gone for the night. Then I would feel silence and peace spread through the house. Such a profound peace, knowing that Robert and my children, those I loved most, were fed and safe and close to me.

Now sometimes on lonely evenings I sit in the dark and try to recreate that sense of total peace, but it doesn't come to me. I can't hear the breathing of my sons or their occasional turning in their beds, can't feel their energy, can't imagine their dream-keepers protecting them from terror or evil. I can't love them as closely as I once did—that's for their own families to do now.

But I can protect the land around me, or at least I imagine that I can. I walk outside to the porch swing and sit in the dusk, feeling the breeze on my arms, watching the bats emerge to feed, hearing the last chirrups of wood pewees returning to their nests and the occasional high-pitched howling of coyote pups. I can imagine the strings that tie them all together, plants feeding the fawns curling up in the woods, caterpillars on milkweeds feeding the songbirds, which in turn feed the owls. All part of a web of molecules and energy that circles around and around, sufficient and complete. I want to put a bubble over this woodland and eliminate any threat: herbicide drift from nearby farm fields, stream waters heavy with nitrates, exotic beetles that kill trees in a single growing season, extreme winds and drought and heavy rainfall. I want to be competent enough to exclude danger, just as I once did with my sleeping boys. But of course I cannot guarantee a safe future. My eyes and spirit grow heavy. I know that tomorrow I will find the energy to once again share my vision of active engagement with the natural world. But tonight I am weary. I need some time off. And so I walk inside and close the door.

FIVE

Memoir
Learning, 1965–1975

IT IS SPRING 1966. MY MOTHER DIED LAST FALL, AND I'VE BEEN at a small liberal arts college ever since, living in a homey dorm with friends who share classes, meals, and late-night talks. Friends whose thoughts and problems have temporarily pulled me out of despondency, friends who care about me and whom I care about, although many days I'm not sure that I care much about myself or what I am doing. How can I when the world around me seems dull and lifeless, when food has no appeal, when I don't hear birds sing or the wind blow?

I feel too tired to wonder about such questions. Sometimes I'm too tired to care about my classes, although amazingly I continue to do well. I am a good student who knows how to follow directions.

Then one day the girl across the hall—a casual acquaintance— calls to me, "I'm walking to the Arb. Come along. It's great outside today." And without thinking, I rise from my desk and fall in beside her, strolling the half mile to the campus arboretum, a strip of land with a shifting creek bordered on both sides by clumps of trees and grassy patches sporting wildflowers—bluebells, forget-me-nots, lilies of the valley. Halfway there her boyfriend joins us, and when we arrive, the two of them disappear down a secluded trail.

Feeling abandoned, I collapse onto a hillside and lie down in the grass—something I haven't done for over a year—and escape into a deep sleep. When I awake, the sun is descending toward the horizon. But I barely notice because right next to my head, I spot an ant climbing a blade of grass while carrying a large seed, an ant who again and again drops the seed before it reaches the top, descends the grass blade, picks up the seed, and restarts its upward climb. Simple repetition. Singular dedication.

I find myself smiling at the ant, and then laughing, and then, with the sun's heat warming my face and the spring breezes cooling it, with kids calling in the distance and bicycles whirring down a nearby trail, with hawks circling high above and cedar waxwings pecking the few remaining chokecherries from nearby trees, I realize that a transformation is under way. For the first time in many months, I am noticing that the grass is green, the ant is black, the seed is tan, and all are waving in breezes that sing through the trees. Color, sound, and motion are returning. Life is moving forward.

And so the natural world, which had trained and inspired me, which had been a mainstay through youth, asked me to return from a land of dull monochrome and invited me to reenter the world of color, of vitality, of life.

I accepted. The next morning I glimpsed the campus dog, an obese beagle who wandered from one dorm to another, head-down in a garbage can with only her tail showing, sticking straight up and wagging. I couldn't stop laughing. That afternoon I threw my shoes into the back of the closet. I wanted to feel grass and rocks under my feet. That night, I stood in velvety blackness on the campus square, listening to a tight cluster of college dropouts talk about why they were walking across the country protesting the war in Vietnam. I accepted the candle they offered and marched with them to the city border.

Little by little I realized that I was where I wanted to be: alive, studying the complexities of animals, plants, and natural systems and relishing the spread of my biology courses—evolution, animal physiology, microbiology, genetics, vascular and nonvascular plants. I learned the life cycles of ferns and mosses, mastered the cellular metabolic pathways that animals use to generate energy, and read about the fox-sized three-toed progenitor of today's horse, Eohippus, with its small brain and arched back.

But I needed a focus, one that looked at the bigger picture, one that would take me from the laboratory outside into the natural world. Thinking that I wanted to learn more about the workings of interacting organisms, I applied for and received a summer scholarship to study at a field research station in the Rocky Mountains high above Boulder, Colorado. So that June and July I spent days hiking from one aspen clump to another, collecting data on the trees and understory plants. I realized that the casual observation of plants I had begun in childhood had a name: ecology, the study of interactions between organisms and the environment. My lifelong love of nature now had a channel to follow. My mind had found its passion.

That summer I discovered another passion. I met Robert on a blind date. He had just graduated from a college back east. We joined another couple and went to eat at a trendy log-walled restaurant in an old mining town. We devoured peanut soup and roast duck, stuffed avocados and apples with blue cheese. When smoke from the fireplace became cloying, I excused myself and went outside to walk through the village. Suddenly he was there with me, smiling, asking me questions about myself. Telling me about how he was in training for a stint as a physicist in Antarctica. We walked the darkened road together, talking, until the other couple came searching for us, ready to call an end to the evening.

The next few weeks, I kept meeting Robert in unexpected places. I'm analyzing soil samples in a Boulder laboratory; he walks in the door. I'm hiking back from a remote aspen clone; he's coming toward me up the trail. Soon we were planning joint rendezvous. One late afternoon we carried sleeping bags and pads up to the tundra and slept under the stars. That night Robert introduced me to the immense, pointing out dying stars and giving them names: white dwarfs, black holes, supernova remnants. The next morning, I introduced him to the minute: tiny-flowered moss-pinks, alpine phlox, alpine avens. By the end of the summer, we were inseparable.

What did it mean to me to fall in love? I wanted to be with Robert constantly. His vitality energized me. His ability to plunge into pursuits where he'd see nature at its extremes—wilderness backpacks, whitewater rafting trips, backcountry ski trips—gave me the courage to do the same. He made me laugh. It seemed that the world was opening through his love for me. I felt that he filled in the ground base that had dissolved when I lost my childhood home, that he created a new rhythm and balance in my life.

The next year, I finished college, and Robert headed for Antarctica. Soon after he returned, we were married in a small Wisconsin town in the same church where my parents had married thirty years before. By the fall of 1971, we were both enrolled in graduate school at the University of Colorado, I in plant ecology, he in astronomy.

During our time in Colorado, we lived in the mountains above Boulder in a small log cabin dwarfed by ponderosa pine trees with broad, rounded crowns and cinnamon-colored bark. Driving the quarter-mile dirt entrance lane, we saw the cabin crouched below us, low and nestled into the land, its reddish brown logs matching the surrounding ponderosa. Farther downslope to the left, an expansive meadow swept to the base of rocky outcrops in the distance. To the right, a shrubby uphill slope gave a clear view of glacier-studded mountaintops several miles to the west, which on winter days shot down an icy wind that slashed through the conifers.

Our cabin, built decades before by a miner, had not been modernized. Therefore no electricity. No running water. No telephone. It did have a pot-bellied stove in the corner for heat, a two-holed outhouse for relieving ourselves, flickering propane lamps for light. The structure preached simplicity, just as my mother's life had years before, and we, in our youth and idealism, settled in.

Soon I was hauling water from the well in the meadow to wash up, traipsing to the outhouse with a candle-lantern at night, and making applesauce from the fruits of a gnarled roadside tree seeded long ago by a tossed apple core. Our lives mimicked the quiet landscape. We slowed down and listened more, in autumn seeking the glimmer of yellow-leaved aspens that shimmered like candles in the darkening forest, in winter stopping to watch the towering ponderosa as they caught the snow. The cabin rapidly became a true home, the first I'd had since my mother's death. The animals and plants, which constantly drew me outside, became my new neighbors.

The mountain landscape provided plenty of views of forest-dwelling animals. One spring, a Williamson's sapsucker woke us each morning by drumming on a rusting tin can capping a nearby fencepost. Once, upon waking, I glanced up to catch a golden eagle soar, then bank just above the bedroom window. Another time, opening the door in a winter snowstorm, a coyote stood two feet from me, peering around my legs into the warmth. A bushy-tailed wood rat established a nest under the cabin; we watched it come in to feed from our dog's bowl during the day and were awakened at night by its random visits. Our final Colorado summer, at precisely 11:03 each morning, a goshawk, normally a secretive and uncommon raptor, soared fast and low past the cabin. I could set my watch by its predictable, elegantly executed hunting route.

As I observed the intricacy of these animals' lives, my respect for survival in the wild grew. One morning I opened the kitchen door and alarmed a Cooper's hawk hulking over a fresh-caught baby rabbit. The startled raptor lifted skyward too rapidly to grab the rabbit twitching in the grass. I watched the hawk flap away, then headed out to check the rabbit, but by then it was limp and still. Feeling for the hawk's loss of a meal, I carried the rabbit down to the meadow and laid it on a rock in the open, hoping that the hawk, now prowling just above the nearby forest edge, would drop down to reclaim its feast.

The animals were captivating, but I was more attracted to the wildflowers that stretched in every direction, replacing the pocket-sized gardens of my Madison youth with unimaginable profusion. In spring and summer I pulled on boots, threw a canteen into a satchel along with an apple, plant guide, and notebook, slung the bag over my shoulder, and headed out to get to know the flowers and grasses that formed the matrix of mountain life. I introduced myself to the early-spring lavender blossoms of pasque flowers, three-petaled purplish spiderworts, the uncommon wood lily, and the splendid miner's candle with its tall showy stalk of white flowers.

The distant mountaintops tempted us to come up and hike. But that was for weekends. During the week, I moved in the other direction—down to campus—where I was busy with classes and research.

My coursework emphasized the patterns and processes of plant communities. I learned about ponderosa pine proliferating at the base of the mountains, ceding to Douglas fir as one climbs upward and temperatures cool, both fading into fir and spruce at the highest altitudes. About the rich grasslands that underlie mature ponderosa pine woodlands, so different from the sparse, scattered wildflowers found under denser, higher conifers. About the fragility of the tundra draped over the mountaintops, which survives the scantiest growing season.-

My blossoming knowledge of plant relationships was reinforced by observations around our home. Sun-filled ponderosa groves proliferated on level land near the cabin. But if I wandered onto sheltered north-facing slopes, I entered cool, dark, dense forests of Douglas fir. Meadow grasses covered the low-lying lands east of the cabin. I waded through their ephemeral ponds in the springtime, delighting in the abundance and brilliance of wild iris blossoms.

My favorite place was the aspen grove that thrived on the moist, rich soils at the meadow's edge near our well. The aspens' white bark set off their sparkling leaves, which quivered with even the slightest breeze. Together with the sprinkling of columbines, wild geraniums, lilies, and lupines in flower, they created an oasis of twinkling light, color, and delicacy.

In summertime, I came to the aspen grove to bathe, dragging in a discarded watering tank, filling it with water from the well, and leaving it to warm until midday. Then I returned to plunge, lather, plunge again, then leap out and wrap myself in a blanket, my shivering completing the refreshing cleanse.

As I came to understand patterns of plant growth and senescence, adaptation and evolution in wild lands that seemed to stretch on forever, I felt as if I was becoming one with the natural order. I recognized that I was being given a vision that was unavailable to many, one of a timeless world where plants and animals followed inbred patterns unhampered by human interference, where nature remained intact and fully functional, capable of maintaining itself indefinitely. I treasured the gift of that vision.

I also recognized that these principles were played out on an immense scale that regulated the world. Plants and animals do not cover the globe helter-skelter. They live in identifiable communities that have been fine-tuned for thousands of years, with plants developing physiological adaptations to particular climates and soils and animals adapting to what plants provide.

Healthy communities deliver ecosystem services, which as a group comprise the planet's life-support systems, services such as filtering and storing fresh water, providing homes for pollinators and insect-controlling bats and birds, cleansing the air, generating rich soils, decomposing wastes, and soaking up carbon dioxide in trade for the oxygen we breathe. Thus, healthy natural ecosystems create a world that is self-renewing and resilient, ultimately and infinitely sustainable. A beneficent world that is trustworthy, knowable, and orderly—the same kind of world I had inhabited as a child.

But wait. Even as I lived there, I saw that my idyllic daily life in the Colorado mountains did not reflect ongoing changes in the larger world. This was the early 1970s. The air and water, forests and meadows in many places were not in good shape. Environmental deterioration was on the upswing. Across the country, public concern was giving rise to a new and energetic environmental movement.

And so, even as I was studying nature's integrity, I began discovering how out-of-control growth of many types was spreading throughout the landscape, threatening the health of the natural world. I learned that a major shift had occurred since World War II. While I was a naïve child, "more" and "bigger" became a national mantra. More and bigger homes, buildings, cars, cities. The U.S. population was growing larger and moving to the suburbs, which were filling with ever-larger houses that sprawled over neighboring farmland, houses that held new and larger appliances, all of which demanded more and still more electricity that came mostly from growing numbers of power plants burning fossil fuels. Urban mass transit systems floundered as soaring numbers of cars took to the road, creating a major escalation in the nation's use of petroleum.

In the countryside, farmers increasingly used synthetic pesticides, fertilizers, and feed additives to boost production.

As the U.S. population and per-person consumption grew, fossil fuel use soared exponentially. Resources were depleted. Native plants and animals dropped in number. And toxic wastes multiplied. Local problems inflated into regional dilemmas, and regional problems spread around the globe.

And meanwhile, the unwanted wastes of all this proliferation—raw sewage, urban runoff, agricultural and industrial chemicals, toxins, particulates and sulfur dioxide and nitrogen oxides from burning fossil fuels, and diverse industrial effluents—were spewing into the air and gushing into rivers and lakes. People protested, but industries, electrical generating stations, municipalities, and individuals continued to pollute the air and water with impunity, for what they were doing was perfectly legal.

Once dumped, these pollutants began their treachery: people developed respiratory and heart problems; masses of fish died in toxin-laden rivers foaming with detergents; raptor eggs contaminated by DDT were crushed by incubating parents; airborne sulfur and nitrogen oxides turned into acids that rained down on gardens, lakes, and forests; large cities smoldered under a sickly yellow smog that contained ozone, which aggravated asthma and reduced lung function; rivers stank from sewage and industrial waste; algal blooms fertilized by city sewage and farm runoff turned lakes into pea soup; lead added to gasoline entered the air and caused developmental delays and learning difficulties in young children.

In January of 1969, an oil well offshore of Santa Barbara, California, blew out, spilling an estimated 100,000 barrels of crude oil—the largest U.S. oil spill to date—which infiltrated surrounding ocean waters, killing untold numbers of marine mammals and birds. Several months later, about the time I was handed my college diploma, an inches-thick oil slick on the Cuyahoga River flowing through Cleveland, one of the most polluted rivers in the U.S., burst into flames. The river had caught fire over a dozen times before, but this burn was widely reported by the press. These two major and highly visible disasters generated significant public outrage. Even the most reluctant citizens had to concede that the misuse of nature had overstepped its bounds.

Finally, with these two calamities, the people of the United States, both through private action and through their governments at all levels, took steps to rein in the many forms of runaway growth, constrain environmental catastrophes, and restore nature's health. On January 1, 1970, the National Environmental Policy Act was signed into law, requiring that federal agencies consider the environmental impacts of their actions. In December of that year, the U.S. Environmental Protection Agency was created as a legal, regulatory, and research agency for environmental issues. And between those two governmental actions, on April 22, 1970, the first Earth Day—a privately organized day of protest—brought 20 million people into the streets. One out of every ten people then in the U.S. The largest demonstration in American history.

This launch of the modern environmental movement generated a spate of legislation directed toward righting particular environmental wrongs. Over the next several years, bills were created and amended to regulate pesticide use, toxic substances, air pollution, water pollution, drinking water, mining, marine mammals, fisheries, coastal zones, oceans, vehicular exhaust, endangered species, hazardous waste management, federal-lands management, and more. Things started to happen. Catalytic converters were attached to vehicle tailpipes, scrubbers were added to industrial and electrical generating plant smokestacks, and sewage treatment plants were built in cities and towns across the country. Workers in hazmat suits started to clean up toxic waste sites. In 1972, the United Nations established its Environment Programme, creating an international voice for addressing environmental issues. That same year, the U.N. Conference on the Human Environment—the first major summit of its kind—was held in Stockholm.

Because of these efforts and more recent legislation, we no longer accept that soot or smog might be discoloring our lungs, that it's all right if rainwater kills fish or turns forests brown, that raw sewage is allowed to float through rivers and lakes, or that environmental toxins like lead and mercury could be poisoning our children. On the whole, we live in a different world, one that's cleaner, healthier, and more beautiful because individually and collectively, we took action. Who would ever want to go back to the times when the opposite was true?

During this period, we came to accept that our planet had limits. We could not engage in unfettered expansion and resource depletion without major consequences. We also believed that once a problem was recognized and defined, it could be solved. These were heady times.

Back then we correctly identified two major drivers of environmental degradation: accelerating human population growth (which is closely linked to increased resource consumption), and the loss of biodiversity (which reduces ecological resilience and Earth's self-renewing abilities).

However, back in the 1970s, we were unaware that a larger problem was starting to threaten our planet: a silent swelling of greenhouse gases. It was true that since 1958, climate scientists had routinely measured the rise of atmospheric carbon dioxide. And also true that they understood that this gas could retain heat and raise Earth's surface temperatures. But in 1970, the increase in atmospheric carbon dioxide seemed relatively small, and global average temperature had changed little for several decades. Nearly everyone pushed the possible results of global warming into future centuries and future generations—well beyond the time people then alive would be affected. Increasing carbon dioxide was something that was invisible and happening far away. Out of sight and out of mind. If only we had paid closer attention, I now think, to the ever-higher levels of atmospheric carbon dioxide. If only we had recognized this gas's power and acted then to curb its increase. If only . . .

But, as is always true, more immediate problems claimed our attention. Perhaps that was what had happened with my mother as well. She may have kept tending the family's daily problems even as she felt changes that were undermining her health. I'll never know. I didn't think about those sorts of things then, although I did wonder what my life would have been like if Mom hadn't died, she who had been security and home to me.

Although her absence sometimes haunted my dreams, I don't remember thinking about her illness. Or the fact that cancer cells might be silently proliferating in my own body, as they surely had for years in hers. If such thoughts had come to mind, I would have shoved them deep into the recesses of my mind. It was inconceivable that my body might be following my mother's disassembling, even though I was daily learning about ecosystem illnesses, pesticides building invisibly in the waters, pollutants drifting silently through blue skies, natural systems approaching a tipping point. Even though, unrecognized by us, increasing carbon dioxide was preventing heat from escaping Earth's atmosphere.

But why dwell on potential problems before being forced to do so? Our days were full and good. I was relishing life with someone I loved, along with our shared home, the studies that stretched my mind, regular hikes through forests and across boulder fields. I focused on predictable, reliable patterns that governed Earth's health. In spite of my growing knowledge of environmental problems, I assumed that humanity could never irreversibly alter two of Earth's largest entities, the globe's atmosphere and its oceans, nor could we ever destabilize something as huge and complex as our planet's climate system. And I never considered that my body would ever turn against itself as my mother's had done.

Robert and I sit outside our cabin in rickety wooden chairs with green peeling paint. We're facing east, looking out over the meadow. It's early morning. We don't say much. There's nothing that needs saying. Our only task is to feel the morning's sunshine and spring-cooled breezes on our faces, to witness the butter-yellow flecks of golden banner flowers waving nearby, to inhale the piney scents of ponderosas warming in the new day's sunlight, to hear the rasp of the blue-black Steller's jays. We are in a daze, still half asleep.

A flock of pine siskins is feeding in nearby trees, clinging to the branch tips and twittering incessantly. A pair of circling red-tailed hawks floats over the meadow below. In the distance a great-horned owl, awake even though it's daytime, calls crisp and clear. Robert casually reaches over and takes my hand. Soon he will head down to campus. I will stay here and work on what will become my first book—a guide to Colorado ecosystems. But at the moment, lost in the mystery, there is no expectation of should-dos or timeframes. Our thoughts are timeless. They float vaguely around one belief: if all that we did in life was to learn the songs sung by other species and watch this complicated interlocking natural world drift past, it would be enough. We would lack for nothing.

PART III

Summer

SIX

Weather & Climate Journal
July–September, 2012

JULY 1 ❧ Summertime. A time of quieting in the woods when the babies that abound everywhere demand food and care. Young downy woodpeckers have been coming to the feeder and learning to assert their rights to sunflower seeds. They are far more subdued than the families of red-headed woodpeckers that swoop down en masse, then rise and dip as a group, their young marked by gray-brown heads. Deer mice are proliferating near the garbage can, building in numbers that I know will push them into the woodshed and garage when the weather chills. Sometimes a mother skunk leads a string of babies to feast at the compost pile. Very cute, from a distance. Walking in the woods yesterday, I nearly stepped on two fawns, one after the other. They lay motionless, so I didn't see them until they leapt up in front of me and sprinted away, looking back as if to ask whether I was dangerous. I knew their mothers were nearby, watching.

I often see babies on the road. Last week a young chipmunk was sitting there on its haunches, front feet up, turning its head this way and that. It didn't know to flee an approaching car, so I put on the blinkers and got out, clapping my hands until it finally ran into the roadside shrubs. I did the same with a young barred owl a few days later. A foot tall but still half fluff, it wasn't yet adept at flying. Again, blinkers on, clapping my hands until finally it half ran, half flopped into the nearby brush.

The owl reminded me of the night many years ago when Matt and I saw a good-sized rounded hump moving across the road. I jammed on the car brakes, and we jumped out to see a mother badger herd her three cubs into tall roadside grasses. The mother turned back to bare her teeth and growl as her babies escaped.

A few years ago, a snarl of snakes crossed the same roadway, migrating from our neighbor's pasture to their hibernation site in our woods. Young brownsnakes, they were only half as large as the normally foot-long adults. Each day for a week, five, eight, sometimes ten snakes were flattened by cars. What could I do but watch and count?

A young tree frog lives on the deck. If I don't close the front door tightly, it hops inside the house, and I find it in the front hall or kitchen. I'm learning to watch where I step, remembering the night I annihilated a full-grown toad. Young Andy had brought it inside. The untimely landing of my foot was not pleasant for the toad or for me. I remember the years when our three little boys would run around the woods chasing bands of tiny toads, each the size of a fingernail, leaping this way and that in an attempt to escape. Those that were caught were put into a jar that (on my insistence) would be emptied before bedtime. I wasn't so lucky when Chris found a nest of deer mice and snuck the nearly grown babies into the house in an outmoded gerbil cage. They promptly escaped, and catching them with our hands was impossible. They were too fast. We had no recourse but to trap them. Just as I had no recourse yesterday when Sidney proudly ran up to me and dropped a baby rabbit at my feet, one that mercifully was dead upon arrival.

Insects too are appearing in miniature forms. I find young bright green katydids on the front door at night. Soon I'll see tiny walking sticks crawling about. I'll put them on the trunk of an oak so they can climb into the canopy, eat leaves, and grow to adults thinner than a pencil but four inches long. I'm less conciliatory about the masses of ants and ant eggs that I find under rocks or pieces of wood. Immediately upon discovery, each adult ant grabs a white egg and runs.

So many babies, so much overflowing life. Only a small portion of these young will live to maturity and reproduce. It's meant to be that way. If all the newborn animals lived to adulthood, we would be wallowing through them, and none of them would have the resources to stay alive. Our woods, our planet, can support only a certain number of deer, woodpeckers, frogs, and even ants, and although the world's carrying capacity is somewhat malleable, it is not infinite. We humans, one of the few species that produces young year-round, would do well to learn this lesson.

JULY 2 ∾ Several days ago, I was looking forward to taking Sidney for an afternoon walk when I heard the tornado sirens go off. I turned on the radio, which immediately blurted out a severe storm warning: heavy rain and hail on the way, dangerous winds up to 80 miles an hour. I studied the radar website on my computer. A deep red blotch was moving toward our woods. I brought in the laundry and took flashlight and computer into the basement. Then I watched and waited. A bit of rain, a little wind. The electricity flickered on and off, as if in warning. Then nothing happened. Then a little more rain and wind, followed by more nothing.

I've been told that people will start to take climate change seriously when it interferes with their everyday lives and livelihoods. When they can't do the things they need to do because of high temperatures or erratic storms. That afternoon, sitting in the basement, I agreed. I couldn't do anything except sit and wait. I yelled at the computer screen, telling the red blotch to move through and finish its dirty work. But the red blotch approached very slowly, its intensity throbbing as it came toward our house.

It seems as though half the news this summer concerns severe weather in the U.S. The same was true last year, 2011, which was perhaps the most extreme weather year to date since reliable record keeping began in the 1800s: drought, heat waves, wildfires fueled by the intense heat and drought-desiccated vegetation, tornadoes, and tremendous floods, many of these record-breaking events. The year 2011 set a record for having the most billion-dollar-plus disasters of any year in U.S. history, with fourteen such disasters totaling over $55 billion in damages; 2011 was also the world's costliest year on record for natural disasters, with total global losses of over $380 billion.

And those, I'm sure, were just the biggest and most obvious

expenses. I was in the basement waiting for the storm to hit because the day before, my department's air conditioning had been turned off as a university-wide cost-saving decision. People in offices around me dripped and dribbled away as the day progressed and temperatures rose, slipping off to nearby coffee shops or home, but I was determined to stick the day out, even though my head was too hot and foggy to get much done. When I finally left, I vowed to work at home the following day.

Climate change is becoming enormously expensive in so many ways. I make a short list: costs of recovery from intense weather events, repairing damage to infrastructure such as heat-buckled roads, cancellations and lost work time due to extreme weather, addressing increased illness, fighting invasive species that are spreading with the warmth, loss of nature and the ecosystem services it provides such as cleansing water and air and building soils, constructing safeguards such as seawalls, dealing with increased social upheaval and rising numbers of environmental refugees. The list could be endless. My unproductive day in a very hot office and the following afternoon in our home's basement were a loss to the university. But that cost is small compared to these many other expenses.

Comprehensive analyses conclude that the cost of dealing with climate change by reducing carbon emissions would be a small fraction of the expense of damages imposed by unabated climate change. What's more, shifting the world to a low-carbon path could produce trillions of dollars of benefits annually. Who's to say that we can't afford to stopper the planet's rising temperatures by developing carbon-free energy sources? How can we afford *not* to do so?

As I sat in the basement watching my computer screen, the throbbing red blotch finally dissolved, and the skies lightened. The dangerous storm had dissipated before reaching our home. This time, I was one of the lucky ones.

JULY 3 ◑ Several days ago, on June 29, one of the most destructive fast-moving thunderstorm complexes in North American history roared from Illinois across the Appalachians to the Mid-Atlantic coast. Hurricane-force winds covered a broad swath 700 miles long in a very short period of time, hitting many communities without warning. The massive storm—a derecho, a powerful, long-lasting straight-line windstorm—was unprecedented and unparalleled. Its power was multiplied by the extensive extreme heat wave blanketing the eastern U.S., with temperatures in the 90s and 100s. In addition to fueling the storm, the record-high temperatures increased the difficulties of living through and dealing with the wind's destruction, especially for the over 4 million people who lost electricity to cool their homes and store and prepare food. After the storm roared through the heavily populated Washington, D.C.–Baltimore metropolitan area and blew out to sea, the nation's capital and suburbs were described as being in post-apocalypse mode, with about a quarter of all households having lost electricity. Early damage estimates for the derecho were $3 to $4 billion.

This year's heat waves and their spinoffs remind us that Earth's sweltering temperatures—the most obvious consequence of rising greenhouse gases—are not the only results of climate change. Heat is thermal energy, and along with global average temperatures, the amount of atmospheric energy has been steadily rising. That thermal energy needs to go somewhere; and both weather patterns and detailed computer models tell us that it's fueling greater atmospheric instability and turbulence. This leads to faster wind speeds, more powerful thunderstorms, and greater weather unpredictability. Some types of storms are becoming larger and more severe, erratic, unprecedented, and unusual. "Weather on steroids," as some reporters state.

The rise in extreme precipitation events and flooding is only one such example. In addition, tropical cyclones—hurricanes, typhoons, and other such storms fueled by warming ocean waters around the globe—are growing stronger, although they have not necessarily increased in number. Peak wind speeds are increasing. These events are already intensifying more rapidly than had been predicted.

Climate models predict that in coming decades, as greenhouse-gas concentrations rise further and the growing heat energy is dissipated in progressively more unpleasant manners, today's extreme events will become more frequent and commonplace. Hurricanes are predicted to become even more intense, heat waves will become hotter, droughts drier, and downpours will drop more water. Ocean storm surges will rise further. More and more people and communities will suffer from weather events that are increasingly the worst, the biggest, the hottest, the wettest, the wildest, the most bizarre, the most destructive, the most costly. Weather's rising deviation from the long-term norms will confound attempts to plan and establish safeguards.

It's not a pretty picture. To me, it's a terrifying one. Our planet is clearly giving us a message. "What we're seeing is a window into what global warming really looks like," stated one earth scientist, referring to this year's weather panoply. "It looks like heat. It looks like fires." Other climate scientists explain that while it's too early to delineate specific causes for any individual heat wave, drought, flood, or windstorm, these are the kinds of extremes expected to increase as the earth gets warmer.

Sometimes I find myself feeling smug about escaping the year's most extreme weather and its spinoffs, being glad that I live far from rising oceans and hurricane zones, far from western evergreen forests turning into tinderboxes. Yet I know that these events affect me even now, here in Iowa. A week ago, 346 homes in Colorado Springs burned in one night in the worst wildfire in Colorado's history; the previous week, 259 homes were lost in a Fort Collins conflagration. The news this morning reported that smoke from Colorado wildfires is now floating over Iowa. At the same time, heat in southern states is pushing northward over the central U.S. I can't be too smug if I look at all the facts: what affects one of us affects us all, in one way or another. Encircled by a ring of extreme events, all of which may be related to a warming world, I feel them as a gradually tightening noose. I know that my time must come.

JULY 5 ∿ The last few days, once again, it's been very hot, temperatures in the upper 90s, sometimes over 100. If I am active outside,

I drip sweat within ten minutes. The sun scorches my skin. I turn red even though I'm doused with sunscreen.

And so I've been spending a lot of time inside, where I'm cool and dry. But this morning, before the air turned blistering, I ventured onto the porch and couldn't pull myself back inside, everything was so alive. Nuthatches at the feeder. The resonant call of a rose-breasted grosbeak. Flickers' more piercing calls. A house wren in the distance—I could imagine it flitting from a tree trunk to the ground to grab an insect. The gentle pecking of baby downy woodpeckers. The tentative chirrup of a tree frog. A young hummingbird visited the feeder—so tiny! The air seemed to be still, but every once in a while a puff of air blew across the deck, a quiet midsummer zephyr.

Inside the house the noise is constant, the fans and the dehumidifier emitting an ongoing hum. White noise, not the rainbow of sound I hear outside. I'd like to open the house to these songs, to the subtly vibrating energy. But I have things to worry about. I don't want our clothes smelling musty. I don't want our leather and antique furniture growing mildew. I own so many things that I spend my life caring for. So I live in split worlds, but mostly inside. The house sometimes feels like a casket, but a comfortably cool one.

JULY 7 Ꮗ Yesterday I did errands in the midday sun and came home exhausted and achy, unable to focus or do much of anything. I went to bed early. I think I must have been reacting to the 104-degree temperatures and intense, unrelenting sunshine. It's hard to stay out of the sun when doing errands at midday—and even walking from the car across the black parking lot to the grocery store gave me a headache that lasted into the night.

Temperatures are not necessarily breaking the all-time records for Iowa. During the 1930s Dust Bowl, Keokuk reached an all-time state high of 118 degrees. But the number of recent days in the high 90s to low 100s has to be unusual. And you don't have to break the record to be too hot.

Climate change is predicted to produce more hot spells like this one with fewer cooling interludes. I'll be surprised if the legacy of the March average temperature, 30 degrees above the norm, is not carrying through the season to produce an all-time high average temperature for the year. My friends without air conditioning bemoan the fact that temperatures aren't dropping during the night. We need cooler air. I'm looking forward to the low 90s temperatures predicted for the coming week.

Climate-change models predict that Earth's rising temperatures will push both ends of the water continuum, magnifying the extremes. Greater heat leads to more extreme rainfall, but greater heat also intensifies natural drought cycles. Droughts become more severe because higher temperatures amplify evaporation, which then sucks moisture from already-parched terrain. Thus, in years that are hot and dry, the landscape becomes drier and hotter still.

Already, the year seems to be demonstrating this principle. In the last few weeks, drought has claimed half of Iowa, including this part of the state, and the drought is spreading and becoming more severe both here and across the country. Only the far northern and eastern states have escaped the plight.

Iowa has been notably short of rain in the last few months. Now, even if we have a fleeting rainstorm, any precipitation that falls evaporates quickly into the hot skies. But other conditions have also contributed to Iowa's current situation, starting with the very dry late summer and fall last year, which depleted the soil moisture. Western Iowa in particular was already abnormally dry at the beginning of 2012. Then March's high temperatures spiraled evaporation upward. Now July's heat is further baking Iowa's soils and magnifying the drought. The same is true across the country.

In coming years, in the U.S., climate change's rising temperatures are expected to intensify natural drought cycles even more, so that droughts will become more significant in many areas and will magnify water scarcity and wildfire problems. Western states in particular are likely to become drier, with drought intensity increasing especially in the Southwest.

JULY 10 ∾ Last night, cooler air dropped down from the north. Walking Sidney, Robert and I commented on how fresh and crisp the 84-degree air felt. You do get used to things.

And then, at 4:30 this morning, I woke up and went out on the deck. The moon hung directly above the house. A single bullfrog droned from a distant pond; otherwise all was still. I realized that I was outside in an early-morning sound gap—after nighttime insects had ceased their serenades but before birdsong had started. Then a distant barred owl called to its mate, who answered from a tree next to the house, its single-noted scream so close and shrill that it sounded like a knife severing the air. Every minute or so, I heard the flutter of a bat passing over my head, and I could see bats in the sky above me finishing their nighttime feast. Pea-sized acorns dropped from trees high above to ping off the roof. I've noted the ground covered with them lately. I think these acorns are aborting because of the drought. Many mammals reabsorb their fetuses if they are starving. Why shouldn't oaks drop their acorns if they have no water? A few minutes later, the eastern wood pewee started its dawn song and a cardinal answered, then a whip-poor-will. The first sounds of the new day, emerging 45 minutes before the morning's first light.

JULY 13 ∾ The heat has returned. The drought continues to spread. The radio announced that it's getting worse fast and that relief is months away. Now nearly the entire middle section of the nation, from eastern Ohio to California, is solidly entrenched in drought, a dramatic increase in just the last week. The drought footprint covers nearly two-thirds of the country. In much of Iowa, dry conditions have morphed to true drought, although the most severely affected regions remain to the south of Iowa. This intensification is happening at the same time that farmers are receiving federal aid for crops suffering from the untimely April frost.

Because of the drought, over 1,000 counties across the Corn Belt have been declared natural disaster areas, the largest single such designation on record. U.S. corn production forecasts have been cut by 12 percent, soybean forecasts by 5 percent. A quarter of the state is now under a burn ban: no open fires are allowed, including those in outdoor grills. Even though I water the flower boxes every day, my plants wilt within a few hours.

JULY 14 ∾ Greenland's ice sheet is again in the news, and for good reason. If Greenland's mountains of ice were released, sea levels around the globe would eventually rise 23 feet. And in the last week, a heat dome over the island initiated thawing of 97 percent of the island's surface ice sheet. (The norm, in any given summer, is for half of the ice sheet to surface-thaw.) This year's extraordinary melt occurred rapidly, spreading across the island in four days, even up and over Greenland's summits nearly two miles above sea level, initiating intense runoff.

The heat dome was short-lived. Within a few days it started dissipating, and the melting slowed and stopped. But with unprecedented events such as these, glaciologists feel that more changes are definitely under way. And those changes could have major global implications. Unlike the Arctic Ocean's floating sea ice, which is already a part of the oceans and thus, when it melts, does little to raise ocean levels, Greenland's ice is nearly all on land. If the entire mass of that ice were released into the surrounding oceans over coming centuries, the melt-water would swamp coastal areas around the globe.

Another possible long-term result: our planet's weather is governed by major ocean currents such as the Gulf Stream, as well as high-altitude air streams like the polar jet stream. If Greenland's melt were rapid, the release of large quantities of fresh water could slow or halt the Gulf Stream, which brings warm waters into the North Atlantic. The elimination of these tepid inflows would act as a cooling influence on the climate in Europe and eastern North America. This prospect is more than theoretical: studies show that this process occurred at the end of the last Ice Age, initiating a North Atlantic cold period that lasted over a thousand years.

Scientists believe it very unlikely that such a major slowdown process will occur this century. So I should not live long enough to see such changes. And yet, when I read about them, I feel my body tensing and my stomach clenching in fear. I force myself to close my eyes and take a deep breath, and remind myself that neither of these massive changes is imminent. However, I know that rising temperatures will continue to whittle away at the ice, and that much remains unknown about the ice sheets and their rates of change. The melting of Greenland could require thousands of years. But even a partial Greenland melt would raise the global sea level significantly. And there could be surprises. The ice sheets are proving to be more sensitive to climate than was previously believed, and we know that in the distant past, collapsing ice sheets have raised ocean levels in just a few centuries. Once self-reinforcing feedback loops are established and Greenland's melting is seriously under way, it would be virtually unstoppable.

At the end of May, for the first time in recorded history, atmospheric carbon dioxide concentrations spiked at 400 ppm at several Arctic sites. They did not remain that high for the entire day but, as with Greenland's melt event, implications for the future are clear.

JULY 17 ∾ The grandkids are here visiting. Right now they are playing with Legos in the living room. I love it when they come. The house feels more alive, more purposeful, as if it's nourished by their youth and energy. Sidney loves it too; she follows the kids around, asking if she can be one of the gang and nuzzling their pockets for hidden scraps of food.

Normally they'd be outside exploring, but not today. Something has died close to the house. The smell pervades the air—you can't track it to a source. The heat only adds to the insult: whoever is rotting out there is doing so with gusto. We'll have to avoid the stench until decomposition has completed its job.

I can't complain about the heat: temperatures rise to 100 degrees nearly every midsummer somewhere in Iowa. We always have days when we retreat to our home's shelter, close the curtains, and seek dark corners for shade and coolness. But there have been so many very hot days this year—weeks at a time with heat indexes well into the 100s, temperatures that feel like 102, 109, 124, 115. Day after day, with no cooling down at night. These very hot days and nights used to be scattered and were the exception. Now the exception is becoming the rule.

This change toward greater warmth in all seasons is robbing me of some of my greatest pleasures. I love stepping into a bracing wind and bundling up against the cold. Even in midsummer I want the early mornings to feel and smell fresh, not wilted like my plants in the flower boxes.

This afternoon I'll take the grandkids into town to the swimming pool. I know that every time I drive, I am in a small way worsening the climate-change problem. But I live in the country, and I need to do errands and get to work. And while I have at times biked the eight miles into town, today, when the asphalt is melting and bubbling in the heat and intense sunshine, bicycling feels nearly impossible to me.

JULY 18 ∽ Stories of drought's effects on agriculture are becoming front-page news. The drought is becoming more severe just at a critical time for corn development—pollination. High temperatures greatly reduce the pollen count so that fewer kernels grow on each corncob. Low moisture intensifies this effect, causing yields to plummet. Soybeans too need moisture in mid-July to plump out their developing pods. Iowa's current crops were planted with hopes of near-record yields; now it's feared that if we don't get some relief from the heat and drought in the next week, yields will drop significantly.

Livestock also are suffering. Farmers have reported losses of thousands of chickens. With the summer's heat and drought, cattle and hog farmers are dealing with poor pastures and decreasing hay production. High temperatures also can lower milk production in dairy cattle and lessen weight gain and breeding efficiency in beef cattle and hogs. And, as projected corn harvests decline, the cost of livestock feed rises. Some farmers are feeding hay now that they should be keeping for next winter. Already there's talk about farmers culling their cattle herds due to insufficient feed. In California the heat is affecting vegetables, and field workers are being sent home due to danger of heat stroke. All these agricultural shortages raise the specter of increases in retail food prices, as well as loss of billions of dollars from decreased U.S. agricultural exports.

In coming years, as the globe's warming climate pushes drought intensity still higher, we are likely to see more agricultural failures. Fortunately, agriculture on the whole is considered to be more adaptable to changing climate than many sectors, and some crops may even benefit from climate change, at least in the short term. Research shows that adding carbon dioxide to the atmosphere stimulates the productivity of certain crops such as soybeans. The warming planet's lengthening of the growing season also raises yields by, for example, allowing earlier planting or even two crops per year.

But the broad effects of climate change are rarely straightforward or simple. Higher carbon dioxide levels benefit corn only a bit, and benefits may fade as carbon dioxide levels rise above moderate amounts. The higher temperatures that stretch out the growing season also decrease the growth and yield of wheat and rice, as well as corn and soybeans. And they further compromise agriculture by encouraging undesirable, yield-limiting agricultural weeds, diseases, insects, and new pest species that are spreading northward. Detrimental pests are likewise encouraged by the higher atmospheric and soil moisture that commonly accompany rising temperatures; Iowa's farmers are already using more fungicides in response to fungal growth stimulated by rising moisture.

Perhaps most importantly, extreme weather events will increasingly influence crop yields. This year has demonstrated the grand disruptions that such events can cause to fruit production: between the April freeze and summertime drought, Iowa is losing virtually its entire 2012 apple crop. Add to these stressors the increasingly intense rains and accompanying erosion, floods, and winds, and net gains from a longer growing season or rising atmospheric carbon dioxide start to fade. Some climate problems may be overcome by new crop strains that better tolerate weather extremes or by different farming practices, but with weather's divergence from long-term norms, farmers will find it more and more difficult to plan appropriately.

The net result? According to the consensus of recent studies, until approximately 2040, shifts in crop growth and farming practices should allow U.S. agriculture to be relatively resilient or perhaps even benefit from climate change. (Unfortunately the opposite will be true in the tropics, where both dry periods and periods of heavy rainfall are expected to intensify.) However, by midcentury, as climate change strengthens, heat and precipitation extremes are likely to override agricultural benefits. By around 2050, yields of major U.S. crops and livestock productivity are projected to decline. The global picture is similar, with gradually intensifying challenges to agriculture as this century unfolds. Not all the expert analyses agree with this picture, but most do, and the risks are profound.

This timing is unfortunately correlated with a predicted rise of the world's population by approximately 30 percent, from this year's 7 billion to 9 or 10 billion people by 2050. In future years, feeding the added 2.5-or-so billion people will present challenges regardless of weather. Thus food security will increasingly dominate international affairs, complemented by water security as higher temperatures magnify water stresses.

JULY 24 ∾ Dry conditions across the U.S. have not expanded in the last few weeks, but they have intensified. Examining the government's drought maps, I realize that extreme drought is now extending its inflated tentacles across the nation's midsection. Parts of the midcontinent now fall into the most intense drought category, exceptional drought. All of Iowa is now rated as being in severe or extreme drought, with more intense drought encircling the state on all sides except to the north.

This morning I watched a young hummingbird trying to access the red sugary liquid in the hummingbird feeder, a glass tube with feeding holes near the bottom. The hummer didn't realize that it could insert its bill into these holes. Instead, it kept trying to peck at the red liquid behind the glass, flying forward—hitting hard—retreating—over and over again. Every once in a while, it poked its long bill into one of the feeding holes, but it needed several tries before figuring out that it could drink the liquid sugar through these holes—this was definitely a learned behavior.

So too with a young downy woodpecker, who learned how to drink from the hummers' feeder by watching the older downy do so. The young woodpecker sat on a nearby tree, its head cocked, staring at the mature bird, who has been drinking from this feeder for the past few years. Finally the young downy flew down, took a few pecks, figured out where to insert its bill, and was hooked. Now that I have two woodpeckers who will regularly feed with the hummingbirds, I'll be filling the feeder even more often than before.

Our woodland creek has dried up, and the understory wildflowers are not producing seeds as they should—a sign that our woodland's plants are being stressed by the heat and dry soils. Yet I'm amazed at how good most of our trees and wildflowers look, their roots apparently finding moisture in soil that appears waterless to me. The plants are aided by cooler temperatures in the shady woods—which are usually three or four degrees cooler than on the sunny road—but in addition the native woodland plants are adapted to live through dry periods. Most are perennials that develop a permanent, deep root system capable of plying distant soils for any available water. Using these well-developed roots, the leaves of most woodland plants have remained green and supple, their stems standing erect in the early morning light. A few, such as the tall joe-pye weeds and woodland sunflowers, may droop as the day's heat rises, their lanky stems bending earthward like shepherd's crooks. But later in the afternoon, when temperatures cool and intense sunlight fades, they manage to recover and again stand upright.

Nearby prairies, also populated by native perennial plants, are thriving. Prairie blossoms line our county roads with abundant flowers in pinks, lavenders, reds, and golden yellows. Prairie plants are survivors that flourish in the dry heat, their roots stretching down over ten feet to find hidden waters. For thousands of years, prairies have used these deep root systems to survive.

While our woods look good, garden flowers planted in nearby cities are turning yellow and shriveling in the heat. Many city trees also are not doing well, their leaves turning red or brown and falling. They aren't adapted to this dry heat. And shallow-rooted lawns have dried to a brown crisp, except where trees or shrubs offer a bit of shade. Homeowners are advised to give their lawns a good soaking if they are brown for over a month. Ironically, this watering need is arising just as some Iowa cities are posting water-use restrictions.

Meanwhile other locations around the world are suffering from the opposite extreme. Torrential downpours and flash floods are threatening the London Olympics as I write, and a few days ago an 18-inch rain hit parts of Beijing, China, inundating streets, killing dozens, forcing evacuations of 60,000, cancelling 500 flights, stranding more than 80,000 travelers, and causing over $1.6 billion in damages.

JULY 26 ℘ Bracing myself against the heat, I trudged up to the road to find the newest edition of the journal *Science* jammed in our mailbox. Its arrival was fortuitous: rocking in the porch chair while drinking lemonade, I read of new laboratory research that revealed a potential link between climate change and ozone in the upper atmosphere, where the ozone filters out ultraviolet radiation that otherwise could burn our skin, multiply rates of skin cancer, and damage crops.

The research showed that massive storms could pump water vapor miles upward into the normally dry stratosphere, where the moisture then would destroy protective ozone by invigorating residues of CFCs, human-produced chemicals that are now banned. The result would be ozone holes—portions of the sky lacking ozone's crucial protective filtration—that might be found over places like Iowa.

This connection between climate change and dangerous ozone holes has yet to be demonstrated in nature. The paper is a warning, a plea for more research and monitoring of atmospheric conditions, so that we can answer a question no one had even thought of asking. It's one of those unpredicted and unexpected possibilities that shows us how much we yet have to learn about climate change.

After reading the article, I tried to push its implications aside, but I had a hard time doing so. A few years ago, during a normal eye check, my optometrist said I have the slightest beginning of cataracts "from a normal lifetime of exposure to UV." Not good, I thought, but what I feared more was the increasing UV light initiating yet another bout of out-of-control cell division on my body's surface. I can use sunglasses as well as sun-creams to protect myself from the sun's rays. But what, I wondered, about the many others with fewer resources or less inclination to shelter their bodies? And what about all the other species, especially the frogs and toads whose skin is so much more sensitive than my own?

JULY 28 ∾ It rained three nights ago, a thunderstorm spilling three-quarters of an inch of water on our woods, not the slow steady rain that soaks the soils. We've had afternoon thunderstorms since then. Rains have cooled the air, sending temperatures down into the mid-80s, a reprieve from 100-degree-plus temperatures before these storms.

A newspaper article today stated that more Iowa farmers are installing irrigation equipment, an unusual trend here where summertime rainfall usually is plentiful. The irrigation is prompted by the drought in combination with corn prices approaching record highs of eight dollars a bushel. One farm manager was quoted as describing bright green, uniform plants on his irrigated acres, but yellowish green to sickly gray corn on the rest of his land. Meanwhile the condition of Iowa's corn crop as a whole continues to decline—from 62 percent in good to excellent condition on July 1 to only 20 percent in that condition today. Nearly half of Iowa's crop is now poor to very poor. Some farmers are reportedly plowing under their corn, thus losing their huge investment in seed and applied fertilizers and chemicals as well as their labor.

Other continents have been struck more intensely by extreme

weather in recent years. But this year, we are the ones suffering from such weather events, and people seem to be taking note. There are many editorials attributing the summer's strange weather to rising greenhouse gases. Some climate skeptics are publicly refuting their earlier positions: one prominent former skeptic is even claiming that human-induced climate change is stronger than reports had predicted.

And new groups are popping up, one being Climate Parents, a group that is hoping to push for efforts and policies that will "protect our children and communities from the heat waves, droughts, storms, and other impacts of ongoing climate change." The group cites the reasons why many of us are practicing "soft denial" of climate change: we know about its perils, but we fail to act because we don't understand the science and because the problem is too big and too depressing. This group is asking parents to wake up and shake off what it calls the paralysis of despair.

AUGUST 3 ℘ Late July's rainy, cooling reprieve was short-lived. August seems to be a continuation of July's dry heat, at least so far. Stepping out the front door, I feel as if I'm walking into a windy oven that desiccates anything within reach.

I am seeing many fewer frogs and toads than usual this year, and no snakes. Amazingly chipmunks and squirrels remain active, collecting sunflower seeds that fall from the feeder and stashing them in the flower boxes, where they germinate. Giant sunflowers trying to grow amid petite impatiens; the combination doesn't work well.

Streamflows across the state are dropping, and farm ponds near the house are shrinking since they haven't had any fresh inflows all summer. With the soils so dry and creeks disappearing, I wonder where smaller woodland animals will find water to drink. Some desert animals can survive on moisture from plants that they eat— and some from dew. But I don't have any such confidence for the woodland animals. And so I've been letting the garden hose run at a trickle and watching the birds come to drink. And I've placed water bowls out around the lawn for whatever creatures might need them.

Often in the morning the bowls are empty. Today I went out at dawn to check them and looking up saw four bats fly off, I assume retreating to sleep away the day. I was glad to see them since the number of bats in the woods seems to be diminishing, perhaps because the dry conditions are reducing insect populations.

AUGUST 7 ⟿ Examining the Iowa weather summaries for last month, it's obvious that July pushed the limits for heat and drought: statewide, we had twenty one days with temperatures of 90 degrees or higher, almost as many 90-plus days as we usually have in an entire year. During the same period, rainfall was scant. Average total precipitation for July was a bit over an inch, about a quarter of what we'd normally get.

Extremes like this help explain the 60,000 dead fish found in mid-July over a 42-mile stretch of the Des Moines River. The cause of death: 97-degree water, hotter than Iowa's fisheries biologists had ever measured before. The majority of fish killed were sturgeon worth nearly $10 million because of the caviar they produce. Fish are also dying in other midwestern rivers from extreme water temperatures, as well as lowering river levels and insufficient oxygen due to the drought and heat. Our neighbor's pond has lost all its fish. If the weather moderates, he'll restock next year.

Problematic midwestern rivers and lakes are not unique. Water bodies around the world are suffering in the face of higher temperatures and rising evaporation rates, along with increased water demand. Some of the world's largest lakes, rivers, and seas are growing smaller with each season.

AUGUST 20 ⟿ Very hot temperatures are supposed to return in a few days, but for the last twenty days, here in our woods, the end of the summer has turned out to be far more pleasant than summer's beginning. Temperatures have been moderate; we rarely need the air conditioner. Sporadic rainstorms have fallen long and gentle.

I love these nighttime rains, the soothing lullabies they play on the roof, the vapors that rise with the morning sun as mists float through the trees, quiet and mysterious. The rise in moisture and lower temperatures are leaving their mark. Many lawns are starting to green up, and once again I hear the drone of distant lawnmowers as neighbors cut the grass. The flower boxes are glorious, with blossoms becoming more numerous and lasting longer.

However, while showers across most of Iowa are more frequent and substantial than in July, statewide August's rainfall continues to be below normal, and the air remains unusually dry. I've read that the rains are slowing the decline of Iowa's crops, but not improving them. Iowa's usual green uniformity has morphed into a patchwork of greens and browns, with plants and soils reacting to the drought in their own unique manner. Estimates of the size of this year's corn and soybean crops continue to drop.

Looking at drought maps, I see that despite our weather's moderation, drought conditions in the nation's center have continued to expand and intensify during the last three weeks. Extreme and exceptional drought, the most intense drought categories, now claim most of Iowa as well as states to the east, south, and west.

Drought's ongoing dominance becomes obvious when I take note of roadside prairie plants growing near our home. Throughout the summer they have been doing well despite the dryness, and in places these plants continue to flourish. But elsewhere, they are so stressed that they are withering and turning brown. Fortunately, these plants are going into dormancy, not dying; the massive, drought-adapted root systems will shoot out leaves and flowers again next summer. I suppose that the decrease in prairie flowers and seed may help explain the large number of hungry birds, especially hummingbirds, at the feeders.

I'm wondering if this summer's drought and high temperatures will lead to an early leaf-drop. Along the road, I've seen sugar maples and crabapple trees that are already turning red and willows with brown foliage. Leaves of silver maples, cottonwoods, box elders, and other trees that normally grow in wet soils are yellowing. Even here in our woods, where the soils are shaded and roots reach deep, bushes are dried to a crisp and the leaves of some trees are starting to wither. The ground remains hard and dry. The edges of oak leaves are scorched and brown. I believe that this year's strange weather has been just too much for them. Since we had May's blossoms flowering in March, I suppose it makes sense to start October's leaf-fall in August. But I worry that nature has been pushed so hard that some elements may not be able to rebound.

Climate has always been on the move, and plants, animals, and entire communities have migrated in response. During the last 2.7 million years, as glaciers repeatedly advanced and retreated across our midcontinent, grasses and wildflowers were constantly on the go, seeding new homelands in rhythm with the pulsing temperatures and glaciers' movements. The plants that form our modern tallgrass prairies started to arrive back in Iowa a mere 9,000 years ago. More recently, approximately 5,500 years ago, a warming and drying climate favored prairies and shoved oak savannas and woodlands several hundred miles eastward; 3,000 years ago, a moister climate crept from the east back into the Midwest and pulled the oaklands westward across the Mississippi River. Oaks have dominated our Iowa woodland for thousands of years, but not forever.

In the last several decades, as temperatures have risen, many species around the world have been observed farther north—or higher on mountains—than in the past. One example: nearly 60 percent of all wintering North American birds have shifted their ranges significantly northward in the last forty years—including the purple finches I sometimes see at the feeders.

These species' ability to adapt to climate change through migration gives hope for their survival. Unfortunately, not all species will be able to do so. The landscape is now too dissected by croplands, highways, cities, and other human land uses to provide easy migration routes. And plant species with long lifespans and poor seed dispersal—trees like the slow-growing oaks that require decades before they produce acorns—may not move fast enough to keep up with today's racing rate of climate change.

Another complication: with the climate continuing to change, species may be moving into another site just as that site is morphing into something else. Perhaps most vulnerable are plants and animals that live in the Arctic (such as the polar bear) or high mountains (the rabbit-like pika) that have no more northerly or higher, cooler place to move. Already, mature polar bears are becoming visibly thinner, and their cubs are born smaller and have lower survival rates. Without ice floes, which they use to hunt seals, wild polar bears may become restricted to small sections of the Arctic by later this century as their numbers drop dramatically. Seals that nurse their young on snow-covered ice floes are also at risk, as are walruses that sometimes crush one another as they crowd onto shrinking ice. Even tiny plants floating in the far-north's icy waters are changing. The algae growing there proliferate as the thinning ice transmits more light. Then they fall to the seafloor, where they deplete oxygen and alter the food web.

In coming years, we can expect to see ongoing changes in the ranges of many species. One example: if current emissions trends continue and temperatures rise as expected, the northern Minnesota forest types we canoe past during our summer vacations—birch and aspen woodlands, spruce and fir forests—are predicted to disappear from the eastern U.S. by the century's end, although they should remain in Canada. Pines would also disappear from U.S. Northwoods.

Anticipating similar ongoing changes in urban areas, city foresters now are planting roadside trees tolerant of greater heat. But it will be impossible for us to relocate most of the earth's life-forms. I think, for example, about the fungi occupying our woodland, the birds that migrate here from South America, and the spring bloomers so intricately tied to the warming of our woods' soils and spring rains. How will they fare in the coming heat?

SEPTEMBER 4 ∾ The end of summer claims perhaps the quietest weather. We're past the normal flood and peak tornado seasons and are wedged between springtime's heavy rains and winter's cold and snow. With this hush to the weather, the coming of autumn is unobtrusive and unassuming—nothing untoward is expected. Days are soft, lazy, and comfortable.

This fall promises to be such a time of peace, stillness, and beauty, a time of recollection and closing, although the woods' preparations for the coming winter are arriving too fast this year. Many of the woodland trees are already tinged with yellow, some are losing leaves, and acorns continue to fall from the oaks. Many of the acorns are stunted and will not be fertile, but some are nicely filled out. They litter the deck until squirrels come to carry them away. Some of the understory plants have shriveled and dried, leaving bare-soiled patches. Digging holes with my trowel, all that I find is dun-colored dust, as if the soils have lost cohesion. The occasional rains are not sufficient to wet them to any depth or to bring the creeks up in the slightest.

All these signs speak of the summer's drought, which has been slightly eased but not erased by August's occasional rains. The entire state remains locked in severe and extreme drought. Very hot weather continues to plague Iowa intermittently and energize evaporation. Today it's 97 degrees and muggy. By later this week we're supposed to have a reprieve, with temperatures cooling to September norms in the 70s during the day and 50s at night. Even with lower temperatures, the drought is likely to write its ongoing legacy on the land for months to come.

I walk out into the early morning mist, choosing to overlook these seasonal aberrations and enjoy the woodland surprises I find whenever I diverge from the path: lavender spikes of lobelia alongside the creek, a spate of creamy yellow chanterelle mushrooms with an aroma hinting of apricots, the many grasses now going to seed: bottlebrush, silky wild rye, wood reed, broad-leaved panic grass. More obvious are the fall-blooming elm-leaved goldenrods that spread through our woods like swaths of sunshine, their deep yellow flower plumes interrupted by patches of knee-high white snakeroot blossoms.

Animals too continue to be obvious. Sometimes a rafter of wild turkeys explodes from shrubs at my feet, although more often Sidney runs ahead and scatters them. Birds remain abundant, but they are far quieter than they were several months ago when establishing territories. Now instead of a choir of voices, there's a single distant rattle of a woodpecker. The hushed yanking of an isolated nuthatch. A lone jay calling. Wood pewees still emit crystalline notes, but less insistently and frequently than before.

Replacing abundant birdsong is the late-summer singing of male insects trying to attract mates. The day-singing cicadas, whose long throbbing buzzes were so evident earlier in summer, are now starting to fade away, even as katydids are singing more prominently from late night until early morning. Crickets are reaching their seasonal peak. Their on-off trill is soft and comforting, less insistent than the harsh rasping of cicadas or the metallic rattle of katydids.

Since I was young, crickets have soothed me from midsummer into autumn by rubbing their wings to make gentle churring songs through night and day. They have ushered in the evening, sung me to sleep, and serenaded my dreams, their rhythmic strumming announcing that the winter's cold stillness is approaching. To me any insect song is a gift. But peace comes from the crickets, the crickets and the slant of the rays of the early morning sun, now originating from the southeast rather than from due east as was true a few months ago.

SEPTEMBER 7 ∾ It rained hard and long last night. Today I take joy in the freshly washed blue of the sky, with puffy cloud cushions lit from below by the rising sun. I marvel at the slant of the sun's rays through the woodland mist. The sparkling world has a sense of newness to it, of creation restored, even though now, in late summer, many tree leaves have been tattered by munching insects and are weighted down by knobby galls. This morning, all that I see is crisp and moist, faultless and beautiful. I sometimes wonder where I get this ability to look at the world each day with hope and positive expectations. I wonder what I would do if I lost this vision.

SEPTEMBER 14 ∾ If life flows into and through the forest in early summer, then late summer seems like life's ebb. Plants and animals have produced offspring to carry the species forward, and now they can relax. For animals, that means no more calling of mates or territorial displays, no more nest-building or hustling to feed hungry baby mouths. Now animals focus on storing food for winter consumption, or for fattening their bodies for the coming cold, or for migrating long distances to warmer climes.

Meanwhile the deep green tree leaves continue to create complex carbohydrate molecules and ship them down to roots where they will be stored until the spring, when they'll flow upward to engender new leaves and tree blossoms—unless they are sugar maples tapped by my neighbor, who will boil down the spring sap he's collected to make maple syrup.

The fruits of reproductive efforts are everywhere. Young bats have now joined the adults zipping through the dusk sky and circling the house from one deck light to another. Moths of all sizes continue to flutter into window screens and fly in the front door whenever we open it, and hummingbirds are constantly buzzing the feeders and chasing away butterflies that have been clustering there. I brush proliferating spider webs from my face whenever walking through the woods. And we had a rare fruit fly attack in the house last week when I brought in a basket of fresh-picked apples, which—on our lone apple tree that escaped the April freeze—are not only abundant this year but also huge.

This kind of response is common among plants: when environmental conditions challenge a plant's survival, it responds by producing more fruits, nuts, or seeds than usual. The wild raspberries and black walnuts too have been prolific, as have oaks. The white oak acorns are already sprouting robust roots that will continue to grow through winter, anchoring the young trees with a twelve-inch taproot within a year. Red oak acorns have a different approach: they sprout in the spring and then, if conditions are good, will grow faster than the white oaks. Both types of acorns are attracting chipmunks that manage to carry five or six back to their burrows in their expandable cheek pouches and the squirrels that all day bury the acorns for winter consumption. Those dug up and eaten will maintain the squirrels through the winter; those that are forgotten will sprout into trees. The abundance of acorns this fall means an abundance of baby chipmunks, squirrels, and oaks next spring. It's all part of the regeneration cycle.

Usually I'm so focused on the land that I barely pay attention to the creeks and lakes near our home. But last week it was impossible to ignore them. The farm ponds were covered shore to shore with a bright green scum: algal blooms, massive proliferations of algae fed by excessive nutrients washed into the abnormally warm water.

Blooms of blue-green algae, a species that produces potent toxins, can cause severe illness and death in people and cattle. One such bloom recently appeared around the Apostle Islands in Lake Superior, where Robert and I kayaked last summer. Had the bloom occurred when we were there, we may have cancelled our trip. This huge, cold, wavy lake is normally immune to such problems, but Lake Superior is one of the planet's fastest-warming lakes. In recent decades, harmful algal blooms have increased in frequency, severity, and geographic distribution both in the Great Lakes and around the world.

Pollen levels remain off the charts. This doesn't bother me, but my neighbor (who lives to be out in her garden) has been having horrible sinus infections that are not responding to antibiotics. Her doctor has told her to stay inside until the first hard frost, which could still be over a month away. "I'm under house arrest," she jokes. She's one of many friends who are new sufferers from allergies, asthma, or other pollen-related illnesses. Rising temperatures are inducing plants to produce pollen earlier and more abundantly, thus intensifying and extending exposures; the rising warmth also encourages new pollen sources to migrate northward.

A number of additional health problems are associated with climate change. Most obvious are responses to high heat, heat stress and heat stroke, and injuries and illnesses traced to other extreme weather events. Less obvious health challenges include the degradation of air quality as temperatures rise, which increases respiratory stress. Waterborne diseases also increase with greater warmth, as do food poisonings.

This summer tick populations around our home exploded, and in the last few months, three of our neighbors contracted Lyme disease from tick bites. In coming years, here in the Midwest, warming winters are expected to further magnify diseases transmitted by ticks and insects that are no longer controlled by winter's extreme cold. In addition, new infectious diseases and their vectors will thrive and move poleward, including illnesses normally restricted to the tropics. In recent months, outbreaks of West Nile virus have intensified in parts of the U.S. because increased heat and moisture have created exceptional mosquito breeding conditions. Climate is not the only factor influencing the spread of infectious disease, but its role should only increase over time as the climate warms further, complicating attempts to address health challenges and further belaboring the public health system.

SEPTEMBER 15 ∿ Because our home is surrounded by a diverse natural area, I need to establish a boundary between my life and the other lives surrounding me. I try to keep that boundary close to the walls of the house: this side of the wall is my life with all its accouterments, my kitchen and books and furniture, my bed and blankets. You others stay on the other side.

For the most part the animals, and certainly the plants, respect that boundary. But occasionally it is crossed with intent. Last week, I started to notice mouse droppings in the basement. I haphazardly set a few traps with peanut butter, not really believing that we had a mouse, not really caring. Until I started to notice its caches of birdseed in shoes stored in the basement and later saw a small gray animal streak pass me while I was doing the laundry. Then—the final blow—the mouse (it must have been a hefty fellow) nudged a jar of olive oil off the basement storage shelf, and I spent two hours cleaning up the mess. I set more mouse traps and baited them with everything a mouse might enjoy: peanut butter with intermixed hot dog, dog food, sunflower seeds, and oatmeal with a dab of chocolate on top. And sure enough, in the morning I had the mouse in a trap. But it wasn't dead; its torso was caught near the hips.

When the mouse saw me, it raised its body and looked into my eyes, as if pleading for release. This wasn't a house mouse, a species that came to America on ships centuries ago. We don't have these "city mice" here in the woods. It was a native deer mouse, a cute fellow with a yielding white belly and large round eyes and ears. What to do? I freed it in the compost pile, thinking that it could live out its last days with easy access to food. And I sprinkled a bootful of peanuts near its mouth. It was the least I could do. Didn't I, after all, invade its woodland territory, rather than vice versa?

Over the years, we've had many other animals cross the boundary line and enter our woodland home. The blind tree frog that the grandkids fed two summers ago, patiently holding flies near its mouth until it opened up and ate. The baby raccoon that Matt bottle-fed when he was young. The baby squirrels that one family dog or another would bring to the house and drop at our feet. Injured birds who occupied our screen porch. Most of the animals lived for a time, but I cannot think of any who reentered nature to continue a long life. Wild animals are best left where they are born.

Regardless of how much we tried to do for these creatures, they did much more for us. Each allowed us to glimpse a very different way of successfully living on our planet. I like to think that by opening us to another world, each animal visitor also stretched our leanings toward tolerance and acceptance.

And perhaps each taught us a deeper way of viewing all manifestations of life. I think of the American white pelicans now flocking on the reservoir near our house. They arrive by the thousands, resting here to feed en route to their southerly wintering grounds. Immense birds with a nine-foot wingspan, they have large heads and huge heavy bills that give them an appropriately prehistoric look: fossils date pelicans back at least 30 million years.

These seasonal visitors return me to a time when the earth was so much younger. Yet here they are, a few miles from our modern home, forming expanses of white on the water, catching the waves, scooping fishes into their baggy throat pouches and tossing their heads back to swallow. When updrafts form, the birds rise and dozens soar as one being, irregular white patches in the blue sky, birds the color of purity. I used to watch them and want to be one with them, to soar and catch the wind, to be part of a single airborne community, but now I am glad to stand here on the ground and dream of earlier times instead.

SEPTEMBER 16 ❧ Fall migration is a lazy drawn-out affair, with birds moving through more slowly than in the spring, when they are on a mission to speed north and breed. In autumn, they linger, foraging for insects, wolfing down seeds, devouring small fruits until weather forces them farther south. Then, on a favorable flight day, perhaps one with good tailwinds, the birds continue their journey.

This morning I noted eastern bluebirds clustering in a shrubby field nearby and a kettle of turkey vultures circling the updrafts. Flocks of cedar waxwings will soon clean my neighbor's crabapple trees of their red berries. Canada geese are again flying in small vees rather than in pairs, as they were when breeding. I sometimes spot good-sized flocks of them in my neighbor's pasture. I like the way they share the field, the cattle on one end and the geese on the other. Wild turkeys do the same thing. It seems reasonable to me: the land is neither totally for us, nor totally for them. It's such a different unwritten law than the one governing Iowa's expansive croplands, where one species (usually corn) is meant to dominate. I haven't seen many monarch butterflies yet this fall, but they too should be on the move soon. A few years ago, the neighbor's apple tree was draped in their black-striped orange wings for a night.

As autumn progresses, the leaves of the elms, ashes, cherries, and hickories in the woods and the hazelnuts and dogwoods underneath them are turning into gold. The countryside around me also, the fencerow saplings and shrubs and the remnant prairie plants along roadsides, the dried grasses in fields, all mirror the deep gold of the sun on the horizon when it spills its rays to the north and south. And all this golden life is shimmering and twinkling, the leaves on tree branches constantly jiggling until they are swept by a gust into the air, there to perform their final dance as they drift and blow downward to the ground to cover and recolor the brown earth. This brightness in the surrounding world cheers me tremendously, makes me feel as privileged as the fairytale queen who spun hay into true gold. But I am far richer than she was, I think.

SEPTEMBER 19 ∽ We're having a short cold snap, a few days where temperatures fall into the 40s at night. The remaining dark greens of the summer world are now fading into yellows and or-anges as the chlorophylls in leaves disintegrate and pigments that have been there all summer, the carotenoids, can be seen for the first time. It happens gradually, the green disappearing and yellow tones taking over, so that one day you look and say, "That tree is yellow, not green." Red is also coming on, but only in select plants like sumac and sugar maple. And of course poison ivy. It carpets the fields with a deep maroon where it's extensive. Browns are more prevalent than usual this year. Some entire trees have shriveled into brown. Oak leaves, despite their heat-scorched edges, remain mostly forest-green, but they look desiccated, as if they would crumble into dust if touched.

It's the time to watch for snakes on the road. They come to the black asphalt surface to warm their cold-blooded bodies as the weather cools. Hopefully I find them before they are hit by cars. I shush them off onto the verge, giving them a warning as I do so, one I know they don't understand.

I can't help but ponder the deer mouse with the crushed hind-quarters living in the compost pile, dragging itself from carrot trim-mings to discarded nuts or noodles. What a cruel fate, to do the most natural, the most necessary act in the world: to open your mouth to take a bite to eat and then feel the stiff wire snap across your torso. In a way, it's like our human situation here on Earth: we do what we must to feed our families, but modern agriculture is a major emitter of greenhouse gases. Unless we grow our own food or shop with extreme care and knowledge, we raise the level of atmospheric carbon dioxide with each bite we take. It's as if the ramifications of that carbon dioxide—the stronger winds, larger storm surges, intense damaging downpours—were a spring-loaded trap that might at any time snap on us.

Robert and I try to lessen greenhouse-gas production through intentionally purchasing locally grown foods, which are easy to find here in Iowa, and by cutting back on red meat consumption. Cattle digesting their grass produce significant quantities of the potent greenhouse-gas methane, as do their wastes when they decompose. And cattle ranches across the tropics are a major cause of deforestation; preserving tropical rainforests is crucial to keeping our climate stabilized. When we do eat red meat, we buy it from local grass-fed beef sources. Funny how thinking about that one small injured mouse—one of hundreds in our woodland I'm sure—is nudging me to consider making more lifestyle changes.

SEPTEMBER 21 ∾ This year the Arctic clearly stands out as the region where climate change is striking first and most intensely. Several days ago, newspapers announced that Arctic Ocean sea ice reached its lowest annual extent since satellite surveillance began in 1979. On September 16, ice cover dropped to less than a quarter of its wintertime maximum. An amazing 4.6 million square miles of ice disappeared since last March, leaving only 1.32 million square miles intact. This late-summer low, perhaps unprecedented in human history, is about half of the 1979–2000 average minimum ice cover.

Arctic sea ice also is thinning dramatically. It's been estimated that more sea ice has melted in the last twenty years than in the previous 10,000. Much of this ice re-forms during the Arctic's frigid, dark winters, but an increasing fraction is newly formed, and this younger sea ice is more vulnerable to melting than older ice. All of these changes are accelerating and occurring faster than models had predicted. People living in the Arctic are not immune to the changes: indigenous villages are increasingly battered by wind-driven waves that erode the coastline, forcing coastal communities to succumb or relocate.

Melting of the Arctic also is raising strong concerns because of its implications for global weather patterns. The frigid Arctic air helps control global climate through, for example, governing large-scale upper-atmospheric circulation patterns. Those global weather patterns can be disrupted and reshaped by the warming of the planet's ice box. Slowing of the polar jet stream, which may have been a factor in this year's extreme weather events, is the most immediate example.

Why the intense and accelerating ice loss in the Arctic? Certainly oceanic and atmospheric heat is key here, where air temperatures are rising faster than anywhere else on the globe—over 3.5 degrees since the mid-1980s, more than twice the average temperature rise of the entire globe.

But other factors also are governing the far-north's strong and rapid response to climate change. Consider Arctic amplification: Light-colored ice reflects the sun's incoming radiation back into space, but once ice starts melting, it exposes dark-colored water that absorbs (rather than reflects) heat radiation. Such absorption further warms the oceans and causes more melting of surrounding sea ice, which allows further absorption of radiation, and so forth. Global warming is magnified.

Amplification is a powerful feedback loop that is now spilling from Arctic waters onto surrounding snow-covered lands. Rising temperatures are melting more snow earlier each year, causing frozen Arctic soils, or permafrost, to melt. This is threatening buildings and roads in Alaska and other far-northern lands and is producing drunken forests of tipping trees. But the melting permafrost also is starting to release tens of billions of tons of carbon stored in the frozen ground since the last Ice Age. That carbon is entering the atmosphere as both carbon dioxide and methane. Faster, earlier snowmelt exposes dark soils that absorb sunlight and magnify the cycle of heating and melting. This feedback loop could ratchet climate change up to a whole new level.

With the alarming swiftness of sea-ice retreat in the past five years, many climate scientists now state that Arctic melting is our first identifiable climate-change tipping point. That is, with self-reinforcing feedback loops coming into play, the melting has passed a point of no return and is taking on a life of its own, over which we have no control.

A few years ago, climate scientists predicted that the summertime Arctic could be ice-free by 2050. With this year's record melting event, that date has moved forward to 2030, and some predict ice-free Arctic summers even sooner. Whenever this occurs, we'll have the first summertime Arctic Ocean entirely free of ice in human history.

SEPTEMBER 22 ∾ Today is the autumnal equinox, the day when the sun is directly above the equator and all places on Earth have twelve hours of sunshine and twelve hours of darkness. A day to celebrate similitude. Yet I find myself reacting against this concept. All my studying about climate change is getting to me. I don't want every place on Earth to be the same. I want ice in the Arctic and sweltering heat at the equator. I want predictable differences, each location on our planet having its distinctive character expressed within given ranges from year to year.

This fall, I'm not getting what I want. The weather report is predicting record lows for tonight. A high likelihood of frost, several weeks before the normal first frost. I tell myself to appreciate the chill in the air.

Meanwhile, in the mountains above our son Andy's home in Tacoma, Washington, state health officials are warning residents to stay inside because air pollution levels are off the charts. Lightning strikes in the tinder-dry forests started several fires that have filled the air with so much smoke that human health is now threatened. State health officials are handing out face masks to those who must go outside.

I know that soon the forest leaves will start to fall en masse, and when they do, the woods will open up and I'll see deer paths that were hidden from me before, routes through the tangles of growth that seemed to prohibit passage. It happens every fall: the thick woods that all summer overwhelmed me and held me back lose their leaves and become more transparent, welcoming me to move forward into new worlds that once seemed unimaginable.

SEPTEMBER 23 ❧ The woods are full of dozens of migrating birds this morning, flitting from plant to plant, a carnival of lives in motion. Small flocks of sparrows stocking up on insects and seeds. Drab-colored warblers. And yesterday, a dozen northern flickers perched upright in the top of a dead tree below our house, absorbing the sun's warmth. They have been clustering here in the woods for several days, I assume pausing during their southward flight.

Taking my usual slow morning walk, stopping to see what's still in flower, bending low to touch the occasional fall-blooming violet, then looking up toward the falling leaves, I glimpse a bald eagle streaking through the trees twenty feet above my head, then lifting its body to the sky. I see bald eagles regularly, but never this close. Was today's eagle perhaps on the chase?

Raising my eyes to admire its white tail and head glinting in the sunshine, I note a small vee of maybe fifteen American white pelicans high above, circling round, catching the updrafts formed as sunshine warms the ground below. When seen at one angle, they are solid white harbingers of perfection. Then, wheeling in unison, shifting in the light, their black flight feathers become dominant, and the birds are transformed. White, to black, round and round, to white, to black, to white.

And then, while focusing on the pelicans, mesmerized by their whirling bodies, I spot hundreds of circling specks so high in the sky that I have to crane my neck and strain to see them—a kettle of broad-winged hawks carried by the atmosphere's currents, traveling thousands of miles to South America for the winter.

I relish the woods in this season, when color becomes so vibrant that it overrides form, and birds again become abundantly obvious. But today I also feel a sadness thinking about animals departing, leaves falling, a chill setting in, and closing the windows against the creeping cold. The line between me and the woods will become firmer, the walls of our house more solid and exclusive, a barrier to the natural world. I need to prepare myself for the coming separation.

Glancing up, I see the flock of flickers again in the treetop near the house, rapping for bugs in the dead wood, reminding me to live for the day without fear of tomorrow. Then at dusk, when I'm walking along the lake near our house, several other images also remind me of the beauty of the moment. Two, three—no, four—flocks, each with dozens of pelicans, glide a few feet above the water, coming in to roost for the night. Then a white moon in a pale blue sky hangs low over a red clump of sumac. Then a fifth flock of pelicans coasts directly overhead. And then—as if making sure I get the message—a barred owl swoops so close that if I had lifted my arms, I could have touched its belly.

Memoir
Mothering, 1975–1997

SEVEN

IT'S EARLY SPRING, 1977. ROBERT AND I ARE SITTING ON A LOG
stretching over a creek flowing through a sixteen-acre woodland,
about eight miles north of Iowa City, where we both work. My hands
rest on my protruding belly, which extends farther every week as
our first child grows within me. We swing our legs in the air and
gaze into the trickling water below, lifting our eyes occasionally to
the fern-covered hillsides, smugly thinking how fortunate we are
to be the land's new owners. The forest envelops us: we can hear
a neighbor's dog in the distance and the low purr of an occasional
passing car, but otherwise it's only birds and rustling leaves and
the occasional chatter of a squirrel. And some other sound I can't
quite define—something that we heard a few times in our Colorado
mountain cabin as well. I've heard it said that a well-functioning,
intact wilderness sings to those who can hear the song. Could this
be that primitive melody?

We had moved to Iowa nearly two years earlier, after Robert
graduated and accepted a faculty position at the University of Iowa.
It was an excellent position for him, and it brought us closer to my
aging father who had remarried, retired, and was once again living
in Madison, a few hours' drive away. Soon after arriving, we started
searching for land in the country, somewhere with the same raw
and vigorous wildness that we'd treasured in Colorado.

This wasn't easy to find in Iowa, with its miles upon miles of
corn and soybeans. We visited disintegrating farmhouses and trampled, overgrown tracts that seemed gray, weary, used up. Then one
weekend we drove down a curvy road and noticed a handwritten

"for sale" sign tacked to a tree on the edge of a wooded plot. We stopped, exited the car, and penetrated a leafy green veil. All was hushed. We walked into a land of oaks and hickories towering far above us and diverse sedges and wildflowers covering the leafy forest floor. Within a few steps from the road, we were transported to a different time and place, a world where wild things called and all appeared fresh and new, a world that seemed far greater than our comprehension. We walked for a while, then returned home and called the penciled-in number on the sign. A week later, we submitted a bid for the land.

Now, several months later, we are in our woods considering our next step. We would like to be living here when our baby is born, so we need a house. But, what to build? A cluster of butterflies flits past and distracts me. My thoughts shift, and I picture myself showing our baby insects like these and the beetles and small red mushrooms I notice at the base of a nearby log. And the purple and pink spring wildflowers with fuzzy stems growing nearby. I imagine our toddler waking to dawn songs of eastern phoebes, whiling away days hearing eastern towhees call in the brush, and drifting to sleep to the hooting of owls.

I want our child to fall in love with the natural world, with its perfection, fullness, and beauty, as I did. And here our child will have an entire woodland to explore, so much more than the wild patches of my Madison neighborhood. I want the woods to be our child's teacher. But also a place to play and stretch the imagination. I see myself walking with our youngster into the woods, looking to the north, and pretending that Ice Age mammoths still live nearby. "Listen!" I'll say. "Do you hear them snorting and clomping their feet? So loud! Are they coming this way? Are you excited?"

"Connie—Con!" Robert's voice calls me back to the present. "Stay focused. What about the house?"

I start by listing the basics. "We don't have much money."

"I'll take the summer off, hire some graduate students. We can get something built, but it will have to be small."

"Small is fine," I respond. "I want it to be warm and loving, like my Madison home was," thinking back to the protective shell my mother had created for my sister and me.

Robert—who is trying to make decisions rather than talk emotions—looks askance. "Tell me specifics."

"It needs to reflect our values," I respond idealistically. Sitting on the log, I have a notion that we can meld into this woodland without leaving a disruptive footprint. I choose to ignore the resources we'll use to build our house and our assumed dependence on cars to get us to work and to the grocery store. I'm unwilling to face the trade-offs inherent in every decision we are making.

Robert returns to specifics. "We'll build something like our Colorado cabin. Tucked into the woods, designed to be cooled by the shade in summer and heated by the sun in winter. We'll add a wood-burning furnace—no lack of fuel," he murmurs as we glance at branches that have fallen from trees. "Too shady here for solar panels, but if we keep it small and insulate it well, we shouldn't use much electricity."

We keep talking, that day and for weeks after. We plan a structure of about 1,200 square feet plus a basement, big enough for two adequate bedrooms, a living room with a music alcove, and a kitchen with a good-sized eating table at one end. A bathroom and a pocket office with our books and a desk. Enough, but nothing extra.

We don't want to disrupt the woodland plants more than we need to, so we'll park the car up near the road and walk to the house on a narrow entrance drive. We'll have a well, but we want to minimize our water use. Here we plan something unusual: a composting toilet that does not require water for flushing. The toilet will decompose wastes in a fiberglass holding tank in the basement, with odors venting through the roof.

Within weeks, we hire a contractor to dig the basement hole and pour its concrete walls and floor. By the end of the university's spring semester, Robert and his students are framing in walls. I join them each day after work, but my growing size limits me to smaller jobs: sealing the cement, sanding trim pieces. By August, we have a roof, outer walls covered with siding, and framed-in inner walls.

We've installed enough furniture and kitchen appliances to make the dwelling livable.

One evening, while on my hands and knees installing the bedroom flooring, I feel the first twinges of labor. I keep working: the pain is mild, and I know this is the beginning of a long process. But the next time Robert comes to check on me, I tell him, "It's started. Time to see our baby!"

"Are you OK? Do you want to stop?" he asks with concern, gazing at the floor tiles scattered around me.

"Let me do a little more, and then let's go to bed," I respond, until the next contraction starts and I change my mind. "Let's go to bed now."

We sleep fitfully through the night, with Robert timing contractions when he's awake. Finally, at dawn, I stumble up the path to the car, and we drive to the hospital as the sun, a yellow globe, emerges on the horizon.

A few days later, our first son, Christopher, came home to a wooden shell without windows or doors. During the day, woodland birds flew from one window-hole to another. At night, bats flitted through chasing insects attracted by our lamps. I covered Chris with a mosquito net to keep these visitors away.

By October, the house was enclosed and fully functional. It took years to complete the inside finish work, but I barely noticed the unstained woodwork because by then I was engrossed in caring for our children. When Chris was three, our second son, Andrew, was born out of the belly of a 747 jet that carried him here from Korea. Arriving as a nineteen-month old toddler, he jumped off the plane's exit ramp and started chasing Chris around the Minneapolis airport. Matthew, the baby of the family, was born when Andy was almost four.

Three little boys running through the woods. Always running.

"Here's one!" yells Chris, and his brothers scurry over to stare at the jar he's filling with baby toads, which he later releases. The next evening they are at it again, this time making a flashlight by filling jars with fireflies that blink on and off. "Cars," announces preschooler Matt, letting me know that he's going to drive his toys up and down the dirt trail to the pond, constructing garages from leaves and sticks along the way.

Three inquisitive, active boys. For over twenty years, their care was my primary concern. I fed them a diet of quiet days with sun shining through the windows beckoning them into the woods and evenings rocking on the porch swing watching the bats come out to eat. I whispered stories about the flowers blooming at their feet and the animals who lived just beyond their sight. I read them evening tales of greatness, legends and myths, and then tucked them into beds surrounded by blackness, where dreams of goodness and possibility surrounded them. They woke to wind whishing in the oaks, clouds racing across the skies, the muted pecking of birds at feeders outside their windows. This is how I idealistically remember those years.

Early one morning, young Matt calls me into his bedroom. "Look, Mom, one is going down, one up. Why?" He's watching an upward-spiraling brown creeper and downward-facing white-breasted nuthatch simultaneously plying the bark on the hickory outside his window. He is learning to search for order and pattern in a world that supports abundant life, just as I had learned many years before.

When the boys were small, they started the day by snuggling into bed with us and staring out the large bedside window at the oaks waving far above their heads. They leapt from our bed to dash outside into their larger home, the woods, to build stick dams in the creek, complain about wood nettles, learn to avoid nests of ground wasps, and live with poison ivy. They dug up worms and millipedes and peeled bark from rotting logs to pry out beetles.

Some days they'd "help" me tend the vegetable garden near the road, Andy sticking in seedlings, toddler Matt stumbling and breaking them. Later in the summer, we ate beans and tomatoes direct from the vine. In the evening when darkness spread, I wrapped the boys in blankets, took them out onto the deck, and sang to them while owls hooted in the distance. Although the owls were not always distant. When Chris was a year old, I came into the kitchen to see him wobbling on a chair, peering out the window into the eyes of a baby owl, who was perched on a deck post perhaps eight feet away, returning the stare.

As the boys grew older, they bundled up in the winter and crafted sledding runs through the woods, around trees, and over snow ramps, or they joined neighbors hitting a hockey puck around the frozen pond. When the drifts were large enough, they pocketed them with caves and pretended they were living in snow houses. In summer, they read to the sound of gentle rains on the roof. I noticed they were starting to learn respect and empathy when I overheard Andy lecturing Matt, "Don't poke at that caterpillar, Matt. How would you like it if *you* were a worm and someone poked at you?"

Our three little boys grew into sweating teenagers with stinky socks and stomachs that were always empty. "When's dinner?" Matt would call out forty-five minutes after eating lunch.

During the 1990s, when the boys were first learning to drive, I sometimes questioned my sanity and survival.

I stumble out of bed to answer the phone at 6 A.M. "Mutels? Police department."

"Yes?" I reply, too sleepy to for lucid thought. Then I realize that it must be about Chris, who had called at ten the night before, saying the roads were too icy to drive home. He was going to sleep at his debate partner's house. "Yes?" I reply again, this time in a panic.

"Your Civic is blocking the high school entrance road. Can't be moved. Blown front tire. We need you to tow it. Immediately." We call the family where Chris is staying. They wake him, and he admits sliding into the curb and walking away from the undrivable car. We later discover the front axle has been bent and sell the car for parts.

Andy announces his first car accident with the words, "The good thing is that no one got hurt." He announces the next one by saying, "It doesn't look so good anymore, but it still works." And then, after we thought we were done with ruined cars, Matt, who has just gotten his license, carefully steers into the garage and, once inside, mistakenly jams on the gas instead of the brakes, catapulting the car through the rear garage wall.

Cars and their untimely movements were not the only problems. I found a cluster of marijuana plants growing in our roadside ditch and remembered a hushed phone call about growing weed. Another time I entered the house when the smell was unmistakable: Chris was teaching his little brother to smoke. And yet another time we returned from a weekend away—just Robert and me off for a few much-needed, carefully planned days, with all the boys safely shuttled to responsible friends' houses—and walked into a beer party. Our boys were not there, but one of them later confessed that he had rented our house out to his friends. "Five dollars a head," he told us about his profits.

There were many more times when we didn't know whether to laugh or cry, scream or just give up. But now, looking back at the years when the boys were young, trying to remember what those times felt like, I create an idyllic scene: I see my arms encircling a broad, shallow, warm sea. The sea is my love, and the boys are wading in it, splashing, playing, and chasing each other. How I cherished those times! The rawness of the boys' young bodies and their actions. Everything was up front. Hunger. Laughter. Anger and tears. Intense preoccupation. Young lives lived with passion and direction. I could almost see the earth's energy rising in their healthy bodies, beating through their hearts and energizing their muscles.

These were the years when the cycle of seasons was predictably beneficent, with each season dependably bringing its own pleasures. I recall well the incredible peace I felt at night when the boys were asleep in bed. Hidden under bedcovers in a woods in the center of the country, I believed they were immune from distant problems. Nothing could harm them. They were safe, at least for the day, and all was right with the world.

But even then I knew this conceit was an illusion. In the 1980s, while I was serving piles of grilled cheese sandwiches and cutting up dozens of apples, I was well aware that changes were occurring high in the atmosphere, distant powerful changes we could not see. The signs were strong, and they were increasing.

The use of fossil fuels had climbed steeply since the end of World War II, with U.S. use of petroleum nearly quadrupling between 1945 and 1980 and natural gas use increasing over fivefold. In that period, the burning of these two fossil fuels massively overwhelmed the use of all other U.S. energy sources.

With that surge, greater amounts of carbon dioxide were added to the atmosphere each year; most of the rise since 1900 to the present has occurred since 1980. Soon danger points were being exceeded: in 1988, atmospheric carbon dioxide levels first topped 350 ppm—a level identified by many climate scientists as the maximum for sustaining climate patterns to which human life and society are adapted.

Mirroring these increases in carbon dioxide, in 1980 the planet's temperature started a clear, ongoing, upward march. Most of the current 1.4-degree global temperature rise has occurred since that year. In addition, the 1980s was, at the time, the hottest decade on record. That decade some scientists became increasingly concerned about climate change, their research and opinions growing more definitive. Toward the end of the decade, they began to demand action to waylay the threat of imminent and rapid warming, taking their arguments to the general public and to politicians, a few of whom took up the cause. Congressional hearings were held and a number of climate bills were discussed—including a tax on carbon emissions. News media started covering the subject, especially during the very hot summer of 1988—the same year that NASA scientist James Hansen first testified about climate change before the U.S. Congress. That same year, the United Nations created its Intergovernmental Panel on Climate Change to strive toward international consensus on climate-change policy. The IPCC released its first report in 1990. At last, climate change seemed to be rising to the fore and getting attention.

But that hope was ephemeral. In 1989, the well-funded Global Climate Coalition, representing industries with profits tied to fossil fuels, was formed to lobby against greenhouse-gas regulations. The politicization of climate change had taken flight, and accompanied by strong pro-industry interests in Washington, it squelched any hope of a national energy policy that could help mitigate climate change.

Now, I think, if only. If only we had stayed on track and passed a science-based energy policy that limited carbon dioxide emissions, the world we now inhabit would be so much safer. It would have been much easier to effect that change back then, the results far better.

And we could have done so. We had the necessary tools at the ready, and in the 1980s and 1990s we used them to address two other environmental problems involving invisible atmospheric gases.

Remember the ozone hole? It ascended into public consciousness in 1985, when human-generated chemicals, primarily CFCs, were shown to be thinning the protective ozone layer high in the sky. This thinning was increasing the transmission of skin-damaging ultraviolet light to Earth's surface and thus raising the possibility of skin cancers and cataracts. Despite vigorous opposition from skeptics and major corporations producing CFCs, the U.S. in 1987 became one of dozens of nations signing an international agreement, the Montreal Protocol, to phase out ozone-depleting chemicals. This agreement is credited with avoiding hundreds of millions of skin cancers and tens of millions of cases of eye cataracts in Americans who would be born between 1985 and 2100, with financial benefits far outweighing the costs and without the dire economic hardships that skeptics had predicted.

And then there was acid rain, a product largely of atmospheric moisture combining with sulfur dioxide from coal-fired power plants, producing sulfuric acid that fell to the ground with rain and other precipitation. The results of this acidic deposition, including injured and killed forest plants and fish in the eastern U.S., were increasingly recognized in the 1970s and 1980s.

In 1990, Clean Air Act legislation pioneered a cap-and-trade program to halve sulfur dioxide emissions through market-based incentives. The Environmental Protection Agency, by limiting the amount of sulfur each coal-burning power plant could emit, encouraged power plants to explore creative methods for reducing sulfur emissions, for example, through installing smokestack scrubbers. Those plants that were slow in reducing their emissions would need to purchase emissions rights from power plants that had worked innovatively to lower their emissions. The Acid Rain Program has saved an estimated $50 billion annually in public health costs. Sulfur dioxide emissions have fallen dramatically, and rainfall has dropped in acidity. Some lakes and forests are showing signs of recovery.

International consensus banning harmful chemicals. Cap-and-trade limitations of destructive smokestack gases. The U.S. successfully used both these tools in the late 1900s. We showed they can work well.

Why have some fought so hard against their application to carbon dioxide emissions, which arguably pose a far greater threat? If only we had started real action on the climate-change problem in the late 1980s, perhaps we wouldn't now be seeing as much rapid melting in the Arctic or such intense early-spring rainfalls in Iowa.

If only I had realized in the 1980s, while I was folding laundry and washing dishes, that insidious changes were occurring inside my own body. It's springtime 1985. I am sitting in a surgeon's office with one-year-old Matt on my lap. The older boys are in school. Robert sits next to me, thumbing through a magazine without reading it. A few days before, during my annual physical, the doctor noted small areas of calcification on my mammogram. He called me immediately. "I'm making an appointment for a biopsy." So here we are.

"Connie?" the nurse calls, fixing her eyes more on Matt than on me—sandy-haired Matt with his pudgy cheeks, who is tugging at my arm and fingering my watch. I squeeze him, hand him to Robert, and enter the examination room. During the biopsy the nurse cringes as the red of my blood pools with white milk spurting from severed milk ducts. The next day, we learn that the abnormalities are what we all had feared: malignant. A mastectomy is scheduled for three days hence.

I return home to stare out of the kitchen window at the woodland stretching into the distance. Strange, but a few days before, it had shown the first colorful signs of spring. Now all I can see are hues of gray. No color at all. Even more strange, I notice that March breezes are tugging at tree branches holding flittering birds. But all such sounds are muted. The next few days, my stomach does not feel right. I don't sleep well. I have to force myself to eat. Sometimes I cannot contain my tears. I turn aside so the boys won't notice them falling. The evening before the surgery, feeling raw and vulnerable, imagining myself nothing more than compromised flesh and blood, I rock the older boys and tell them I love them, then nurse Matt one last time and snuggle him to sleep. Then I go to lie sleepless on a terror-soaked bed.

The next morning Robert drives me to the hospital and holds my hand until I am wheeled into the operating room, where a mask is clamped over my nose and mouth and I sink into oblivion. I awake to nausea, vomiting, and a red searing pain in my chest so intense that it burns away any desire to live. I lie like a mummy wrapped in hospital sheets for three days, trying to hold still (moving sets off the nausea) and watching my serum drip from a tube stringing from my chest into a plastic drain bag. The breast that used to feed my baby is gone, replaced with a thick gauze bandage spotted with dried blood—a sign of all I have lost.

Things did not get easier after I returned home, at least not at first. The sharp pain faded to a dull ache and the nausea subsided, but I was exhausted. I wanted to nap after the smallest task, like putting peanut butter sandwiches on the lunch table. I snapped at the kids for no reason. I yearned to curl up in a warm, quiet, dark corner and enter oblivion.

Why the fatigue, the bad temper, the depression? I told myself that healing from major surgery was hard. And learning I had cancer was a shock, everything happened so fast. I also could see that my cancer had reopened my well of grief about Mom's cancer and death.

But underneath all this, I knew, was the unspoken dread that I was following my mother's course toward death. I was terrified that my young boys would be left alone as I had been, that their orderly, predictable, trustworthy lives would vanish. That they would need to fend for themselves through all the chaotic changes to come. Of course, Robert would still be there. But I knew the robust, nurturing love of a dependable mother and home, and I knew what it meant to lose these. I sat in the living room watching the boys, who were oblivious to my anguish, build cities out of blocks and arrange their tiny cars inside.

The spring dragged into summer, pulling me reluctantly along. The myriad lives in our woodland worked to draw me outside myself, but I did not respond. It wasn't until autumn, the season of senescence when plants die back and the woodland becomes more transparent, that I felt the tension and fear softening. Finally, on a windy Saturday morning in October, they blew away. While the boys were playing with Legos in the living room and I was vacantly gazing out the kitchen window at blackbirds flocking and geese flying south overhead, the truth came to me: I was not my mother. I was not dying.

I was a healthy thirty-eight-year-old woman who had faced cancer and, at least for now, had won. A fog lifted from my brain, and I heard a replay of the words the doctor had spoken months before, when he was standing beside the hospital bed. "We moved fast and we caught your cancer early. It was contained. Your lymph nodes were clean. You have every chance for a healthy life."

Why hadn't those words registered before? I didn't know—nor did I now care, because that day I started to feel energy for the first time since my diagnosis. "Let's go for a walk and take our lunch along," I called to the boys, "and maybe we can see a movie tonight!" They looked up at me in amazement, then dropped their toys and ran to the door.

Over the next several months, I embarked on a new educational course, one attuned to my body's needs. I started reading about cancer prevention and discovered a large palette of proactive choices. I adopted a low-fat, mostly whole-grains-and-vegetables diet stressing foods with antioxidants like broccoli, spinach, and kale. Then I reinstituted regular exercise, something I'd given up when the children had joined our family. Weight was not a problem, but stress was. I learned to meditate and, more importantly, started doing it. I read about the mind-body connection and how emotions can affect the immune system. When I lay down to rest, I pictured health and strength flowing through my body. I considered what it meant to take care not only of my family but also of myself and decided I needed to move more slowly and demand less of myself. Take time to sit with a cup of tea and stare out the window, snuggle and read with the kids, cultivate friendships and a support network. And I was religious about regular medical checkups.

In these ways, I worked to help my body repel the chaos, the pain, the unpredictability of another bout with cancer. These actions were my attempts to circumvent a repeat of the fear in the night and the emotional storms—the radical departures from normal life that cancer had precipitated. What I wanted, of course, was a life I could count on, a life like the one I had lost.

But nothing could ever again be as it was before. My body had changed, as had my life, which now felt weighted down with new requirements and demands on my time. For example, planning and fixing two dinners—one new-diet for myself and one old-diet for the rest of the family, whose food preferences remained unchanged. However, I kept going, and eventually I realized that in exchange for inconveniences such as these, I and my family had been gifted with a positive, hopeful future.

Because cancer was caught early and treated aggressively, I had choices my mother never had. And this made all the difference. I determined to remain vigilant in order to stay alive and continue providing support for my children. I had learned that recognizing problems early and immediately doing whatever I could to solve them gave me a chance at a full life—a lesson I have since applied to many other aspects of life, including most recently my consideration of climate change.

It's 1989, four years after my surgery. The boys are trotting up the lane to catch the school bus, Andy pulling little Matt along by the hand. I watch them from the doorway until the bus disappears down the road. Then I take a few minutes to sit at the kitchen table and relax with a cup of tea before heading into town. The rising sun lights the room as daydreams of past, present, and future times glide through my mind. To my right, a family antique, a cherry cupboard made by my great-great-grandfather, holds my mother's Sunday dishes that I now use on holidays. Someday, I imagine I'll offer these to my boys and their wives. Behind me, the wall is decorated with photographs of my family. In coming years, I trust that I will add photos of the next generation. To my left, a door leads outside onto a screened porch, where we'll have dinner tonight and talk about the day. In front of me, birds peck at the seeds I've just added to the feeder, juncos and chickadees and woodpeckers and nuthatches, creatures who instinctively trust that their world will not change, unaware of the fact that changes are already on the way.

Suddenly, a single bird startles from the feeder and rises skyward.

PART IV

Autumn

EIGHT

Weather & Climate Journal
October–December, 2012

OCTOBER 1 ◡ Autumn creeps into the woods on baby steps. I note the changes more by what's disappearing than by what remains. Many of the taller plants have melted back into the soil, so that as a whole the woodland understory is shorter than before. Soon I'll again be able to walk through the woods with ease, and I will forget how in summer I need waders to penetrate the dense vegetation.

Migrating birds have been drifting through, raptors soaring singly or in small groups above the reservoir near our home, and large flocks of geese and ducks settling on the water to rest and feed. October will also bring dark-eyed juncos back from their breeding grounds in the Northwoods. Meanwhile other birds will leave— blackbirds, for example, which are forming large mixed flocks, the red-wingeds mingling with brown-headed cowbirds and grackles, the starlings joining in, all staging for their southward flight. The bats have either found a local site to hibernate or migrated south to where they can feed through the winter. One night I was mesmerized by them circling the house and snapping up bugs attracted by houselights; the next, they were absent, just like that.

When temperatures drop below freezing, the songs of crickets and katydids will cease, their music replaced by the rustling of drying leaves and the trees' last great annual show, when their leaves turn russet and red, yellow and orange and brown. If temperatures hold, the multicolored leaves could stay on their branches for weeks, changing the trees into bright lollipops on stick trunks. But at some point, hopefully on a day with bright skies and a brisk freshness in the air, the winds will rise and leaves will fly in a snowstorm of color and dance, twisting and twirling as they soar and circle and drift to the ground. Then I'll kick my way through their thick layers, just as I did when I was a kid. As a fire-prevention precaution, I'll rake them away from the house, forming the gigantic piles that my boys used to love for jumping and tossing.

I accept these days of quieting not as stories of diminishment but rather as part of the great cycle of life. I know that the seeds of life remain—the tubers of perennial plants hiding in the soils alongside hibernating toads and insect grubs, the migratory birds and bats seeking out safety and warmth in southern locales. These seasonal disappearances are orderly, sequential, predictable processes that speak of the maintenance of life.

The patterns may be muted in coming years. Already many of Earth's species are fading under the press of expanding human needs. Climate change intensifies existing stresses—polluted air or water, habitat destruction—and also adds stresses of its own. Often overlooked is an increase in health problems. For example, the moose in northern Minnesota, where we love to canoe, are suffering rapid declines in part because of massive tick infestations—over 100,000 ticks can be found on some animals. Why? Today's shorter, warmer winters with less snow allow ticks to soar in number, and their infestations produce anemic "ghost moose" carrying multiple deadly parasites.

Plants and animals confronted with intensified climate change and its effects will have two options: adapt, or migrate to an area where the climate better suits their needs. Some species will do one or both of these with ease, but unfortunately stresses may be building too fast for other native species to adjust or move to safety. Those species may simply disappear.

No one can say exactly how high extinction rates may go—estimates predict that 10 to 50 percent or even more of all current plants and animals could be gone by 2100 if current emissions trends continue.

It follows that rising extinction rates could cause extreme

disruption of the planet's natural communities, thus decreasing the natural world's stability and its capacity to provide life-sustaining services—things like cleansing the water and air, moderating drought and floods, forming soils, recycling nutrients, providing pollinators for our crops, and decomposing wastes. Humanity's needs are intertwined with those of nature's creatures and natural systems. They need our protection. We need their services. Their survival depends on us and ours depends on them.

Nature's practical services are crucial, but there's also something deeper at risk. Years ago, I read of a tribal boy whose tropical-rainforest home was threatened by oil development. When asked what the loss of the birds, monkeys, sloths, and other animals would mean to him, he replied, "I would be lonely without them."

I think of this now and of how my evening begins with a certain midsized tree frog surfacing from a flower pot on our deck, creeping along the deck railing, and leaping onto our kitchen window, where it hangs perpendicular to the ground, catching insects attracted by the light inside. And with a pair of bats emerging from the bark of the hickory tree just outside our bedroom window, stretching their wings, and rising into the darkening sky. If they disappeared, how would I time my summer evenings, I wonder?

I fear the gradual graying of the world, the dissolving of the delightful freshness of a new spring day, the fading away of the color of songbirds and butterflies, the twinkling out of first one woodland wildflower, then another, each loss a diminution of the whole. How do we put a value on quality of life? If these degradations come to pass, what will nourish the human spirit? There are some losses that I cannot fathom. Rather than contemplate them, I try to use my days to quietly push the world in other directions.

Yesterday I dug a cluster of delicate lily-like bellwort plants from a path where they were getting trampled, then divided the roots and replanted them in a safer spot. The plants were entering winter senescence, the bellwort leaves about to fall from the stems, so I was amazed by what I saw protruding from the root clusters: dozens of inch-long robust white sprouts extending upward, ready to pierce the soil surface early next spring and produce yellow flowers in abundance. I never anticipated that there could be so much life hidden underneath this one small patch of drying leaves, so much anticipation of the future, so much dedication to producing beauty in abundance.

OCTOBER 12 ∾ Last night I made yogurt, as I do every week. I heat milk before I go to bed, let it cool, add some powdered milk and starter from the previous batch, and pour it all into my yogurt maker to incubate overnight. By morning, the liquid has become a thick gel, creamy white, glassy-smooth. Milk recreated. Perfection. I dip in a spoon to savor the first bite. Once again it's delicious, a bit tart but ever so good.

Waking to this vision, this taste, reminds me of how much we depend on transformation, on raw or unwanted substance being reformed into something healthy and good. The woodlands do this day after day, year after year, taking the sticks and leaves that fall from tree crowns and the smaller plants that brown and wither in the fall and reducing their substance to raw materials that are reincorporated into new life. I see this as the natural world made new, over and over again. I think of the process as nature's way of repeatedly forgiving us, of giving us another chance. How strong, our need for forgiveness.

OCTOBER 18 ∾ I've been out raking leaves. It feels too soon to be doing this, but leaves started turning in a major way after a hard frost on September 23, about three weeks earlier than usual. Soon afterward the countryside became a collage of intense yellows, oranges, and brilliant reds, with many trees changing color in quick succession. The bright hues did not last long. The foliage change was followed by weeks of large temperature fluctuations—sunny hot days interspersed with much colder times. And by periods of strong winds, when leaves flew through the air, transforming the woodland sky into a rainstorm of color. It seemed like a race through a spectacular but early, short autumn. Was this because of the ongoing drought? Or because the trees leafed out so early last spring? I can only guess.

By mid-October the oak leaves had mostly turned bronze, brown, and reddish gold, and all it took was a few more days of strong winds and thunderstorms to cascade them down in droves. Now the trees are nearly bare. Time to rake the leaves off the lawn and entrance path. I pile them high, then load them onto a tarp and drag them far into the woods where I spread them thin.

I'm used to raking a few weeks later, when days are as crisp and cool, clear and crunchy as a fresh-picked apple, or when the usually chilly fall days give way to a brief reprieve of warmth, the last of the year, a time we call Indian summer. I pull on old jeans and sneakers, maybe a sweatshirt, and head outside. I usually rake during the day, when I'm serenaded by woodpeckers and watch the chipmunks and squirrels dart ahead of me into the woods, collecting nuts and stashing them underground. But I prefer to rake by moonlight, when I see little but feel the closing of the woodland, the leaves withering, the understory plants shrinking to soil-bound root systems, and the animals disappearing to hidden winter beds.

OCTOBER 25 ♋ This morning, a strong cold front brought rain as well as thousands of migratory birds. The woods were full of them. Cedar waxwings, various sparrows and blackbirds, purple finches, towhees, many birds I couldn't identify, winged lives on the move, chased south by the coming winter.

NOVEMBER 1 ♋ This past weekend, the news was rife with warnings about an unusually large hurricane following the Gulf Stream northward from the Caribbean. The storm hit land near Atlantic City, New Jersey, yesterday evening. One of the worst storms ever to strike the U.S. One of the largest hurricanes ever to hit the Atlantic coastline. Some people are calling it Superstorm Sandy. Others, Frankenstorm.

I sat glued to the computer for hours, listening to reports of the hurricane's advance and character, watching picture after picture of the devastation. Sandy was unusual in many ways. For one thing, it was huge, covering a good share of the eastern continent, with tropical-storm-strength winds blowing over an area a thousand miles in diameter. For another, it took an uncommon route, turning sharply westward from the Atlantic onto the coast, and then heading toward the Midwest, rather than heading eastward out to sea as Atlantic hurricanes normally do. And one more thing—once on land, Sandy merged with an eastward-moving cold system, forming a hybrid storm whose size, energy, reach, and destructive power were all magnified. A "monstrous hybrid vortex," some are saying. Sandy continued to spin west and north, finally losing energy and disintegrating in Wisconsin and Canada.

Along its way, Sandy produced heavy rains and (at upper elevations) blizzards from Virginia to Rhode Island and strong winds that blew westward all the way to Chicago. The hurricane broke multiple weather records. It affected half the states in the U.S.; virtually every state east of the Mississippi River felt its impact.

But Sandy maximized its damage by landing in one of the nation's most heavily populated regions. Residents of New York City and the nearby New Jersey and Connecticut coastlines suffered the most. Storm surge waters, supplemented by high tides, large pounding waves, heavy rains, and sustained winds of 80 miles per hour (and gusting higher) wreaked havoc. Ocean waters rose to record levels in New York City, flooding streets across lower Manhattan and filling subway and commuter tunnels with corrosive salt water.

Newscasters are predicting that Sandy will become one of the most expensive hurricanes on record, second only to Katrina in 2005. Damages will run in the tens of billions. But the costs are far greater than monetary. They include nearly 150 Americans killed, thousands unaccounted for or trapped in flooded homes, hundreds of thousands evacuated. Sick and elderly residents isolated without medicines, food, or heat. At least 650,000 U.S. homes damaged or destroyed. Electrical power gone for 8.5 million people; some places, it may not be restored for weeks or months. Schools, factories, and stores closed, hospitals evacuated, the New York Stock Exchange barred, 20,000 commercial flights cancelled. Lower Manhattan silent, dark, and under water. Fires ravaging the tattered remains of other communities.

What caused this massive wreckage? Was this superstorm related to climate change, and if so, how? Multiple links between the two are starting to be made, with two of the links being unequivocal. For one, sea level around New York City is about a foot higher than it was a century ago because of melting ice sheets and thermal expansion of ocean waters. In addition, apply to Sandy the warmer atmosphere's ability to hold more of the moisture evaporated from warming oceans. That moisture is then drawn into storms and dumped out in heavier rainfalls, which are deposited on the higher seas. These combined factors elevated Sandy's storm surge and its flood potential well above what it would have been a century ago.

A third climate-change feature probably increased the storm's severity: unusually high sea-surface temperatures. Hurricanes are fed by warm oceans, and this October, along the East Coast, sea surface temperatures were up to five degrees warmer than normal. Much of that rise may have been from natural variability, but climate change also has been raising ocean surface temperatures since the 1970s, and this is thought to have contributed a notable fraction of the energy that fed the storm.

The fourth and most tenuous linkage to climate change involves, once again, the weakening of the polar jet stream. Several analyses have suggested that the jet stream is more often forming persistent, sluggish loops that block the normal movement of weather systems. A very strong high-pressure atmospheric blocking pattern over Greenland helped turn Sandy west, onto the Atlantic coastline, where it merged with the eastward-moving winter storm.

So—what caused Sandy? While global warming may not have created Sandy, it could have intensified Sandy's massive size, and it added at least a foot to the storm surge, which enhanced flooding damage substantially. Climate change took an existing weather event and put it on steroids, thus magnifying the storm's most disastrous inclinations.

While the multifaceted effects of this storm have yet to be assessed, we know that the recovery will be long and difficult. Now efforts are focusing on finding the dead and guaranteeing that the living have food, water, shelter, and heat, difficult commodities to provide without electricity or transportation networks. And then, once immediate needs are met, decision-makers will need to turn to the rising seas, consider the atmosphere's growing thermal energy and rising moisture content, and ask how to prepare for the still-larger storms that are sure to come.

NOVEMBER 3 ❧ I was reading at the kitchen table yesterday evening when I heard a rumble and then a huge crash—the sound of multiple branches breaking followed by a tremendous thump. The noise came from south of the house, so I guessed that it was one of the two-foot-diameter red oaks near the creekbed falling to the ground. A cluster of four such trees died years ago from oak wilt. Robert wanted to fell them for firewood, but I pleaded to let them stand, citing the advantages of dead trunks for wildlife. And indeed they have provided many benefits. I've watched pileated woodpeckers excavating nesting holes in these trees, holes then enlarged and used by squirrels and later occupied by wood ducks. Barred owls too have nested here. And of course there were many smaller occupants, red-headed and red-bellied woodpeckers, nuthatches, flying squirrels, the thousands of insects that broke down the tree's fibers. In winter, I'm sure that clusters of chickadees filled unoccupied excavations, roosting communally for warmth, puffing out their feathers and cuddling into a single ball.

All these memories filled my mind when I rose this morning as the dawn sky was outlining the upper branches of the woodland trees with a muted yellow. I walked directly onto the deck. My assumption was correct: there at the bottom of the slope was the white bark-free trunk of a woodland giant lying on the ground, its splintered branches flung in all directions. The tree was shattered.

The fall of the tree did not sadden me. Dead trees are supposed to crash down after living a long life, as this one did. But today, looking down on a splintered tree, I found myself shivering. I couldn't help but fixate on the hush before the fall. The previous evening's deep stillness, when the world outside my window was peacefully sleeping and there was no sign of anything amiss, even though for years the necessary prerequisites of this final demise had been quietly accumulating—the tree's roots rotting away, its massive trunk becoming riddled with animal and insect holes, the tips of its branches breaking off in the wind. When the accumulated conditions were sufficient, the tree fell. Not in a windstorm or under the weight of heavy snowfall, but in the middle of a still night.

As I stood in the dawn and looked down, my mind traveled back to the day before my cancer diagnosis when I nursed my infant son and sang him to sleep, not suspecting that even as I did so, my body's cells were wildly proliferating. Then I thought of the hour before the ripping line-winds struck the eastern U.S. this past summer. And the moment before Sandy's storm surge slammed into the continent's coast and assaulted our nation's largest city. As with the oak, the prerequisites had been mounting—the atmosphere accumulating thermal energy and moisture, the sea warming and its waters rising, the jet stream slowing and looping. The carbon dioxide invisibly accumulating in the summer skies, the Arctic ice pack slipping away. If only we had long ago recognized the warning signs of these ongoing processes and acted on them, would we have deflated their multiplying impacts?

The climatic prerequisites continue to accumulate, one upon another, but I wonder toward what end? We can model some of the changes to come as climatic balances tip further toward instability. But what key considerations are shaping the future?

Within the current century, the timeframe addressed by most climate-change studies, we know some but not all determinants. For example, we know that we have gone too far to eliminate climate-change repercussions. We also know that in coming years, many types of extreme weather will become more intense. The greater the future greenhouse-gas emissions and the more the temperature rises, the worse the problems will become.

And we know that because carbon dioxide has a long tail, we cannot exclude all future climate change. A quarter of the human-produced carbon dioxide that's accumulated in the atmosphere today will remain a thousand years from now. It will continue to trap infrared radiation and further raise Earth's temperature for thousands of years to come. The excess fossil-fuel-generated heat that's been stored deep in the oceans will also raise future air temperatures, as that heat over long time periods rebalances with the atmosphere. Today, given these two factors and current atmospheric emissions, we are already committed to a future global average temperature rise of about a degree. Future greenhouse-gas emissions will raise that commitment still higher.

A few more factors: we know that climate change is not totally predictable, and since humans have never before struggled with a warming planet, we do not fully comprehend where today's changes will take us. Why, for example, are many climate-change problems expressing themselves faster than scientists had predicted? And what of climate-change spinoffs such as unstoppable feedback loops or tipping points slipping out of control—how and when will these come into play? We appear to have crossed one tipping point already, leading to the rapid melting and probable dissolution of Arctic ice, a melt that is already changing the planet's ability to reflect incoming sunlight and that seems to be altering our continent's weather.

I now see that we will be struggling with climate change and its repercussions, including some that we cannot foresee, for the indefinite future. But how much will our increasingly hot, humid, turbulent skies shape the years to come?

To answer this question, I need to know how high future temperatures will rise. I spread out a newly published graph on the table before me. The graph charts global-average surface temperatures, actual and predicted, from 1900 to 2100. It starts with a single gently rising line that traces actual temperature measurements to around 2010.

Beyond that date, the single line splits into multiple lines of different colors, representing possible temperature futures based on different emissions scenarios. All these lines trend upward and become steeper, with the most dramatic line shooting skyward within a few decades. This last line represents our current trajectory, the place we are going if we don't rapidly reduce current greenhouse-gas emissions. This is our business-as-usual scenario, the one that could by midcentury spin us beyond the 3.6-degree temperature increase that's considered the maximum safe rise for avoiding dangerous impacts on the climate system. This line could take us beyond a 10-degree average temperature increase by 2100, a full seven times our current 1.4-degree rise. And this is where we are now headed.

I look away from the graph and read about what such dramatic temperature increases would mean. With current business-as-usual emissions, by 2100 many locations in the U.S. would have 75, 100, or more days every year with temperatures above 100 degrees, compared to fewer than 20 such days per year in the recent past. Within the same time span, extreme precipitation events would be multiplied by five—five gully washers cutting new channels through our woods, for every one such rainfall we have today.

But the report that stuns me the most describes the potential emergence of extreme, unprecedented, and continuous heat waves sweeping across the globe in the 2030s to 2050s, much sooner than was previously predicted. Possibly within my own lifetime. With this departure from today's seasonal norms, the average annual air temperatures across many parts of the globe would be hotter than the most extreme annual temperatures we've experienced in the past 150 years. We would still have heat waves and cold spells, thunderstorms and snow, summer and winter, but in another very real sense, Earth's climate would change beyond recognition, making the world that I and my ancestors have known a thing of the past.

Something in me rejects this possibility as absurd. Neither our physiology nor our lifestyles, social patterns, or infrastructure are adapted to such heat. And yet this future diagnosis is not fiction. Here is the newly published research report in front of me, a massive analysis of numerous climate models.

My eyes return to the graph to search for more hopeful futures.

Two future-temperature lines rise less steeply. These reflect what would happen if nations meet their current emissions-reduction pledges: temperatures would rise more gently than with the business-as-usual scenario, but they would still exceed the 3.6-degree safe limit.

Then I notice two more lines tucked underneath the others, closer to the bottom of the graph. These lines describe a future with temperatures remaining below the 3.6-degree limit. They represent low emissions scenarios that reduce the use of fossil fuels dramatically and soon. Can such temperature futures be achieved? Yes indeed, the accompanying text states. It is both technically and economically possible. Numerous studies have shown the feasibility of low-emissions scenarios that combine multiple factors including energy conservation, new technologies, and shifts to renewable energy sources.

Gazing at the graph, two facts become clear. First, without major changes soon, our current temperature increase and its resulting problems will be a mere shadow of what's to come as climate change overwhelms all aspects of human life. We have only just begun to feel the repercussions of climate change: we are today in a position likely to be envied by future generations.

Second—and here's the main point—we still have options. There is still time. The size and extent of future climate change depend on what we do next. While we cannot eliminate climate change, we can govern its sway over our lives. Future temperature increases will be determined almost entirely by how much more carbon dioxide is emitted. Whether we ignore this fact or work to control proliferating emissions is within our control. Every year, every day, we are deciding which line to inscribe on the graph that defines Earth's and humanity's future.

NOVEMBER 4 ❧ I finally went down to examine the large oak that fell below the house. The trunk had cracked open from the impact of the fall, and broken branches had been thrown some distance. A ball of roots and dirt remained at the base. Then I noted motion near the upper end of the trunk, which lay like an opened book on the ground, displaying all that had been inside. Bees. A bee hive, with row upon row of yellow honeycomb lining the tree's formerly hidden inner recesses.

My first reaction was total delight. A wild bee hive in our woods, secluded in the top of a tree that I had observed daily for the past several years, a hidden treasure of golden sweetness, of wax combs dripping honey!

Then I looked more closely and saw that this was more a story of death than life. The exposed hive had been ravaged by raccoons and skunks. Chunks of honeycomb had been pulled from the trunk and scattered on the ground. The waxy tree innards were littered with dead bees. The living bees that I was watching were robber bees from another hive, attracted by the smell of honey. Only a few days before, the hive had been a complex living community creating intricately designed wax cells filled with honey and pollen. Now it was a ruin. I called my neighbor, a beekeeper, who came to salvage the remaining honeycomb. He'll use it to make lotions and candles that he sells at the farmers' market.

Back in the house, I turned on the radio and listened to reports about the ongoing devastation of Sandy. Six days after the storm struck, over 1.5 million homes and businesses in New York and New Jersey remain without electricity, and temperatures are dropping. A major snowstorm may hit the ravaged area in a few days. Relief agencies have set up warming shelters and are handing out blankets. Gasoline shortages are severe because fuel can't be delivered to gas stations, and many stations don't have electricity to operate their pumps. Drivers are standing in lines several blocks long, sometimes for hours. Tempers are rising, as are fears of lawlessness and looting. The storm victims are cold and miserable.

The focus on Sandy is forcing me to think about one of climate change's most serious threats: sea-level rise. This is a subject that I usually ignore, living as I do far from any oceans. But the ongoing suffering on the East Coast is putting a face on the future. I've read that in coming years, rising ocean levels will displace hundreds of millions of people in low-lying countries like Bangladesh; inundate major cities such as Miami; obliterate small island nations such as the Maldives; and confront all seaside locations with ever-higher storm surges and catastrophic coastal flooding.

Global sea levels have increased fairly steadily over the past 130 years, and the rate of the upsurge is now accelerating. In the last two decades, since 1993, sea level rise has been almost double the rate of the preceding 80 years. That's led to a mean global sea level rise of eight inches in the twentieth century—a rise that is unevenly expressed around the world (consider the twelve-inch rise in the New York area; studies have shown that sea levels along portions of the U.S. Atlantic coast are rising three to four times faster than the global average).

Climate change has contributed to the oceans' rise in two manners. First, water from melting ice sheets and continental glaciers has increased the absolute amount of water in the oceans. Second, because average ocean global surface temperatures have risen about 0.8 degrees between 1971 and 2010 and because water expands as it warms, oceanic waters now occupy more space.

Both factors are expected to increase in coming years. Current estimates predict that the world's oceans will rise on average 10 to 32 inches by the end of this century, with regional variations in the exact amount. Some models indicate greater near-term rises. The estimates assume that while much of Earth's ice will continue to melt at a steady or increasing pace, large-scale or rapid ice loss from Greenland or the West Antarctic Ice Shelf is possible and could raise sea levels by another foot or more this century. While both are now melting, dramatic ice loss from these locations is not expected before 2100, but it is not impossible. The risk of huge ice losses rises greatly in coming centuries.

Putting sea-level predictions into perspective, a rise of 27 inches would submerge 70 percent of the Miami area. Much higher rises would obliterate the southern third of Florida and swamp many cities along the U.S.'s densely populated East Coast. Today's greenhouse-gas emissions are committing us to bigger sea-level rises far into the future. If we don't massively cut greenhouse-gas emissions, within a few hundred years, most of the world's coastal cities could be largely or completely under water. With 80 percent of the world's population living within a few hundred miles of an ocean coastline, a large proportion of Earth's future inhabitants are at risk of losing their dwellings or facing waves of environmental refugees fleeing the coasts.

NOVEMBER 7 ᐇ Yesterday President Obama was elected for his second term. In his acceptance speech, he stated, "We want our children to live in an America . . . that isn't threatened by the destructive power of a warming planet." I hope these words give hope to parents living in New Jersey and Long Island, where today a new storm is bringing snow, sleet, and winds up to 60 miles per hour. The storm is threatening to produce additional power outages on Long Island, where 200,000 remain powerless from Hurricane Sandy. In nearby New York City, the need for shelter remains overwhelming; between 20,000 and 40,000 people have lost their homes or can't yet return to them. Many more are trying to live in dark, increasingly cold apartments without functional utilities, as the city plunges further into frigid darkness. The international aid agency Doctors Without Borders is helping Sandy's isolated victims, many of whom are elderly. This is the first time ever that the organization, which normally serves war-torn countries, has set up emergency clinics in the U.S.

NOVEMBER 11 ᐇ Yesterday, bright sunshine lit the clear, windy, blue sky and soaked the landscape, turning the drying woodland into a collage of dull tans and browns. Today a steady drizzle swirls clouds of mist among the trees. Brilliance has been lost, but not beauty. I had forgotten how lovely the late-autumn woods become when only a few understory plants remain upright and their colors stand out against the carpet of oak leaves, glistening with moisture under a gray sky—the maroon of leafy raspberry canes, the bright yellow of aster stems topped by white puffs of seeds, the bright green of catbrier vines and tall woodland grasses, and even the rust-colored leaves clinging to ironwoods and some oaks, the last trees in the forest to lose their foliage. On sunny fall days, I barely notice these late-fall outliers. But on gray rainy days like today, the various shades of reds and rusts, yellows and greens, even muted browns and grays all light up in a way that outshines the sun, as if each remaining leaf and stem were glowing with its own inner energy. These days I appreciate the nuance and detail that are easy to miss when I move too fast. These days I believe that yes, the meek, the hidden, the simple lives shall indeed inherit the earth.

As the days grow shorter and darker, I find myself hunkering down into a smaller world, a world that doesn't extend much beyond the house, the woods, and my immediate daily activities. Or maybe my autumn world is deeper rather than smaller—a world where inner voices are more important than outer life. I think in metaphor rather than fact. Late autumn is a quieter time of the year, a less physical time. A restful season. I think I need the coming winter to counterbalance the outward-oriented summertime, when I'm working in the woods nearly every day. I believe that my planet, swinging from day to night, from summer to winter, from glacial to interglacial period, also needs these times of rest and reclusion, at least here in the temperate zone, where animals and plants have grown accustomed to the seasonal pulsing of life for thousands of years.

NOVEMBER 25 ∾ After a quiet Thanksgiving that Robert and I spent with friends, I am back to my research, this time reading a report about the sea butterflies scientists have found in the oceans surrounding Antarctica. The shells of these tiny mollusks were dissolved and severely deformed. I examine a picture of the beautiful pink creatures. They appear to fly through the water on diaphanous wings. Though small, they comprise a vital food source for certain fish. But the calcium carbonate forming their shells shows extreme dissolution because of ocean acidification—"the other carbon dioxide problem" as some say, referring to the growing concentration of oceanic carbonic acid produced from rising levels of dissolved carbon dioxide.

Researchers have long understood that ocean acidification was likely to harm shell-building sea creatures in coming centuries. But this study, the first showing shell disintegration in ocean-collected sea butterflies, reveals that this ecologically important group of mollusks is already suffering such harm. These distant, disintegrating drifters are also a reminder of how my own actions here, in the middle of the continent, affect life even in distant oceans.

About a third of the carbon dioxide we've released into the air has dissolved in the oceans. This oceanic carbon sink has been beneficial for us since it has removed a good portion of our carbon dioxide emissions from the air, but it has been detrimental to many ocean-dwelling organisms. The waterborne carbon dioxide undergoes chemical reactions that shift the oceans' pH from the alkaline toward the acid range of the scale and decrease calcium carbonate minerals needed by crustaceans, mollusks, and other animals for their shells and skeletons. The shift slows the growth of corals and dissolves the carbon-containing shells of mollusks such as the ethereal sea butterflies.

In addition to soaking up atmospheric carbon dioxide, the oceans have absorbed a whopping 90 percent of the heat energy that's been added to the atmosphere from 1971 to 2010. As with carbon dioxide, the oceans' temperature-buffering action is good for us, but not necessarily for ocean dwellers. Many are struggling to cope with a dramatic rise in the oceans' average global surface temperature of about 0.8 degrees in the top 250 feet of water in that time period. Considering the immense size of the oceans—they cover nearly three-fourths of the globe—this amount of added heat is truly astounding.

The oceans' warming temperatures are already proving their power. Corals, for example, need water that's warm but not too warm; they undergo mass bleaching when water temperatures spike. Warming waters are also pulling mobile marine species northward, with these climate-change-induced shifts occurring more rapidly in oceans than on land. Nearly a billion of the world's poorest people, largely in developing countries, rely heavily on oceans for food, jobs, and revenues. These people would be highly vulnerable to climate change's multiple oceanic effects.

NOVEMBER 29 ❧ I just took Sidney on her usual morning walk through the woods. She snuffled her way through the fallen oak leaves, searching for tasty bits to eat. Parts of dead animals? Animal droppings? I don't want to know.

Woodland leaves were white with a heavy frost. Last night, even though I had added three or four good-sized logs to our wood-burning furnace, the supplementary propane kicked in and woke me when the logs had burned to ash. We need to get more wood in today to replenish the small stack we usually keep in the basement.

Birds are abundant at the feeders, honing in on the blocks of suet. I should put out water for the birds; the creek is frozen solid. Today feels like a normal November day—indeed the entire month would feel normal, except that these cold spurts are interspersed with balmy days warming into the 50s and 60s. After these warm days, night temperatures don't drop below freezing, and when I walk Sidney I slide down a trail of mud. This is not normal for wintertime in Iowa. Last winter, the soils froze to a depth of only a few inches rather than the expected few feet.

News reports remind me that things are not normal elsewhere either. I recently read of a dramatic increase in the speed of Canada's springtime snowmelt. This late-season snow cover is now vanishing faster than Arctic ice. The early disappearance of snow dries the ground sooner, alters river-runoff and fish-spawning patterns, and increases the probability of permafrost melt and larger and more frequent wildfires.

Meanwhile, a tanker loaded with natural gas is on its way through the Arctic Ocean via the Northeast Passage, bound for Japan. In the past five years, traffic through the Northeast Passage has in-creased dramatically in late summer and early fall, for both com-mercial ships and tourist boats. The ships are taking advantage of the

50-percent-plus decrease in Arctic ice thickness since the 1970s—and similar decreases in total late-summer sea-ice volume since 1979.

But this particular tanker voyage, inspired by the extensive ice-melting this past summer, is the first that's so late in the year. Arctic melting is clearly opening a new frontier for use and abuse. Ironically, the melting of sea ice initiated by global warming is expected to lead to new Arctic oil and natural gas exploration, releasing new sources of fossil fuels that would create an amplifying feedback loop and further magnify global warming.

The tanker sails on, even as negotiators from nearly two hundred nations meet at the eighteenth United Nations Climate Change Conference of the Parties, COP18. These annual conferences, now held for nearly two decades, constitute the major international forum for dialogue on stabilizing greenhouse-gas concentrations. In less than that period of time, since 2000, the concentration of atmospheric heat-trapping gases like carbon dioxide has jumped 20 percent.

A number of climate summaries have been published in conjunction with the conference. Just before COP18, the World Bank released *Turn Down the Heat: Why a 4°C Warmer World Must Be Avoided*, a powerful report highlighting worldwide consequences of global warming: without dramatic and rapid emissions reductions, a 7.2°F average temperature rise (equivalent to 4°C) will be reached by or before 2100. This rise would be double the safe upper limit of 3.6 degrees that would avoid dangerous human-caused interference with the climate system.

The report states that a 7.2-degree world "is so different from the current one that it comes with high uncertainty and new risks that threaten our ability to anticipate and plan for future adaptation needs. . . . It would be so dramatically different from today's world that it is hard to describe accurately. . . . Climate change affects everything. . . . There is no certainty that adaptation to a 7.2 degree world is possible. . . . A [7.2-degree] world can, and must, be avoided."

On the second day of COP18, a new U.N. Environment Programme report warned that current climate projections are likely to be too conservative because they don't consider the thawing of far-northern permafrost, which is already accelerating. The release of carbon dioxide and methane from thawed permafrost could significantly amplify global warming.

The following day, the U.N.'s climate agency, the World Meteorological Organization, released its *State of the Global Climate* report, which emphasized changes in the Arctic. "The alarming rate of its melt this year highlighted the far-reaching changes taking place on Earth's oceans and biosphere," stated WMO Secretary-General Michel Jarraud. "Climate change is taking place before our eyes and will continue to do so."

And today, a major new study reported that like Greenland and the Arctic, Antarctica is losing ice mass and its rate of loss is accelerating.

All of these changes are happening faster than climate scientists had expected. Sometimes this information is too much for me. As with Sidney's foragings, I don't want to know the details. I don't want to understand that our possible future may too soon become our present. I can ignore that fact here in our woodland home, and I often choose to do so. Here things seem to be pretty much as they always have been. The shells of my woodland mollusks—tiny land snails—look just fine to me, and I have no permafrost to worry about.

DECEMBER 3 ❧ December 3, and here in the woods it's 72 degrees—72 degrees in December. Unheard of. Probably another record-high temperature. With the wintertime warmth, we do not have to heat our passive solar house at all. But summertime in December? A heavy wet feeling presses in. Because the past few days have been cool at night, moisture has condensed on surfaces everywhere and is now dripping: from the bird feeders, the sides of our house, the leaves. The garage floor is a puddle, and I am concerned that tools we store there might start to rust. I would love to open the windows to the balmy breezes but I daren't. Once again, I won't chance the growth of mildew in the house.

People always comment on the weather. I've noticed that more and more often they say that unseasonably warm days like today are too strange, too unusual for comfort. But some passers-by on the streets still casually remark, "Beautiful day, isn't it?" and I return, "It certainly is warm out," and smile. I don't want to become a doomsdayer. I want to say this: "Warm, yes, but everything comes with a price. Think more broadly. Consider the possible costs."

One such cost is detailed in a new report commissioned by the CIA and other federal agencies on security risks associated with climate change. The eighteen-month study concluded that in coming years, accelerating climate change will place unparalleled strains on American military and intelligence agencies by causing ever more disruptive events—changes in water, food, and energy supplies and public health around the world that could cause internal instability and international conflict. Failed states, famine, flood, disease, wandering environmental refugees, inadequate resources to cope—all are likely future scenarios for our military and humanitarian agencies. Hurricane Sandy provided a preview of what to expect in the near future, the lead author stated, but the damage could get much worse.

DECEMBER 8 ∾ The United Nations' COP18 talks concluded today, claiming only a "modest step forward" but no major achievements. The Kyoto Protocol, the current international agreement for decreasing greenhouse-gas emissions country by country, was set to expire but instead has been extended for eight years, granting time for negotiating a new international agreement. A work plan for those negotiations was developed. Also, discussions were held concerning formation of a Green Climate Fund, with contributions from wealthy nations going to the poorer developing nations, those that will be hurt most by climate change but have contributed least to its development. This subject created considerable dissension, and little progress was made.

Nothing in the conference summaries affected me as much as an impassioned plea, made in response to Super Typhoon Bopha, which hit the Philippines in the past week with winds of 175 miles per hour. The typhoon killed nearly 2,000 people, displaced hundreds of thousands, flattened villages and banana plantations, and brought flooding, mudslides, and misery to many. Upon learning of Bopha, the lead COP18 negotiator for the Philippines made a heartfelt plea for greater dedication to meaningful discussions. "As we sit here in these negotiations, even as we vacillate and procrastinate here, the death toll is rising. . . . I appeal to the whole world, I appeal to leaders from all over the world, to open our eyes to the stark reality that we face," he beseeched, breaking into tears. "I appeal to all, please, no more delays, no more excuses. Please, let [this conference] be remembered as the place where we found the political will to turn things around."

I frequently take off down the trail with Sidney at dusk, returning home when skies blacken. Doing so, I've noticed that there's an instant when moon shadows first appear. One minute the ground surface appears smooth and featureless. The next minute, patterns of twigs and branches draw detailed lacey squiggles across the trail, and the darkening skies draw attention to what was there all along: a full moon up above, shooting its muted rays of light through the trees.

Today I thought that this is what we need regarding climate change. An "aha" moment, a clarity of understanding and recognition, an acceptance of the diagnosis and a willingness to do whatever it takes to control carbon dioxide's rapid multiplication, a decision by both ordinary people and policy makers to make climate change a priority and find a cure. A time when we say, "Now I see. Now I accept. Now I act."

DECEMBER 16 ∾ After all the weather-related destruction of the past year, we're now in recovery mode, which is proving to be more difficult and expensive than originally thought. For example, when Superstorm Sandy struck several weeks ago, damages were estimated at a whopping $30 to $50 billion. But already Congress is considering a $60 billion supplemental relief appropriation, and total expenses may go higher.

While Sandy may be grabbing the headlines, the nation's most long-lasting climate challenge may be recovery from the lack of rain. In 2012, 80 percent of U.S. agricultural land experienced drought. The large drought footprint moderated a bit this fall, but on the whole it has remained remarkably unchanged. Drought still claims nearly two-thirds of the nation, just as it did during the drought's peak in July. This year's drought is the most extensive since the Dust Bowl of the 1930s. Exceptional drought continues to cover much of the Great Plains, with less severe drought extending from California to Illinois. All of Iowa remains droughty, with intensity greatest toward the west. The ground is so chalky-dry now that squirrels in our woods, digging for nuts, raise a plume of gray powder.

I'm starting to see statistics on the drought's effects. Corn and soybean prices rose as their harvests fell 20 and 14 percent respectively below last year's levels, a smaller dip than had been expected. However, the year's reduced grain harvest still cost Iowa farmers over a billion dollars in lost revenue. Now the grain can't be barged as usual down the Mississippi River, which is dangerously narrow and shallow because of near-record low water levels. This important artery for commerce, which ships $7 billion of corn and other goods to markets in a normal December-January period, is starting to shut down because of the drought—a threat that could raise further the prices of commodities. Fortunately, retail food prices have not risen as much as originally forecast, at least not yet.

No price has been placed on the personal hardship of nearly 100 million U.S. residents—almost a third of the nation's population—who this past summer sweated their way through ten or more days of temperatures exceeding 100 degrees.

Concerns now extend to crop conditions in the coming year. Precipitation in 2012 was low for nearly all of Iowa. Two months ago, I read that three years of normal rainfall would be required to recover from this year's drought. Since then, fall rainstorms have replenished some of Iowa's missing soil moisture, but soil conditions remain worse than a year ago, and moisture deficits will extend into 2013.

I know that poorer nations are also struggling to recover. But I sometimes find myself mentally blocking their plight. Dealing with the damage close to home is enough for me. I worry about this intentional blind eye—in myself and in the world as a whole. If extreme weather events are accepted as the norm, will we stop responding to the needs of others with open hearts, checkbooks, and volunteer efforts? When will compassion fatigue dry up our wellsprings of concern as well as our cash donations?

In any case, now, here, our weather is quiet, and I am grateful for this. It's taken me a lifetime to learn that the best days are defined not by the presence of excitement and news but rather by their absence, by boring normalcy. No big storms, no untoward trips to the doctor. These are the times I can dig into work and ideas and live deeply, with love and empathy for others, rather than skating across the surface trying to survive.

Of course, I know that these days and weeks with no extreme weather events are deceptive. The silent multiplication of greenhouse gases continues, every day, every hour. Every minute, the risks of greater future climatic change grows larger. The seductive periods of remission, the times when we cannot see or sense the ongoing changes, when weather is calm and life is pleasant, too easily lull us into inactivity that restrains us from working toward life-giving treatment and preventive action.

DECEMBER 17 ∿ One week until Christmas. The kids and grandkids will arrive tomorrow. Today is the day to make beds, plan dinners, get out decorations, wrap presents, and generally prepare the house for taking our boys back to a time when their wishes could be easily met.

Meanwhile, others have wishes of their own. The squirrels, for example, who woke me this morning by noisily clambering across the roof, trying to drop down onto the hanging bird feeder stuffed with nuts and seeds. Their wish was for easy access.

And me—I have my own wishes. I wish for air cold enough to tend the jet stream and keep it in its rightful place. Cold enough to refreeze the melting permafrost and halt its discharge of potent methane gas. I'm dreaming of frigid air that turns today's drizzles into snow that wipes away the dull grayness and covers our earth—our woodland—with whiteness, newness, and hope.

I'm wishing for icy winds that blow northward-moving invasive insects and plants back to their southerly homelands. And for health for all the species that belong here in our woodland, for the fungi and spiders as well as squirrels, birds, and all the unseen creatures that rustle through the leaves.

I wish for a climate that is as stable and dependable as that of the last ten millennia—the time span when our human species soared into a position of power but not necessarily wise governance. And for people who care enough about our future to decrease their carbon footprint—and demand that the government do this for the nation. It can be done, I keep thinking. We know what to do. We're lacking the will, but not the techniques. And will is something that can be changed.

While I prepare the house for my family's arrival and think about my wishes, I also consider what I want to do with the grandkids. We'll go outside as much as possible. We'll take hikes and look for treasures—feathers, bits of dried mushrooms and lichens, pieces of wood in unusual shapes or colors. Maybe I'll help the grandkids make art works for their parents with these. We'll also make cookies, and maybe a gingerbread house that usually is eaten before we complete it.

I'll take them shopping for food that we'll donate to our local food bank. And they'll pick out a farm animal that our family can buy for children in other lands; this has become a tradition, a small act that I hope helps the grandkids to consider the needs of others. If we have a snowstorm, I'll bundle them up in snowpants and boots and scarves and send them out to sled down the hill and make houses in the lee of the drifts, the way their dads did a few decades ago. There was more snow back then.

At night, we'll cuddle and sing near the fireplace in the living room, and I'll read to them. Then I'll tuck them into bed with flashlights and tell them to hide the flashlights from their parents. "Just read under the covers as long as you want," I'll whisper, figuring that there's no better way to instill a love of reading than to make it a forbidden delicacy. Then, when the house is stilled and the day's events float through my mind and dissolve into dreams, I'll sit in the kitchen and look out the window at the black and the stars and wait for the salvation of my planet, my home.

DECEMBER 26 ∞ The boys and their families departed this morning, and I'm left with a quiet house and memories. For several days last week, when our home was full and busy, we had warnings that a severe blizzard was on the way. Weather reports predicted a major storm centering over eastern Iowa, dumping a foot of snow that would be reworked by strong winds into ground-blizzards and road-blocking drifts. Following the snow and wind, extreme cold would set in. Anticipating the worst, people flooded grocery stores and wiped many items off the shelves. Our local market was chaotic. The parking lots were packed. Advent services at church were cancelled and many offices were closed. The shopping mall, of course, stayed open.

I was looking forward to the snowstorm. I love feeling that I am snowed in, especially with grandkids here to snuggle near the fireplace and read or play games together. But unfortunately, here in our woods, the temperature didn't fall below the requisite 32 degrees. Instead, a steady reading of 33 produced drizzle with occasional mushy sleet and lightning and thunder that crashed through the wintertime woods and thrilled the grandkids. But the earth itself remained dark and wet, at least until the second morning, when for a brief period the temperatures dropped and gave us a few inches of snow. Enough for a white Christmas, enough for me to pretend the winters were the way they used to be, and enough for the kids to find the sleds in the garage and slide down trails they built through the woods. I loved watching them from the kitchen window, laughing and crashing into each other as their dads had done many years ago. For several days now, since that first and only snowfall, the temperatures have remained below freezing so the snow has lingered, although it's developed a crusty hard surface.

Now that our grandkids are gone, I am asking myself whether their grandchildren will have days of playing in the snow. What will a midwestern winter be like beyond year 2100, the year little Ellie would celebrate her eighty-eighth birthday, a time not really so far away? This question is not easily answered. Few climate-change studies look beyond the present century because the uncertainty is large, variables are numerous, and possibilities are diverse. Any prognosis depends not only on the size and timeframe of ongoing carbon emissions but also on the complexities of Earth's response. Still, we can describe a few possibilities.

Here's the best option: A century from now, we could see our global average temperature rise plateau or even start declining back toward historic norms. Repercussions of climate change would not disappear, but we could be looking back at our worst climate-change fears as historic novelty. This could happen if we cut our greenhouse-gas emissions deeply and soon.

In contrast, if we continue magnifying emissions and accumulating thermal energy in the atmosphere, we could enter a hothouse world with weather impacts beyond today's imagination, with extreme events spreading into all aspects of human life and civilization: food production, water supplies, infrastructure, economic viability, transportation, health concerns, national security, lifestyle choices, public safety—everything. In the long-term future, beyond 2100, in addition to intensification of emerging problems such as mass extinctions, major food shortfalls, and extreme coastal flooding, we are likely to see new tipping points activating nonlinear, abrupt climate change—runaway reactions that create inevitable surprises. Reports mention several possibilities: increasing carbon released from soils and permafrost, disruption of ocean circulation patterns, rapid changes in ecosystems, massive die-offs of tropical rainforests, dissolution of coral reefs.

Some potential changes could require centuries to unfold—for example, the transition to an ice-free world or oceanic releases of the potent greenhouse gas methane. The first, culminating in the melting away of Antarctica's ice, would raise sea levels around the globe another 200 feet and would further magnify temperatures by decreasing the planet's reflection of sunlight. These changes would be extremely significant, but the true horror story involves the potential release of immense stores of methane from deep, frigid ocean deposits around the globe. Should either of these changes occur, a new wave of warming would raise temperatures to devastating new highs. If such tipping points are reached, humans could only watch, becoming witnesses to geologic revolution.

Will temperatures continue to rise indefinitely? Yes, as long as greenhouse gases build in the atmosphere. Eventually, we will choose or be forced to abandon fossil fuels as an energy source, and their carbon dioxide emissions will cease. But even then, because of carbon dioxide's extremely long lifetime in the atmosphere and the excess heat stored in the oceans, global average temperatures will continue to go up for several centuries. Even after temperature rises halt, sea levels will likely continue to rise for centuries more because of the oceans' ongoing thermal expansion. In the meantime, for many thousands of years, Earth's oceans and ecosystems will absorb atmospheric carbon dioxide until eventually our planet finds a new equilibrium, with incoming solar energy balancing outgoing radiation. Earth's average temperature will stabilize, although likely not at the levels we now know.

The worst repercussions of a high-emissions world lie a century or more out and extend into the indefinite future—this is clear to me. We are today creating a climate-change crisis for billions of future people. Because of the long period required for the climate to restabilize, climate change and all its spinoffs are for all human purposes permanent and irreversible.

I think about what would be required of all life-forms during the lengthy recovery period while the climate is restabilizing, how birds and trees and people would be required to adapt to tumultuous planetary change. Would our woodland be able to survive the ongoing transitions and demands? Would humanity? Would civilization? The earth has survived transformations larger than this in the distant prehistoric past. I know that our planet will survive again.

But when I think of the people and culture I hold dear, this truth is little comfort to me.

DECEMBER 27 ♫ Several days after the snowstorm, Robert and I took a long walk starting at dusk. We hiked a five-mile circuit on nearby gravel roads. The air was cold. We had to skirt patches of ice and hard-packed snow to avoid falling. High in the atmosphere, ice crystals scattered the rising moon's rays, giving the near-full globe a pinkish halo that grew larger, then smaller as we walked.

Our route took us mostly through expanses of sleepy pastures with occasional small woodlots—nothing approaching our solid expanse of mature oaks, but still picturesque. With the countryside's uninterrupted coating of snow, the fields continued to glow brightly even as dusk gave way to black skies. Outlines of gentle hills became more sharply accentuated. Slopes appeared as hummocks, smooth and white and round as if they were scattered breasts rising from the earth or perhaps gigantic bellies early in pregnancy. It was as if the earth, our planet, was trying to declare its desire to create new life yet one more time, finding still another method of announcing its willingness to nourish and propagate all its millions of life-forms.

DECEMBER 28 ♫ Three days after Christmas. Another frigid Iowa morning. Two finches were huddled on a bird feeder in the predawn darkness, finding protection in its thin cedar sidewalls, their feathers fluffed so they looked like round balls. As the sun rose, the woods turned into a crystalline wonderland with every tree twinkling as if it bore diamonds on its frost-covered branches. I filled the bird feeders to overflowing and scattered abundant seed on the ground at their base, also adding suet to the wire mesh holder, preparing for the birds who would descend once the feeders were bathed in sunlight. Two hawks sat in distant treetops where they were already warmed by the sun's first rays—knowing instinctively how to survive in extreme cold. Unfortunately not everyone does: I found a dead mouse in the middle of the garage yesterday, its small perfect body frozen stiff.

Despite the cold winter nights, I know that the winter solstice is now behind us and that each day the sun's light is becoming a bit more intense, already faintly heralding the springtime resurgence of life. There is something magical in this cycling of the seasons, of knowing that the ice and snow outside the window will melt into ground that's greening with clumps of sedges, needle-shaped leaves of spring beauties, three-lobed leaves of hepatica, umbrella leaves of mayapples and heart-shaped leaves of violets topped by lavender and yellow and white blossoms. I can easily picture the return of the same life-forms that have flourished here for thousands of years, just as Native American mothers and grandmothers must have done before me. With time we learn to assume that nature's patterns are normal, and with that acceptance comes a deep hope: that all aspects of life will follow predictable cycles and that our own personal periods of darkness will circle back to light.

Several years ago, during an intense cold spell, a nearby lake froze solid. While I was walking at night along its shore, I heard a sound like the plucking of a guitar string, a low note coming at irregular intervals, sometimes loud and insistent, sometimes soft and soothing. The loudest notes were accompanied by the melody of rushing water, I assume created by surging currents just under the ice surface. I have witnessed the patterns of flowing water and the breakup of ice in the spring, but never before had I heard icebound water singing such a melody. It was strangely comforting to me to stand in the cold black air, listen, and think of the lake and its water and ice adapting to invisible shifts and changes known only to them.

I've come to see that in many ways, my life has been an intimate dance with nature's cycles and patterns. Others I know are engrossed in other passions, and yet I see us all moving together, collectively carrying forward the inbred tempo and rhythm so naturally that we barely realize it's happening. We have simply assumed that we will follow the globe's cyclical seasonal rhythms until we quietly exit the stage.

Writing these thoughts, I realize that I am one year older than when I started this consideration of changing environments and climate. One year closer to the end of my own straight-line journey through life. I can feel my body becoming less resilient, more frail as I age. I can accept this. Half a lifetime ago, I had serious expectations that cancer would force me to abandon my boys, just as my mother had left me. But thanks to prompt and proactive medical and personal care, I'm here to see our sons with growing children of their own. I've been blessed with health and without deprivation of any sort—I've had food, laughter, a warm home and a safe bed, and family and friends who have known and loved me. And a robust and resilient planet that has twirled through its cyclical paces without any question of failure. What more could I have wanted?

However, in this last year, I've come to see that the planet I depend upon may also be heading out on a one-directional tangent, at least in terms of humans and human society. Several risks could take us there, but the largest danger is climate change and all its interacting possibilities.

And this—the idea that our planet's life-supporting systems might in some significant way be terminal—this I am not ready to accept. Not as a lover of the natural world, with all its delight and diversity. Not as a mother. Not as a grandmother. Not on my watch. Not without a fight.

And so, as the year comes to an end and I sit appreciating the birds at my feeders, my questions focus not on what we should do. We know what we need to do. Instead, I ask myself, why we aren't doing these things already? And what can we do to change this?

NINE

Memoir
Stilling, 1997–2012

OUR BOYS LEFT HOME AROUND THE TURN OF THE CENTURY. Chris entered the Peace Corps in Asia. Andy was in the army in Washington. And Matt was about to graduate from high school and go away to the same liberal arts college I'd attended thirty-five years earlier. Once he left, Robert and I would live alone in the house we had built for sheltering our sons.

Other family members had left our lives as well. My dad had died a decade before and my stepmother a few years later, dissolving my last family links to Madison, the city that had formed me. Robert's parents were gone too, and both of our sisters lived far away.

Departures are hard for me. They spiral me into self-pity and depression. When I feel the downward slide starting, I force myself to switch focus from what I've lost to what I still have, and in this instance, what I had was huge. Yes, our sons would all soon be gone, but I had lived long enough to hug each one goodbye as he left home. None had been left to wander a motherless geography, as I had feared. At age fifty-four, I had outlived my mother by one year, and I was working on stretching that gap.

I might not be recounting this story if doctors had not aggressively treated my cancer and I had not remained vigilant about staving off a recurrence. I had stuck to my reliable diet, exercise, and meditation regimens and regular medical checkups.

But the threat of cancer remained a part of my life and always would. The year before, when I had been fifty-three, my mother's age at her death, weird dreams began creeping into my sleep. Small oval bodies cavorted outside my bedroom window, pounding on the glass to get my attention. Then my mother entered the dreams. She was walking down the path to our home, telling me something I could not hear. About that time the mounting malaise created by these visions was joined by vague discomfort on both sides of my lower abdomen that persevered for months. I felt that these were warning signs I could not ignore. So during my yearly medical exam, when blood tests for ovarian cancer, part of my routine monitoring protocol, came back high, I found myself telling the doctor, "I think I need to have my ovaries removed."

It took some talking to convince her, especially since an ultrasound showed nothing visibly wrong, but when I explained my cancer history and my growing sense that something in my body was changing for the worse, she referred me to a surgeon.

Fifteen years earlier, my breast cancer diagnosis had required a rapid response. The urgency robbed me of time to plan ahead and adjust, producing considerable anguish which I believe contributed to an extended, painful recovery.

Now I wanted to prove to myself that I could do things better. Since my surgery would be a proactive response to a threat of illness, I had choices and time to prepare. I started by stepping up my meditation routine. I talked through my fears with Robert and friends. I also worked on better communicating my concerns to my doctor, especially my dread of repeating the intense nausea and pain that had followed my mastectomy. "We do things better now," she reassured me, and later the anesthesiologist calmed me with similar words about the improved anesthetics she would use.

Even with all my preparations, the last few days before surgery were tense. I was on edge, slept fitfully, and cried easily. I had to remind myself that I was doing the right thing by addressing a potentially life-threatening problem with action, rather than waiting until it was beyond my control. I visualized postsurgery life as a vibrant healthy woman who had extended her lifespan well beyond her mother's. By the time I checked into the hospital, I entered with confidence. I felt that cancer was not in control. I was.

I awoke in the recovery room feeling blurry but miraculously free of pain and vomiting. Robert sat next to me, engrossed in a book. He looked up, smiled, and offered me a sip of water. A few days later I returned home to nap on the sofa while family members padded quietly around me.

A week into my recovery, the doctor called me. "I have a present for you. Your ovaries—well, they were not malignant, but both had cells that were premalignant. Your premonitions were guiding you well. You were sitting on a time bomb. You needed to have your ovaries removed. You did the right thing." When I asked her about follow-up, she instructed, "Just keep doing what you have been doing and you will be fine."

That surgery was performed a dozen years ago. It's now 2012. I'm sitting in our living room, considering the home where we've lived for thirty-five years. Our house has served us well. We've made a few changes, such as updating our appliances for more energy-efficient models and acquiescing to Iowa's growing heat and moisture by installing air conditioning. But on the whole, the house remains modest and efficient.

It's especially satisfying on cloudless winter days with temperatures in the 20s or 30s. Then, as long as the wind is not strong, sunlight pours through the large south-facing windows and warms the house into the 70s. Those days, we don't build a fire in the furnace until the sun goes down.

And the composting toilet? It's almost like a family member, with its own quirks and demands. Such as—fruit fly outbreaks. Solution: we no longer feed the toilet our kitchen wastes; instead, we constructed an outside compost pile. Or—a pile too dry and crusty to readily decompose. Solution: we added an automatic water sprinkling system. Or—the pile degrading too slowly. Solution: we threw in some red composting worms. Now the toilet demands next to no care. Admittedly the boys were embarrassed by it when they were teenagers. But by their twenties, they would boast, "I grew up in a house with a composting toilet!" as if doing so branded them as cool. We figure that in the thirty-five years we've lived here, we've saved about half a million gallons of water that would have been flushed down a conventional toilet.

With the boys gone, I revel in our home's memories and luxury. Some days I marvel at all I have in this well-insulated shell of wood and glass. It's a quiet resting place with half a dozen nooks for curling up and reading, each with its own view of oaks and hickories waving slowly in the wind. Two decks for watching summertime bats come out from the trees to feast at dusk. Three beds and a sofa for napping, each with its own slant of incoming light, its own sense of warmth and security. Our home has the same sense of peace as the home where I grew up.

So why, with my love of our woodland home, do I still sometimes yearn to return to my childhood home? Why, when half waking at dawn, might I sense my sister sleeping nearby and think I hear the thump of Mom kneading bread dough in the kitchen, the click of the door latch as Dad heads out to work, the rattle of the mail chute when Davey Myer comes to play? Why do I imagine myself sitting next to Mom in the living room, gazing into the fire, chatting about everything and nothing, just being together? Why do I thirst for a journey back to those days when the world seemed whole and good, back to a home under the arching elms, a home that no longer exists, the place of safe haven that defined me before the pain of loss, before cancer, before climate change? I know that we are living in a different world now and I am a part of it. The days of innocence are past.

Life has taught me that lesson again and again. Two summers ago when Robert and I were visiting Boulder, we drove up to our old cabin in the mountains. We hadn't been there for many years. We wanted to approach slowly from a distance and soak in memories, so we parked down the road and ambled into the meadow, expecting to wade toward the cabin through a field of flowers and grasses. But the meadow, once vital and expansive, had been invaded by ATV trails, its moist pockets ground into muck. As we drew closer to the cabin, we could see that the resilient ponderosa pines were gone, probably victims of the mountain pine beetle. In their place an assortment of junk cars and appliances had erupted, discards of the current owners who were living in a roughly constructed modern house that loomed above our once-magical cabin. Instead of drawing closer, we turned around and walked back toward the car, the full sun beating on our faces and making us sweat, chained guard dogs growling in the distance.

As we drove away, I thought about how different my life is now than when we lived in the mountains—in some ways richer, in some ways leaner. But, here is what's most important: Robert and I have been able to raise our family well while avoiding the worst calamities. With a mixture of providence and my own efforts to maintain my health, I've managed to thrive in the many ways that are important to me, most especially in my role as a mother and grandmother. And now, the family that I saw as shrinking is growing again. The boys are married and so we've gained three daughters along with five grandchildren, a few months to twelve years old, who trace their heritages to four continents. More richness than I had ever imagined.

My favorite times, the occasions when I feel most alive, are those spent with the grandchildren. Six-year-old Matvei and I walk out into the garden. "Why are we always walking around with these things?" he asks, tugging at the magnifying glass I have strung around his neck. "Because I want you to see the world in different ways," I answer. We find a shrub with ants crawling up and down. Matvei stares, then raises his magnifying glass and scowls as he backs away.

"Those ants, they're eating the little bugs!" He's close to tears.

"No," I say, amazed at his detailed observation. "The ants are milking those little bugs, the way we milk cows. Those bugs are aphids. They feed the ants sugar water, and the ants protect them. Good for everyone!" Matvei sees a lesson in nature's balanced complexities and in animals working together, all wrapped into one.

Later that day, Matvei flops on the bed while baby Ellie crawls under the blankets and giggles. Matvei props himself up on pillows and waits for me to read him stories of myths and legends, of gods and God. I watch his eyes as I read, noting when they glaze over and he's lost in inner worlds. When that happens, I think, "He's hooked!"

and I speak more slowly and quietly, my voice falling to a whisper, hypnotizing him and calling him to visit other worlds and times.

Moses and Noah are walking in our woods in early spring. The boys are stomping in the creek and crawling over logs. Eastern phoebes are calling in the distance. Moses shouts, "Look! Scarlet elf cups!" He points to the cluster of small, brilliantly red cuplike fungi protruding from a patch of moss.

"Good job!" I confirm, praising his correct identification. The boys crowd around and we carefully poke into the litter under the moss, searching for the white fungal threads that mysteriously weave roots and soils into one rich matrix. A cluster of butterflies flits past. The boys are now digging for beetles in the rotting log. And I am noticing the light purple blossoms of hepatica nearby.

"Come here, boys, look at those fuzzy flower stems. Those hairs actually help hold in the plant's warmth, just like your jackets do." Walking back to the house, I ask, "Did you know that huge wooly elephants lived here a long time ago? They were more than twice as tall as your dad. They had thick coats and giant tusks that wound in a circle."

I am trying to feed these kids the same diet of love for the creation that my mother fed me and that I fed their fathers. I want them to treasure this incredibly complex and beautiful planet. I hope to root them in the natural world's diverse abundance and soothing resilience, but also to show them that our planet is a closed system with boundaries and limits. That if we care for our generous natural world, it will be able to take care of us.

I think our grandkids may need this lesson even more than their fathers. With ongoing environmental pressures, our planet is becoming more strained, more fragile, more vulnerable. Who knows what losses our grandkids will face. What stresses. What kind of world they will inhabit. What they'll be forced to live with—and to live without. Will they have the fortitude, resilience, and love to face their fears and act? How well will they adapt? Will they become future ambassadors for the natural world, as I am hoping?

The grandkids and their parents live in distant locations—Chris's family in Switzerland, Andy's in Washington, Matt's in Virginia. Too far away to regularly involve them in my latest passion: restoring our woodland to a healthier state.

Many years ago, I realized that eastern Iowa's oak woodlands, with their clusters of native spring wildflowers, were becoming tracts of the walking dead. Why? Primarily because wildfire, once prevalent across Iowa, had been eliminated during agricultural settlement in the 1800s.

I could see the ongoing transformation on our land. Without fire to thin the trees and open the woods to sunshine, our oak woodland was becoming dark, dense, and somber. The wildflowers I loved were dying out. Sun-hungry oak seedlings were also fading away, which meant that in coming decades the oaks—along with their acorns that feed so much wildlife—would disappear. It was only a matter of time.

I knew that diverse roots and tubers of many understory plants remained in our woodland soils. For years I had set small fires during the dormant season and then watched as native wildflowers returned to the burned patches, increased in size, and spread. Animals also responded positively. One fall day a decade ago, as I was tending flames licking slowly through the oak litter, I heard the muted chirrups of twenty or thirty migrating bluebirds perched in nearby trees watching the flames. Soon the birds began pouncing into the smoking ashes immediately behind the flames, feeding on exposed insects killed by the fire. After an hour of gluttony, they were gone.

These bluebirds had almost certainly never seen an oak woodland burn before. Yet they somehow knew that fire and smoke on a fall afternoon meant food in abundance for their southward migration.

The land and its inhabitants were giving me a message. If we acted in time and imposed the appropriate controls, we could reverse our woodland's terminal trajectory and convert our land back to an open, light, airy, healthy savanna replete with diverse understory vegetation, reproducing oak trees, and animals who knew how to use them.

I remember the excitement of our first large woodland burn, a few Novembers ago. A well-trained burn crew had carefully checked the woods for hazards and raked wide firebreaks, then lit a fire that crackled and crept along one edge of the burn unit through the oak leaves, the lines of red, orange, and yellow flames hugging the ground and turning litter into ash. Then the burn boss yelled, "Let it rip!" and the crew encircled the entire five-acre woodland with a ring fire that was lifted by the wind and took on a life of its own. Flames collided, rhythmically surging forward and ebbing back, then wheeling upward in a whirlwind of pure energy. Standing at the edge and staring into the inferno, I felt I was privy to the inner workings of Earth's elementary powers, the forces of creation and destruction mingling until they became inseparable.

Early the next spring, our woodland let us know that the burn had been a success. First sedges in profusion started shooting thin emerald spears through the ashes. Within weeks, the burned woodland was bursting into fields of deep-pink wild geraniums, which faded into expanses of lavender joe-pye weed dotted with spikes of the rare poke milkweed, plumes of white baneberry and Solomon's seal, and purple-berried blue cohosh, which in autumn yielded to a carpet of mustard-yellow elm-leaved goldenrod.

Faced with the enormity of environmental problems, working to renew our woodland's health and diversity has become my way of making a positive contribution, of joining with others to do something hopeful in the natural world. This is just one small plot of land, but here I can attempt to preserve native biodiversity, ensure the continuation of midwestern oak woodlands, and improve ecological functions. With time, our woodland soils should become deeper and richer in organic matter. Their potential for erosion and loss of nutrients should decline as their water-holding capacity rises. Acorns, nuts, and fruits should feed increasingly diverse native insect and wildlife populations.

Working on our woodland's restoration has taught me both the strength of our ability to return nature to life and health and nature's willingness to respond to our healing actions. We will never be able to recreate the full glory of presettlement times, when millions of now-extinct passenger pigeons flew overhead and elk, bear, wolves, and other long gone animals roamed here, but we can regain a goodly semblance of that ancient integrity.

And what about the world beyond our woodland? How have we fared with the environmental problems I studied in the 1970s as a student in Colorado? A quick look at statistics discloses that we've solved some, even as others have escalated. I suppose it will always be this way, as long as growing numbers of humans claim more resources for their own use.

Visible air and water pollutants have decreased dramatically in the U.S.—raw sewage and industrial by-products in rivers and, in the atmosphere, sulfur dioxide, particulates, lead and other toxic metals, nitrogen oxide, and carbon monoxide. On the land, many toxic waste sites have been cleaned up. Because of decreasing pollutants, hundreds of thousands of lost work and school days, cases of asthma and bronchitis, and premature deaths, plus thousands of cases of cancer and heart disease have been prevented. However, pollutants and pollution-induced health problems have not been eliminated. Most of today's air pollution and consequent health problems are created by the burning of fossil fuels, which is exacerbated by ongoing population growth and increasing consumption.

Other problems also persist, although they are better regulated than before. Pesticides are still ubiquitous, killing millions of birds, fish, and other animals each year. The loss of biodiversity remains problematic both in the U.S. and around the globe. Freshwater availability is a growing concern worldwide, as are the impacts and high control costs of invasive plants and animals.

Agricultural pollutants have become a major water-pollution dilemma, especially in the Midwest. Fertilizers and pesticides from row-cropped fields leach through the soils, sometimes joined by manure from confined animal feeding operations that spills from holding tanks, all eventually running into the Gulf of Mexico, where they create a major dead zone that threatens marine life. In addition, research has been revealing that problematic emerging pollutants—trace amounts of chemicals such as prescription drugs, caffeine, hormones, and veterinary medicines—are now widespread in our waters and may produce unanticipated harmful results.

What about climate change? In the 1980s and 1990s, the subject became a major research field as scientists measured and analyzed the complex physics of Earth's climate. These studies resulted in thousands of peer-reviewed scientific papers. A strong consensus developed that linked rising fossil fuel emissions with the atmosphere's growing heat content and its many adverse climate consequences. Mathematical climate models, which were becoming more consistently and reliably accurate, supported these connections, which were agreed upon by the vast majority of climate scientists.

Sometime in the early 2000s, when atmospheric carbon dioxide was first topping 370 ppm, we quietly passed the point when global warming could be alleviated and recognized that we needed to start adapting to its power. I remember that shift well. Sitting around a table with colleagues involved in climate research, someone slipped the word "adaptation" into our discussions. I was stunned. I confronted him: "Adapt to climate change? Are you giving up on our ability to restrain it?"

"Maybe," he replied quietly, "or maybe I'm just admitting reality. Climate change is here, it's with us now, and it could get much worse."

Indeed. Since that time, the concentration of human-generated atmospheric carbon dioxide has continued to increase a few parts-per-million per year. We may soon approach the point at which increasing greenhouse-gas emissions produce irreversible changes in our climate system. Many questions remain: What tipping points might we exceed and when? How could climate change exacerbate other environmental problems? How can we prevent or learn to live with complications we cannot predict? And the most important question of all: Are we willing to take hard proactive steps to reduce our consumption of fossil fuels and stop their environmental disruptions?

Sometimes I'm tempted to pretend that climate change and all its horrendous threats are not real. But I know that reality doesn't work that way. I had another brush with cancer a few years ago. A melanoma, the bad kind of skin cancer. Again the veil descended. Again the world turned gray, devoid of motion and sound.

But this time the shock and depression did not last long. I had learned the important lesson: deal early with disorderly growth and the solution can be easy and inexpensive, the results good. Because I was aware, alert, and ready to address any bodily changes, when the mole started to morph in color and shape like clouds before a storm, I was in the doctor's office having it removed. Robert was at my side. Our eldest granddaughter Sophia tagged along (she insisted she wanted to see the operation, but of course she couldn't; she could only come in when it was over, and a good thing too, she being squeamish about blood). Stage 1. A simple outpatient surgery. Snip and pull, snip and pull, a deep excision, then stitches, and it was gone. Cancer foiled again.

This time the handling of a cancerous growth seemed so easy that I risk being smug about my handling of the threat. But I shouldn't be. I know that, someday, accident or illness will remove me from my family and from this woodland I love so dearly. Someday, the birds will come to a feeder without seeds. For me, at my age, death is part of the natural order.

I'm not willing to assume the same for our planet. Just as I have worked to thwart cancer's growth, I need to continue working to ensure that Earth will be able to nurture and sustain little Ellie's great-grandchildren—and those life-forms abounding outside my kitchen window, within the protective canopy of the oaks and hickories swaying in the breezes. I ask myself what I can do for those who live here and for all who will come to be in future years. I sit at the kitchen table and wonder.

PART V

The Seasons to Come

TEN

A Weather Review, 2012–2013

THE YEAR 2012 ENDED WITH THE USUAL NEWSPAPER, RADIO, and television reviews of major events. A number of these were weather related. One newspaper sported a full-page photograph of people wading past inundated cars in the nation's largest city, New York. Another considered the "confusing" 2012 hurricane season, with its ten hurricanes and nineteen named storms, many more than the dozen or so of most years. Instead of clustering in late summer, tropical storms occurred from May onward. Hurricanes Isaac, which came ashore onto Louisiana in August, and Sandy took bizarre routes. Sandy then became the biggest storm on record, more than a thousand miles across. It was unclear whether global warming played a role in shaping this unusual season—with climate change, the number of hurricanes is predicted to decrease, not increase, although individual storms are supposed to become more powerful. However, analysts concluded that 70 percent of Atlantic hurricane seasons since 1995 have been busier than the long-term average.

Some news media asked whether 2012's extreme weather—the spring and summer's record-breaking heat, major drought that raised grain and food prices around the globe, and debilitating and costly storms—would finally push our government toward policies that would help reduce greenhouse-gas emissions. James Hansen, a NASA scientist who has voiced concerns about climate change for decades, was quoted as saying that we are now in a planetary emergency. The same article pointed to Germany, with its emphasis on renewable power production, as a sign of hope.

Iowa's wind-power industry stands as another sign of hope. It's one of the state's shining lights, providing tools for renewable energy production while employing thousands of Iowans and in 2012 providing a quarter of the state's electricity, a larger fraction than any other state. In spring 2013, a regional electric power company announced it would spend $1.9 billion to expand wind energy production in Iowa. That major investment will bring even more jobs, and the renewable energy should attract other green industries to Iowa. Within the next several years after 2013, Iowa should be producing half of its electricity from renewable energy sources.

Soon after the close of 2012, analysts were tallying the weather events of the past year, comparing them with U.S. weather records that date back approximately 140 years. Resulting statistics supported the notion that this year truly was unusual:

- The year 2012 was the warmest year on record for the contiguous U.S. and for nineteen states.
- July was the warmest of any month in the U.S. data record.
- Departures from the norm were exceptionally large: the 2012 U.S. average temperature was 55.3 degrees, 3.2 degrees above the annual average and one degree warmer than the previous annual record. Spring had the largest temperature departure from the long-term average for any season on record.
- The years 2004–2012 make up the warmest such period on record.
- Considering all fifty states, over 33,000 daily high-temperature records were broken during the year, compared to approximately 6,200 low-temperature records. The 5:1 ratio of highs to lows greatly exceeded the 2:1 ratio of the last decade.

Many other national records were broken by individual events. For example, the Lower Mississippi River reached near-record-low flow rates; and 2012 was the second worst fire season on record, with 67,000 fires burning 9.3 million acres. Wildfires burned 3.64 million acres in August alone, a record for that month.

With regard to the entire planet, the year strongly confirmed the sustained long-term warming trend, with each decade since 1980 being warmer than the decade before. More specifically,

- The year 2012 was one of ten warmest years globally on record. Every year since 1976 has been warmer than the long-term average.
- Ocean heat content remained at near-record-high levels in surface waters.
- The average sea level reached a record high.

Anomalies were especially strong for northern regions of our planet, where the climate is changing most rapidly. June snow cover in the Northern Hemisphere was the smallest ever recorded. Arctic sea ice by September had shrunk to the smallest extent in recorded history—18 percent below the previous record low. Greenland experienced a record thaw, with 97 percent of the ice sheet's surface exhibiting melting in July, four times the average extent of surface ice-melt. And permafrost in northern Alaska reached record-high temperatures.

One record after another broken, and by atypically large amounts. I've heard it said that 2012 didn't break the temperature records—it obliterated them, setting a new and very high bar. I've also heard it said that living through 2012's extremes was like looking into our future. We need to brace ourselves.

The year's extreme weather was also reflected in 2012's $11 billion plus disasters in the U.S. Only year 2011 (with $14 billion events) exceeded this number. The most expensive of the 2012 events, Superstorm Sandy, cost $65 billion; the year-long drought, $30 to $40 billion. As a group, the disasters caused over $110 billion in damages; some studies say closer to $140 billion. The federal government invested nearly $100 billion helping to clean up the destruction, many times what it spends annually on solving the climate-change problem. The 2012 total costs were second only to those of 2005, when Hurricane Katrina elevated total damages to $160 billion.

Meanwhile, levels of atmospheric carbon dioxide, methane, and nitrous oxide—all major greenhouse gases—continued to climb. Atmospheric carbon dioxide rose by 2.1 ppm in 2012, reaching a global average approaching 394 ppm. The rise was driven by a number of growth factors, including a more than tripling of the number of registered vehicles in the U.S. since the decade I had learned to drive, from approximately 75,000 vehicles in 1960 to 254,000 vehicles in 2012.

In January 2013, the U.S. Global Change Research Program, comprised of thirteen federal agencies, published a review draft of the *Third National Climate Assessment*. This document corroborated predictions of other recent scientific reports, while specifically addressing climate changes in the U.S. If we do not temper our current greenhouse-gas trajectory, by the end of this century the U.S. can expect average temperatures rising between 3.6 and 7.2 degrees, possibly up to 10 degrees; extreme heat waves becoming commonplace; sea levels rising up to four feet; more frequent and stronger downpours; and declining crop yields, insecure food supplies, and the like. The report stressed that climate change is not relegated to the future: we are experiencing its effects now.

As the 2012 statistics were being tallied, 2013 unrolled its own unusual weather. The new year started out wet and cold, which restrained the blossoming of spring wildflowers in our woods until late April, two weeks later than the norm and well over a month later than in 2012.

The late 2013 spring was not a major record-breaker, but on April 17, a local thunderstorm dumped seven inches of rain on our woods and nearby towns in a short time, creating mudslides, widespread flash floods, and impassable roads. Farmlands and city parks lay under several feet of water. In fewer than 24 hours, we received nearly a quarter of the total precipitation we usually get in a full year. Volunteers filled sandbags to protect water treatment plants. The saturated soils filled basements and threatened to collapse sewer pipes and produce sinkholes. As the rain swelled creeks and raced downstream, the Mississippi River, which this past winter was low enough to limit barge traffic, went into flood stage. While one would never hope to repeat such a storm, the rain did help mitigate the extended drought in eastern Iowa, even as western Iowa and about half of the contiguous U.S. remained under drought.

I watched from my office window as this day-long thunderstorm turned the sky black, wishing I were home to see what was happening in the woods. Returning at dusk, I nearly twisted my ankle in gullies eroded into our gravel entrance path. I gazed at the valley bottom below the house. The engorged creek, normally one foot wide, filled the entire 20-foot-wide valley floor. The next morning, I roamed the woods gazing at sights I never dreamed possible: hillsides scoured of plant life, the streambed cut measurably deeper and wider, erosion channels running down slopes that had been protected by leaf litter, downed sticks and tree limbs washed into haphazard heaps. Fortunately the woodland section we had burned a year and a half before fared better because the fire had stimulated protective understory growth. But elsewhere spring wildflowers were clinging to the soil with their few remaining roots, their normally buried bulbs glistening in the sunlight. The path to the pond had become a miniature canyon. Years before, during Iowa's mammoth floods of 1993 and 2008, I had observed the devastation that water can create. But never had I seen our woodland's hillsides, valleys, and plant life so besieged. Animals too. My neighbor, who had been watching three barred owl chicks mature in a hollow tree, reported that the nesting tree had fallen into rushing floodwaters and the chicks had drowned.

Our woodland must have suffered similar fates in the distant past. It will heal. Plants will creep back onto the bared soils. Milder erosion channels will fill with duff, piles of tree limbs will decompose. We will shovel gravel into the gullies in our entrance path. In a year, the signs of this storm will be largely gone. But here's the rub: this type of extreme rainstorm is symptomatic of what's predicted with the increasing heat, moisture, and thermal energy in the atmosphere. This storm foretells the future. Our woods can survive a single extreme downpour—but what if there is one every decade? Or every year? Will the prognosis change? When will the woodland's resilience and healing capacity be exceeded?

A few weeks after April's deluge, May began with a record-breaking midwestern snowstorm, followed a short two weeks later by heat that across the Midwest broke numerous high-temperature records for so early in the year. Sioux City in western Iowa reached 106 degrees, 9 degrees higher than the previous daily maximum and 77 degrees above the city's subfreezing temperatures of two days earlier.

Then widespread and extended rains started to fall. By the end of May, flooding was extensive across the state, including Iowa City. Again the university barricaded buildings along the Iowa River, students were recruited for sandbagging, and I was wondering if I'd need to evacuate my office building as I'd done five years earlier. The large reservoir upstream from Iowa City came within inches of going over its spillway, as had happened in 1993 and 2008. Farmers who in 2012 watched their crops wither during the drought now couldn't finish spring planting because soils were saturated. Iowa had the wettest spring in 141 years of record, with a statewide average of 17.6 inches of precipitation, 7.4 inches above the springtime norm of around 10 inches.

Just when Iowa's floods started to wind down, Central Europe (including Switzerland, where granddaughter Ellie and her parents live) had record heavy rains and the worst flooding in decades, leading to water-filled subways, landslides, evacuations, power outages, missing people, and deaths.

Meanwhile, greenhouse-gas emissions increased at a more rapid rate than ever before. On May 9, 2013, for the first time in over 800,000 years, the average atmospheric carbon dioxide concentration reached 400 ppm for an entire day. In following days the average level dropped, but the trend was clear. This level, which significantly exceeds the "safe" level of 350 ppm, was little noticed by the press.

More prominent was media praise of America's growing success in the production of oil and natural gas from fracking—the hydraulic fracturing of underground rock formations that yield these fossil fuels. Fracking is helping the U.S. decrease its carbon dioxide emissions by switching from coal-fired to cleaner gas-fired power plants, and it may contribute to U.S. energy independence in the next few decades. However, while these developments are widely admired as a source of bridge energy, the crucial question remains: Will fracking and increased use of natural gas truly become bridges to renewable energy sources, or will they merely encourage the U.S. to extend its carbon-based fossil-fuel dependence?

The 2013 weather extremes continued as we rolled into summer. June 2013 became the 340th consecutive month on record with global temperatures above the twentieth-century average. Frequent intense rainstorms lit Iowa's nighttime skies, the thunder rumbling through the woods for hours and making sleep difficult. One night Sidney, seeking comfort, leapt vertically onto our bed, all eighty trembling pounds of her landing splay-legged on top of me and refusing to budge. The next morning, I noticed that the heavy rainfalls were eroding the soils around the piers supporting our second-story deck, threatening its integrity.

A week later, Arizona wildfires fueled by unusually strong winds and drought burned hundreds of homes and killed nineteen firefighters who had been battling the blaze in triple-digit heat, an inferno within an inferno. Temperatures in Death Valley, California, approached 130 degrees that week. The same week, I read of a Swiss glacier, a tourist attraction as well as a nearby town's water supply, being draped in white cloth to reflect sunlight and decrease the glacier's rapid melt rate. How bizarre, I thought, until I understood that this is what we've been reduced to: struggling to protect the little bit we have left.

Around that time, I drove home from Wisconsin on what would have been my father's one-hundredth birthday. I had spent a soothing, contemplative afternoon at the cemetery, trimming shrubs around the family plot, planting flowers at Dad's gravestone, quietly communicating with his spirit and asking it for guidance. At dusk, I started my drive back to Iowa. Speeding along a high ridgeline, I saw that I was approaching a wide belt of roiling black clouds banded on either side by an eerily golden light, a reflection of the setting sun. When I entered the thick rain and churning darkness, the winds hit so hard that I struggled to control the car. All I could do was to cling to the steering wheel and drive forward, entering what appeared to be a river of airborne water. I was terrified. It's here, I thought, an altered climate, a diseased planet, all that I've been dreading. But this is only the beginning. If predictions are right, today's exceptional records will become normal within the next few decades. Things will get worse.

In late June, President Obama announced his new Climate Action Plan, directing the Environmental Protection Agency to establish greenhouse-gas emissions standards for new and existing electrical power plants. These plants emit about 40 percent of the nation's greenhouse gases, so applying limits to the dirtiest plants could greatly reduce total U.S. emissions. The plan also proposed advancing renewable energy technologies, broadly expanding energy efficiency, assisting communities in building resilience against future climate extremes, and working on the international front. Back in August 2012, Obama tightened automobile emissions standards: by 2025, the average fuel efficiency of all new passenger cars sold in the U.S. must be 54.5 miles per gallon, up tremendously from the legislated average of 34.5 miles per gallon required by 2016. The 2025 standards would reduce U.S. oil use by 3 million barrels per day. These all could be important steps toward limiting U.S. greenhouse-gas emissions, but because President Obama is getting little legislative support for his proposals, they will be difficult to implement.

In late August, when Iowa public schools started the fall semester, some opened only to close again due to an extreme heat wave. Temperatures approached or topped 100 degrees, and the heat index far exceeded that mark. High temperatures coupled with little rain led to talk of flash drought. Drying soils rapidly took a toll on corn and soybean development. Predictions of crop yields declined.

As had happened the previous year, our woodland soils baked to a powdery dust. I again put dishes of water outside around the foundation of our house, hoping that frogs, toads, and small mammals would use them as sanctuaries. They did—and birds also drank from them since nearby streams had withered to fetid pools.

Meanwhile, a new study reported significant increases in violent human behavior associated with climate change's higher temperatures, reinforcing several dozen earlier research papers linking higher temperatures and increased rates of violence. And one of the largest wildfires in California's history burned for weeks without containment, destroying hundreds of square miles of tinder-dry forests and threatening Yosemite National Park, as well as thousands of homes and San Francisco's water supply. The number and size of western wildfires forced the U.S. Forest Service to shift its resources from efforts to improve forest health, such as ecological restoration, to fire suppression.

Soon afterward, in mid-September, Florida health officials announced a "pretty serious outbreak" of the tropical disease dengue fever, also known as breakbone fever because of its excruciating joint pain. The mosquito-transmitted disease, for which there is no vaccine, had been eradicated in the U.S. around 1940, but outbreaks started again in the far south in 2001. Warming temperatures are thought to be creating opportunities for dengue fever to flourish and move northward: the current outbreak is 200 miles north of former epicenters.

Dengue fever outbreaks, wildfire infernos, floods and drought, massive rainstorms. By late summer of 2013, the year had seen several environmental crises, but on the whole the U.S. weather was not as extreme as in 2012. Even Arctic sea ice did not melt as much as the previous year, although long-term trends still pointed to an ice-free Arctic within decades.

And then, in mid-September, heavy rains fell in the mountains above Boulder, Colorado, where I had first studied the interactions between people and the environment, where my love of plants and native ecosystems had first defined my profession. It rained more and more. Nine inches in one day, over seventeen inches in a week, and that in a semi-arid region where September rainfall normally averages under two inches. The nine-inch daily amount doubled the previous calendar-day rainfall on record and was nearly twice as much as the previous *monthly* September record. The weekly rainfall easily topped the previous record for any month on record and made 2013 Boulder's wettest year ever. Waves of water, mud, and debris blasted down mountain canyons above the city, washed out roads, and isolated mountain towns, then spread out onto the plains below to destroy other cities and flood agricultural lands. The rains, described as biblical in proportion, were unusual in their four-day duration and the breadth of area affected: storms stretched from New Mexico and Colorado eastward into Kansas, flooding over 2,000 square miles in Colorado alone. Once again, unusual patterns in the jet stream were implicated.

All fall, I had been eagerly awaiting the release of a major new synthesis, the *Fifth Assessment Report of the Intergovernmental Panel on Climate Change*. The IPCC is the internationally accepted authority on climate change. Organized through the United Nations, the IPCC coordinates the efforts of hundreds of climate scientists from around the world, trained professionals who volunteer their time to review thousands of scientific reports and produce a major summary of climate change every five or six years. Its massive reports, thousands of pages long and inches thick when printed, are the most comprehensive and carefully distilled statements of our climate-change knowledge. Would this fifth summary contain new information, I wondered?

The first of four ponderous volumes was released at the end of September. Its conclusions, stated emphatically and with very high certainty, were much like those of other recent reports, with minor variations in statistics. The overwhelming consensus confirms that temperatures of the air and sea are continuing to rise because of human release of greenhouse gases.

By 2100, global average temperatures will rise another 0.5 to 8.6 degrees, depending on the amount of carbon dioxide that continues to be emitted; sea levels will rise another 10 to 32 inches or more; and wet areas will get wetter (with precipitation increasing as much as 50 percent), while dry areas get drier. Put briefly, think more and worse heat waves, more intense rains and droughts, and more powerful hurricanes. The *Fifth Assessment* then presented alternative scenarios whereby extreme weather events could be reduced if we lowered future carbon emissions. The message was clear: global warming is unequivocal, but we can stave off the worst risks by reducing carbon emissions.

The second IPCC volume bluntly outlined future risks exacerbated by global warming: starvation, poverty, flooding, heat waves, droughts, and disease are likely to worsen, and deaths from heat and flooding will rise. Eventually, crop production could drop and drive food prices upward even as population numbers rise and food needs increase. The report described a natural world in turmoil as plants and animals try to escape rising temperatures and extinction rates continue to increase. Economic growth will slow, income will drop worldwide. Rising temperatures and moisture may limit outdoor activities in some areas. Once again, the report stated that these risks can be reduced greatly by lowering emissions, but stressed that current efforts to treat climate change are inadequate compared to the risks.

Overall, this *Fifth Assessment* confirmed what I'd already concluded. We know the science of climate change. We know what's happening and some of the results—we're feeling them already, we see them around us. We also know how to treat this all-encompassing dilemma: we must comprehensively reduce our greenhouse-gas emissions. And we understand many steps we could take, steps that would improve our economy and ultimately save (rather than cost) money. What we lack so far is the political will to act—the strength to push aside short-term and narrow economic interests and to form policies at all levels for the common good, for the health of our children and grandchildren, for the well-being and vigor of our climate and our planet and for all future Earth residents.

The IPCC assessment might have been the year's climate-change apex, had not Super Typhoon Haiyan overwhelmed the Philippines on November 8 with sustained winds approaching 200 miles per hour. Judged by wind speed, Haiyan was the strongest storm on record ever to reach landfall anywhere (although a few other storms at sea have had higher wind speeds). As extreme as those winds were, the accompanying storm surges—some exceeding 20 feet high—are said to have killed more people and done the most damage. Photographs published after the storm showed the flattened wreckage of villages and landscapes roamed by dazed residents, many holding cloths over their noses to block odors of rotting flesh. The storm killed close to 6,000 and displaced a thousand times as many Filipinos. Street scenes were described as desolate, apocalyptic, and fetid. Because of the extent of destruction, relief efforts to deliver water, food, and medical care could not reach those in need for many days.

Climatologists stated that the storm's power was augmented by climate change. Haiyan drew strength from atmospheric heat that had been absorbed by the oceans, heat that extended to the unusual depth of over 300 feet. Other climate-change-related multipliers included winds intensified by the atmospheric heat, heavy precipitation fed by rising atmospheric moisture, and storm surges lifted by global sea level rise. Reports added that cyclones are predicted to become even stronger as ocean temperatures rise further.

Haiyan struck three days before the opening of the COP19 meetings, the annual United Nations Climate Change Conference, where nations gather to work toward stabilizing greenhouse-gas concentrations. Last year, during the COP18 talks, Super Typhoon Bopha had struck the Philippines, leaving behind over $2 billion of destruction. Bopha was at the time the most expensive and deadliest typhoon on record for that nation.

This year, the same soft-spoken Filipino negotiator who had addressed Bopha at the 2012 meeting related Haiyan's unprecedented and staggering devastation. The negotiator emphasized that he spoke for countless Filipinos who could no longer speak for themselves, as well as for orphans and survivors who had lost everything but their lives. He asked whether our inactivity will subject future generations to similar horrors and whether we are willing to accept a future where superstorms become a way of life. "What my country is going through as a result of this extreme climate event is madness," he exclaimed. Then, clearly anguished and breaking into tears, he declared that in solidarity with his fellow storm-struck Filipinos who had no food, he would voluntarily refrain from eating for the remainder of the meetings or until meaningful outcomes were in sight. "The climate crisis is madness. We can stop this madness," he stated as those around him stood and applauded.

When COP19 ended, negotiators rightly claimed to have made real progress in slowing forest destruction in developing nations and thus reducing greenhouse-gas emissions from that source. COP19 also helped to set the stage for a new 2015 global climate agreement. But once again, little progress was made in transferring appropriate technologies and compensation for extreme weather events to developing nations.

I don't deny that every climate negotiation and agreement is important in itself. But watching as extreme events seemed to spread, becoming ever more pervasive, these collective responses from the planet's single international climate-change forum seemed meager indeed—more reactive than proactive. The broader goal of stabilizing greenhouse-gas emissions appeared lost in the details.

Thus the year 2013 ended with continued warnings from researchers but with few major steps taken to shift our planet to safety. Greenhouse-gas emissions and global temperatures continued to steepen their rate of increase. Climate researchers now state that the science of climate change is settled, that we are only waiting for policy changes to catch up with reality. One message is clearer than ever: in the same way that preventive medicine is less expensive than surgical cures and chemotherapy, so reducing emissions is cheaper than paying over and over again for recovery efforts. It is cheaper to reduce emissions than to rebuild cities, cheaper to prevent flooding than to feed hungry masses whose farmland has been washed away.

Here's another message from many climate scientists: *all* weather events, around the globe, are *now* being affected to some degree by climate change. It's not that all major events are caused by climate change—that would be too strong. Weather has always been variable and will remain so; extremes are part of that variability. But weather events are being heightened, their strength magnified, their damages intensified by changes wrought by our warming atmosphere.

This bothers me the most. It leaves me wondering if we are close to losing the ability to opt for planetary remission. As if I and all of humanity are now wanderers on a failing planet, trapped within a system that lacks any certainty of healing and recovery, defining home more by its weaknesses than by its exuberant vigor and health. Is this indeed the case, I ask myself, or are there things we all could, we all should, be doing? Is there still hope?

ELEVEN

The Years to Come

AS I WAS COMPLETING THIS BOOK MANUSCRIPT, IN FEBRUARY of 2015, a massive blizzard struck eastern Iowa. I was not fazed. I hunkered down at home, warm and cozy, sipping my tea, gazing out at the blowing drifts when I wasn't typing away on my computer. I planned to spend the entire day this way. All was perfect.

Until the electricity went out. Probably a line went down, I thought. I knew the power might be out for a while, given the ferocity of the storm. I kept typing away—until my computer battery died. Once I stopped typing, I realized I was getting cold. The electric furnace fan was out, so the heat from our wood-burning furnace largely remained in the basement. How about warming my shivering body with hot soup? The stove didn't work. Calling friends? My cell phone's battery was dead, and our land-line uses electricity. Sewing? Only by hand.

I was cold. Hungry. Bored. All I wanted was electricity. I didn't care where it came from. I just wanted it. A few hours later, when the refrigerator started purring once again and the lights came back on, I cheered.

Fossil fuels are seductively abundant and readily available. Are we addicted to them? How could we not be. They have gifted us with power and mobility, comfort and ease, and affluence beyond compare. Our lives and economy are intertwined with their use.

But all this luxury has come with a hefty price tag: air and water pollution, health risks and premature deaths, national security concerns, environmental degradation from mining and drilling operations, wildlife lost to oil spills. The list goes on.

And—the greatest cost of all—climate change. The problem that is unthinkable, global, irreversible, self-compounding, essentially permanent, without precedent, unpredictable, inescapable, vast across time and space—the problem that touches everyone and affects everything.

Given these realities, I see two choices. We can live for the day, ignoring current and predicted changes and waiting until our heating planet further destabilizes our climate. In my mind, this choice leads to a world where people and nations are constantly reacting to intensifying but unpredictable climate crises that exhaust mental reserves, increase threats, and challenge the national economy. For the present, this is the easy choice. It requires us to do nothing more than to continue with business as usual.

Our other choice is to work proactively to minimize climate change's intensification and ramifications. This choice, although requiring more effort at present, increases humanity's future options even as it lessens the misery and uncertainty that we, our progeny, and all life around the world may face in coming years.

As I envision these alternatives, I picture granddaughter Ellie. Working to better her future is the only way I can look into this baby's trusting eyes, eyes that see only good in the world, eyes that are open to all possibilities. Considering Ellie, I find that the latter choice is my only option.

But what exactly does it mean to minimize climate change?

The basic elements are straightforward. We need to rapidly and significantly cut carbon emissions by moving away from the major source of those emissions—that is, by decreasing and eventually eliminating our use of fossil fuels, with coal, the dirtiest of these, going first. That means switching to renewable energy sources such as wind, solar, hydroelectric, biofuels, and geothermal, which do not raise atmospheric carbon dioxide levels. Some analysts add nuclear power to the mix.

The switch to renewable energy sources must be paired with

energy conservation—increasing the energy efficiency of buildings, appliances, industrial processes, and all forms of transportation. Working to slow the speed of the climate-change process also is crucial. Doing so would provide crucial time for developing new mitigation strategies and would give nature time to adapt. These three broad-range goals—cutting emissions, increasing efficiency, and slowing things down—can be implemented through multiple initiatives: technological innovation, economic investments, governmental policies and legislation, transnational agreements, the acceptance and commitment of citizens to the greater good.

One last element remains crucial: adapting to the impacts of changing weather patterns. Because climate change is already upon us and will remain for the long term, we need to factor its current and predicted effects—rising flood waters, faster winds, higher sea levels and storm surges, shifting precipitation patterns, and the like—into every new policy, infrastructure design, and construction project.

How fast must these changes be implemented? Are we talking years, decades, or centuries? A number of scenarios have been developed for preventing dangerous temperature increases—that is, for keeping the average temperature rise below the 3.6-degree danger zone. Generally speaking, these scenarios require substantial cuts in greenhouse-gas emissions in the next few decades, followed by stabilization and decline to near-zero emissions, producing a carbon-neutral world by 2100 or before.

A sense of urgency underlies all implementation schedules. The more rapidly we decrease fossil fuel emissions, the more effective, less expensive, and easier our greenhouse-gas reduction efforts will be. Failing to lower emissions significantly in the next few decades could render stabilization impossible without severe economic disruption or the need for yet-undeveloped technologies.

Cutting emissions sufficiently means that we will need to leave fossil fuels unused and in the ground. Calculations show that about 80 percent of currently known coal, gas, and oil reserves will need to remain unburned if we are to avoid dangerous climate changes. This fact countermands the current trend of employing new and more extreme technologies, such as fracking, to mine less readily available fossil fuels, technologies that often create additional environmental hazards.

At this point, we possess the technological and economic means to make the necessary energy adjustments and positively shape our climate future—a position that future generations may come to envy if rising climate problems surpass these capabilities. We are well situated to claim the many benefits of moving toward a carbon-neutral society: an invigorated economy, job growth, savings from increased energy efficiency, reduced air pollution and associated health benefits, decreased environmental costs of coal mining and oil drilling and refining, energy security, and, of course, the mitigation of climate change.

Both the possibility and the benefits of adopting renewable energy sources are emphasized by the Solutions Project at Stanford University. This project asserts that a complete switch from fossil fuels to renewables by 2050 is both affordable and achievable with current technologies. Project researchers have outlined transformation pathways to renewables for all energy uses—transportation, electricity, heating, and industry—for every state. By 2050 Iowa, for example, could be powered by about two-thirds wind power and one-quarter solar power (plus a few minor sources), as long as energy efficiency measures decrease demand by about 30 percent. Florida, in contrast, would be mostly powered by the sun, with off-shore wind also figuring in. The Iowa switch to renewables would create approximately 58,000 construction and 24,000 operational jobs over forty years, would save 540 lives annually by cutting air pollution, and could pay for itself in ten years. The average Iowan would save close to $14,000 a year by midcentury through lowered energy, health, and climate costs.

Another hopeful initiative involves slowing the rate of climate change by reducing black carbon—the soot produced in large quantities by coal combustion, small cookstoves in less-developed countries, and diesel engines. Black carbon particles contribute to climate change by absorbing solar heat and, because of their dark, sunlight-absorbing color, by speeding the melting of snow and ice sheets when the soot is deposited on their surfaces. Unlike carbon dioxide, black carbon remains in the atmosphere for only a few days. Thus significantly reducing the amount of black carbon produced would immediately slow climate change, potentially buying us a few precious decades to better address this crisis. The World Bank is now investing a good share of its budget in reducing black carbon emissions.

The move toward a fossil-fuel-free world is already under way, although progress is slower than is needed. That move could be accelerated by putting a price on carbon—that is, creating financial incentives that shift some of the fiscal burden of fossil-fuel use, for example health-care costs, back to the producer or user. Such financial incentives, which would give renewables a market edge, can be applied in a number of ways, one being through cap-and-trade programs such as the U.S.'s successful 1990 initiative to reduce atmospheric sulfur dioxide, which was discussed in chapter 7. Another approach involves placing a carbon tax on fossil-fuel use or production. British Columbia in 2008 implemented a very successful carbon tax that has allowed reductions of corporate and personal income taxes, cut fossil-fuel use, stimulated job creation, and invigorated the economy. Dozens of nations (including China), states, provinces, and cities now use carbon-pricing schemes.

Eliminating the billions of dollars of federal tax incentives given to fossil-fuel producers each year would also stimulate the shift to carbon neutrality, as would switching some of those incentives to renewable-energy development and research, public transit systems, and other climate-friendly initiatives.

At present, fossil-fuel-reduction strategies in the U.S. are largely bottom-up or grass-roots approaches enacted by corporations, smaller governmental bodies, and even individuals and citizen groups. Let's take a look at a few hopeful thoughts, approaches, and efforts now in progress.

In 2012, in the U.S., fossil fuels provided approximately 80 percent of total energy use while renewables remained an unimpressive less-than-10 percent. However, a shift to more renewables is emerging. Renewable energy accounted for nearly 40 percent of all new domestic power capacity installed in 2013, and investment in the U.S. clean energy sector surpassed $100 billion in 2012–2013, stimulating economic development while supporting hundreds of thousands of jobs. Renewable technologies are increasingly cost-competitive with conventional energy sources. Their costs continue to fall, with wind and solar power costs dropping more rapidly than anyone had expected. It's not uncommon now for individuals or businesses to install solar panels that power their homes, produce excess power that's sold back to electric utilities, and in some cases recharge the electric car in the garage.

These systems are part of a move toward distributed energy—energy that is produced in small quantities near or at its site of use, rather than in large central power plants. Distributed systems eliminate energy losses from long-distance transmission and also may be more resilient in the face of extreme weather events.

What do the companies Google, Kohl's Department Stores, Staples, and Whole Foods Market have in common? By 2014, all had achieved carbon neutrality, at least with regard to the electricity that runs their operations and stores. That electricity is derived from their own solar panels or renewable energy purchased from outside sources, with carbon offsets—payments made to reduce greenhouse gases elsewhere—purchased for any remaining electrical needs.

While the federal government has adopted relatively few measures to decrease carbon emissions, especially in light of the need, some states and cities have picked up the slack. California is a model for the nation with its climate-change program, initiated in 2004, which addresses all sectors of the state's economy. Using legislation and regulations, California addresses fossil-fuel emissions through solar panels and other renewable energy efforts, strong emissions reduction standards for passenger vehicles, a cap-and-trade program for greenhouse gases, energy efficiency programs, and additional measures. The state aims to reduce greenhouse-gas emissions to 20 percent of 1990 levels by 2050.

New York boasts an active energy and climate-change program, and it has also adopted the 80-percent-by-2050 emissions-reductions goal, as has Massachusetts. Both states belong to RGGI—the Regional Greenhouse Gas Initiative established in 2005, a program whereby nine eastern states have joined a cap-and-trade incentive system for limiting emissions from power plants. Both New York's and RGGI's programs are credited with spurring economic vitality and creating jobs.

Some cities are diving into similar or more intense initiatives. My college and college town—Oberlin, Ohio—have together joined the Climate Positive Development Program to create one of the first cities in America that removes more carbon from the atmosphere than it adds. The town and college propose to do so by sharply reducing carbon emissions through radical moves toward energy efficiency and renewable energy sources, both of which will boost the local economy and promote sustainability.

Elsewhere, around the world, nations are making similar strong commitments. My favorite example is Switzerland, where Ellie's dad, our son Chris, is part of a large research team to help the country become carbon-neutral by 2050, in transportation as well as electricity and heating. How will Switzerland do so? One possible answer lies in a small pilot power plant near Chris's research lab. Looking beyond the problematic intermittent nature of many renewable energy sources, this pilot plant switches from using one energy source to using another as conditions dictate: solar panels when the sun shines, wind turbines when the wind blows, and biomass combustion when neither is available. The concept is to design the proper mix of renewable energy sources and employ them in a distributed rather than centralized manner, fitting power generation to each village's needs and capabilities. Switzerland's massive energy transition to renewable sources was initiated by governmental policies, is incorporating the efforts of university researchers, and will be carried forward by private industry and market forces.

Sweden is making strides to become the first oil-free nation in the world in terms of heating, power generation, and transportation. Sweden's efforts blend energy conservation measures with development of renewable fuels. Broad political support and strong incentives, including a carbon tax and tax exemptions for biofuels, have fueled tremendous growth of its renewable energy sector. Germany is focused on becoming carbon-neutral in power generation by 2050. Iceland and Norway depend on renewables for almost all their electricity, and Denmark's wind turbines are already fully replacing fossil fuels on especially favorable days.

Indeed, the European Union is on track to meet or exceed its goals of reducing greenhouse-gas emissions by utilizing strong energy efficiency measures, development of renewables, and a cap-and-trade system for factories and power plants. By 2050, the E.U. expects to achieve 80 to 95 percent emissions reductions. Once again, these measures are boosting the economy, creating jobs, and strengthening Europe's competitiveness.

Such major switches are happening only in a handful of countries, but that handful is showing that top-down government-initiated approaches to climate-change mitigation can work and that they can bring multiple economic and employment advantages. Along with the efforts of individuals, researchers, companies, and organizations, they add up to an energizing, exciting, and hopeful whole. But are they cutting greenhouse-gas emissions to a measurable degree?

Looking at global trends, the answer is a disappointing but unquestionable no. The world as a whole is still going in the wrong direction. Rather than declining, the global rate of greenhouse-gas emissions is rising a few percent almost every year. Our world's greenhouse-gas global blanket is becoming thicker and larger. Extending today's emissions trajectories into the future, they steepen at a dizzying pace, taking the world beyond dangerous temperature increases by midcentury or possibly before.

Considering only the U.S., the news is somewhat better. Although greenhouse-gas emissions steadily increased before 2005, between that date and 2013 they decreased by 9 percent, although between 2012 and 2013 emissions again showed an increase of 2 percent. The recent several-year decrease is wonderful news. But the decline in greenhouse-gas emissions was too small and too slow to maintain climate-healthy temperatures. In addition, the decline was produced in part by power plants switching from a dirty fossil-fuel source (coal) to a cleaner one (natural gas), a switch that was correlated with increased exports of unburned coal for use in other countries. What we need instead are solid gains in alternative energy sources that shift us permanently to a carbon-neutral future.

Clearly something more needs to be done—but what?

Remember that climate change has been christened the largest and most significant quandary ever faced by humanity. It is an enormous dilemma with enormous consequences. It requires an enormous response—one that is powerful, rapid, and far-reaching. One that utilizes top-down as well as bottom-up efforts. Climate change ideally deserves a concerted program that brings together research, education, technological development and implementation, supportive policies and programs, and international agreements—such as the Montreal Protocol that was signed by the U.S. and is described in chapter 7. A program that involves individuals, community groups, institutions, businesses, and governments at all levels. I picture something like the U.S.'s remarkable industrial mobilization during World War II. Or perhaps the wartime Manhattan Project, which included building a city in the wilderness that brought together the brightest minds to focus single-mindedly on a project they linked to the survival of civilization, paradoxically creating the first nuclear bomb. Mightn't we similarly gather people and resources together to work wholeheartedly for the survival of a livable climate?

It is true that a large-scale switch to renewables will require tremendous economic and infrastructure renovation, but we've done these things before. In the U.S., inactivity regarding climate change is less a matter of inability than of our will to act. In particular, we are lacking political will power, although entrenched economic interests tied to the use of fossil fuels and power generation, as well as a lack of understanding of climate change, also factor in.

Given these difficulties, how can we come to see climate change as a challenge that creates new possibilities, rather than as a crisis that elicits fear? How can we accept climate-change mitigation and adaptation as a method for stimulating creativity and our economy, even as it builds environmental health and a robust future? As a mechanism for uniting humanity around a common goal? A venue for expressing our commitment to future generations? An opportunity, not an indictment? The energizing challenge of a lifetime? Our historic moment? Our finest hour?

Of course, none of these questions has an easy answer. But there are meaningful ways that each of us could address climate change. Here are a few suggestions.

Keep learning. Stay abreast of this rapidly developing field. Read. Search the web. Attend lectures. Talk with others. Seek knowledgeable, reliable sources and ply them for information. (See Finding More Information at the end of the book for suggestions on evaluating information sources.) Focus on understanding one aspect of the bigger picture and become a well-versed advocate for that subject. Remember to consider hopeful actions as well as climate-change manifestations. Knowledge is empowering. Ongoing learning can help maintain a perspective that feeds appropriate action while avoiding despondency.

Talk with others. Many know little about climate change. Few realize the long-lasting effects of today's fossil-fuel emissions and the need to reduce them soon. Too many think there is nothing they—or anyone—can do. They may not realize that we still have a window of opportunity for shaping the future.

Most people listen best to a trusted friend. Share what you know, what you are doing, your fears and frustrations along with your positive visions. Encourage optimistic exploration of innovative solutions. Generate hope. You may help transform the disengaged into dedicated problem solvers.

Adjust your mindset, but don't be too adaptable. Climate change can be insidious, slowly shifting outlooks as it transforms the environment. Too much acceptance of changing weather patterns can smother initiatives to address climate change. The result: a steadily declining quality of life.

On the other hand, we need to accept that some lifestyle changes may be inevitable. By doing so, we can better direct future changes and choose options more to our liking.

Considering lifestyles, I once again think of Ellie and her family in Switzerland, whose total use of fossil fuels is a fraction of that of a comparable U.S. middle-class family. Ellie's brother walks to a nearby grade school; her sister takes public transportation to a secondary school. Ellie walks with her mom to the market, riding in the pram one way, taking the bus home with groceries. Her dad bicycles half an hour to work or hops onto a fuel-cell-powered, nonpolluting bus. The family lives in an apartment on a modest lot a few blocks from a public forest and operational farm, both crisscrossed by small roads and trails, where parents and children bike, hike, and picnic. There are many ways to live well on this earth without decreasing the ability of future people to do the same.

Returning to concrete suggestions—*act*. Do what you can to reduce your personal carbon footprint, that is, the amount of fossil fuel emissions that support your life. Eat local foods. Fly less. Bicycle and walk more. Better insulate your house. Clad your roof with solar cells. Install energy efficient lightbulbs. Search the web for lists of the many options.

Better still, *calculate your carbon footprint*. Many websites provide carbon-footprint calculators. The better ones consider home size, income, and other factors to produce a targeted list of recommendations for reducing your footprint.

Take the next step. Assess and reduce the carbon footprint of your business, institution, or church. Push for action in your community. Join a climate action group working on a still larger scale. Then share what you are doing. Let your actions be a model for others.

Advocate for larger actions among businesses, industries, institutions, and government at all levels. When actions and policies are positive, applaud those in charge. When negative or absent, encourage those in charge to change. They need to hear that your votes and purchases are shaped by their actions. Share your thoughts through a letter to your local paper.

Contact with elected officials is especially important. Email or phone them or post a message on social media. Combine facts with personal stories about how climate change is affecting you or your community. Keep statements short and to the point. Talk about how a healthy climate and healthy economy walk hand in hand or about how we need more education, research, and technological development as well as climate-friendly policies and programs. Let officials know if you support a carbon tax and binding international agreements. Push for policies that encourage the switch to renewables. Pledge to make one advocacy contact a month or a week. Don't forget that your voice is important and that you have influence. Pressure produces results.

And last—*make climate-change mitigation a priority*. Remember that doing nothing is promoting the status quo; doing nothing allows the further intensification of climate change. Also remember that small actions add up. Voices are rising. Your voice, combined with those of others, can become a powerful generator for healthful change.

We may think of climate change in many ways. As a planetary disease that invisibly intensifies and spreads as we go about our everyday business. Or as a systemic disaster that we already see unfolding but only as a shadow of what is yet to come. We can approach it as a catastrophe that threatens to redefine life on Earth. However we position it, we might ask this obvious question: Why would anyone choose to face this unfurling crisis?

But face it we must—face and address it. Solving this daunting problem won't be easy. There is lots of work to be done. There is no model from the past. There is no single path or plan; multiple solutions are sure to be required. And we are bound to make mistakes.

But in a sense, here is all that matters: at this point, the ultimate magnitude of climate change remains in our hands. We still have choices. We can still address this overwhelming problem and prevent its worst repercussions by decreasing carbon emissions. But we don't have time to waste.

It's that simple.

Do I have faith that this planet's people and nations will pull together to heal the earth's climate? Do I remain hopeful? How could I not, after all I have learned of the creative thought, effort, energy, innovation, and diverse approaches already being directed toward climate change? We Americans may be slow to accept the diagnosis, but once we decide on a course of action, we can move fast. At some point, I believe that we will.

In the meantime, we each can construct and share a vision for the future. Mine is one of high resilience and low risk. A vision of a balanced, self-healing planet with vibrant human societies and healthy, robust, self-perpetuating environments.

As I write these words, I imagine all my grandchildren—Ellie, her siblings, her cousins. What do I want to leave as my legacy for them? Sitting at the kitchen table, gazing out at the birds and the trees, the answer comes easily. I want a place where they can sit in comfort and safety, overlooking a natural world that fills their needs and brings them joy. I want to leave them a world that in some small way is healthier because of my interactions with its processes and creatures. Nothing more, but nothing less.

This is my vision, one person's hopeful legacy. What is yours?

One evening, I walked Sidney at dusk as the sun was dropping in the west and starting to beam through thinning clouds. We took a path through a woodland park near our house. Rising over a ridge, I entered another world. I came upon a patch of hundreds, perhaps a thousand fireflies blinking close to the ground, lighting up the white balls of wild onion flowers and the maidenhair fern fronds as if they were Christmas trees. A thousand tiny blinking lights, on-off, on-off. Of course I had known that there were fireflies in the forest, but if I hadn't been there, in that one spot, just at that instant, just when the dusk seemed to be gaining dominance and overtaking the world, I would not have known the magic of those lights.

Hundreds of brilliant specks of hope and beauty glimmering in the darkening sky.

Finding More Information ∾

EXCELLENT SOURCES of climate-change information are readily available. Books and websites abound, many of which are designed for the lay public, and the subject is increasingly discussed by the news media, although many would argue that it should be covered even more.

But how can you find scientifically accurate information you can trust? Here are some suggestions for doing so:

- Search for science, not ideology or opinion.
- Discount sources that use ad hominem or emotion-based arguments and those that dismiss the scientific record.
- Choose information presented by persons with training and credentials in climate science or by professionals located at a reputable institution.
- Look for information sources that examine long-term climate data collected over large areas; put aside sources that develop conclusions from selected short-term or geographically limited data sets.
- Be skeptical of information produced by sources that profit from discounting climate-change science, for example, corporations that sell fossil fuels.

Many books address specific aspects of climate change such as policy options or personal responses. For straightforward, easy-to-understand explanations of a broad range of topics, I recommend *The Rough Guide to Climate Change* by Robert Henson (Rough Guides, 2011). The book has been updated and republished as *The Thinking Person's Guide to Climate Change* (American Meteorological Society, 2014).

News media, both in print and on the web, are important for tracing unusual weather events and changing expressions of climate change, such as accelerating ice melt. Major national news outlets such as the *New York Times* typically cover significant events well.

Websites and blogs rapidly incorporate new developments and our growing understanding of climate change. In addition to presenting basic information on climate-change mitigation and adaptation, many include descriptions of how climate change is being expressed, suggested actions for combating climate change, and regional as well as national analyses. Some include helpful aids such as materials for educators and students, links to other sites, and interactive features. In addition, most major climate-change reports are now posted on the web. It's easy to wander these websites from topic to topic, getting a sense of current climate observations and research projects under way and discovering interesting details in passing. Search the web and you also will discover the large amount of creative thought and experimentation now being invested in solving climate-change problems. Be sure to keep in mind the tips above on finding trusted sources.

Websites of international organizations such as the World Bank and the United Nations World Meteorological Organization, Environment Programme, and Intergovernmental Panel on Climate Change commonly post significant climate-change analyses and reports, including the IPCC's Climate Change Assessment Reports. These massive, multivolume documents, released about every five to six years, are compiled by several hundred climate scientists from around the globe. They provide the definitive analysis of global climate-change effects, trends, and predicted future expressions.

Websites of many U.S. federal agencies and federally funded research and development centers now incorporate climate-change information. Some of the most comprehensive websites in this realm, with abundant resources for the general public, include the following:

- The Environmental Protection Agency, which discusses regional and national aspects of climate change and includes educational resources, a carbon emissions calculator, and suggestions for reducing your carbon footprint.
- The National Aeronautics and Space Administration, with abundant written, graphical, interactive, and educational resources, climate apps, an extensive listing of possible solutions, and more.
- The National Center for Atmospheric Research, where much of the nation's climate-change research is carried out.
- The National Oceanic and Atmospheric Administration, which includes a National State of the Climate report that summarizes the climate nationally and globally for each year and month. NOAA also hosts the National Climatic Data Center, the world's largest active archive of weather data; use this site to locate diverse data sets and their interpretations.

These websites often include maps and visualizations that are beneficial for understanding climate patterns.

Many other federal agencies include subject-specific climate-change information on their websites: the Department of Defense addresses climate change and national defense; the U.S. Forest Service considers climate change and tree migration; etc. Simply search for the name of an agency followed by "climate change."

The U.S. Global Change Research Program, composed of the research arms of thirteen federal agencies, is charged with guiding the nation's response to climate change. USGCRP published National Climate Assessments in 2000, 2009, and 2014. These important reports, the most detailed climate-change analyses for our nation, detail events, trends, and climate-change effects regionally and for the nation as a whole. If you want to see how climate change will be expressed in your region of the country in coming years, examine this report on the web. The NCA website also includes graphics for PowerPoint use.

The National Academies of Science, comprised of the nation's most esteemed scientists and engineers, and its affiliate, the National Research Council, regularly publish and post reports on varied aspects of climate change, written to inform the public and provide scientific information for policy decisions.

Many states now post information on regional climate change, although the amount of detail varies from state to state. Here in Iowa, the Department of Natural Resources website includes a detailed report on how the state's greenhouse-gas emissions could be reduced and an Iowa climate-change impacts report, and Iowa State University's Climate Science Program posts ongoing analyses of statewide expressions of climate change. States with established climate-change programs, such as California and New York, have well-developed websites that consider climate change and its local effects and describe what the state is doing to ameliorate negative consequences. These sites serve as models of what dedicated governments can do.

Other sites that present a wealth of dependable information include several independent climate blogs, for example, entries posted on Skeptical Science, on the Weather Underground website, and on Real Climate, whose contributors are climate scientists working to provide a quick response and greater context for developing stories. Climate Central, an independent organization of established climate scientists and journalists, focuses on researching and reporting the facts about our changing climate and its impact on the American public. The Center for Climate and Energy Solutions, an independent nonpartisan organization, works to promote energy policies that also protect the global climate. Many conservation and advocacy groups such as the National Audubon Society, World Wildlife Fund, and The Nature Conservancy also include climate-change information on their websites, especially as it pertains to their focus of concern.

The Yale Project on Climate Change Communication regularly posts surveys of public opinion about climate change and useful educational materials. As always, it's good to verify that any claims are grounded in solid, peer-reviewed science.

This is an introduction to the many web resources available. Other excellent sites can be identified on the website "101 Top Web Resources on Climate Change."

Bibliographic Essay ∾

A Sugar Creek Chronicle touches on many of the diverse topics that together comprise climate change. I gathered my information on these subjects from books, peer-reviewed scientific journals and reports, websites, videos, news reports, discussions with university colleagues in climate change or environmental studies, and even my old college textbooks. I used multiple sources for each concept, trend, and prediction and have cited only a small fraction of the total number that I consulted. In all cases, I worked to trace information back to its original publication. References cited herein were the best and most helpful resources I could locate for each topic.

This bibliography focuses on my information sources for significant aspects of climate change. I have not included specific citations for most 2012–2013 weather events and associated news stories, although I did cite analyses of major extreme weather events when these were available. I have also omitted citations for easily located peripheral information such as population statistics. My weather and news information was primarily from print and broadcast reports, particularly those in the *New York Times* and *Washington Post*. I sought multiple accounts of each event and verified the weather details with scientific reports or analyses when possible. All my descriptions of news and weather events are unembellished records based on actual circumstances.

Much of the broad depiction of climate change was written as a synthesis of information from books and major reports that were released during or just before this project. These sources included the following:

- *Third National Climate Assessment: Climate Change Impacts in the United States*, Jerry M. Melillo, T. Richmond, and G. Yohe (eds.), draft 2013, finalized 2014, published by the U.S. Global Change Research Program and posted on its website, doi:10.7930/J0Z31WJ2. This discusses current and predicted effects of climate change throughout the U.S. My descriptions of regional climate change in the U.S. are taken from this report.
- *Turn Down the Heat: Why a 4 °C Warmer World Must Be Avoided*, November 2012, produced for the World Bank and posted on its website. Subsequent reports in this excellent series consider specific regions of the globe.
- *The Rough Guide to Climate Change*, R. Henson, 2011, Rough Guides Ltd., London. In addition to writing this book, Bob Henson was a major source

of expert information, answering my questions and reviewing the science content of this book, offering numerous corrections and educational comments as he did so.

- *Fifth Assessment Report of the Intergovernmental Panel on Climate Change*, R. Pachauri and L. Meyer (eds.), 2013–2014, IPCC. This is the definitive climate-change assessment, prepared over several years by hundreds of climate scientists from around the world. The report consists of three volumes. *The Physical Science Basis*, by Working Group I, documents observed changes in temperature and climate, oceans, the water cycle, global ice, the drivers of these changes, and predictions for the near and long-term future. *Impacts, Adaptation, and Vulnerability*, by Working Group II, details what climate change is doing to life on Earth and how humans and other species are adapting; it also proposes possibilities for managing future risk and building resilience. *Mitigation of Climate Change*, by Working Group III, describes how climate change could be brought under control and the scientific, environmental, economic, and social effects of doing so. These thousand-page-plus volumes are condensed into three *Summary for Policymakers* documents and a *Synthesis Report*. I highly recommend these easily understood summaries. All these reports are accessible on the IPCC website and also are published by Cambridge University Press.
- *Climate Change—Evidence and Causes: An Overview*, E. Wolff and I. Fung (lead authors), 2014, produced jointly by the U.S. National Academy of Sciences and The Royal Society and posted on their websites, also published by the National Academies Press.
- *Global Climate Change Impacts in the United States*, T. Karl, J. Melillo, and T. Peterson (eds.), 2009, produced by the U.S. Global Change Research Program and posted on its website; also published by Cambridge University Press.

I also regularly consulted the climate-change websites of the Environmental Protection Agency and other federal agencies.

These information sources fed into all but the most specific subjects discussed below. Thus I have not provided citations for broad climate-change concepts and processes, impacts and effects, or commonly accepted trends, such as increasingly extreme weather including stronger hurricanes and heat waves, new human health problems, hotter wildfires, rising atmospheric moisture, and species responses to changing climate, or geographic shifts in these trends. Where no citations are provided, readers can assume that information was compiled from several of the above-listed sources.

The following pages include more specific citations for significant topics and data sets, data that are especially important (such as ongoing rises in atmospheric carbon dioxide concentrations), recently published research that may not be easily accessible, significant reports on aspects of climate change such as its military or economic implications, and peripheral subjects that might be particularly interesting to readers. For some entries, I include explanatory comments.

Current Temperatures and Atmospheric Carbon Dioxide Levels

Information on increasing temperature and its effects is given in nearly every climate-change publication, but a few clarifications are needed. The current figure of 1.4 degrees (0.8°C) rise in average surface air temperature, discussed in most detail in the preface and the March 19 journal entry, is derived by comparing temperatures in recent years, 2003–2012, to temperatures in 1850–1900. One might also use the estimated linear trend from 1880 to 2012; doing so, the current temperature rise would be slightly higher, a bit over 1.5 degrees. Readers may see that higher rise in other publications.

Another explanation. The 3.6 degree (2°C) temperature-rise safe limit, discussed in the March 19 journal entry and elsewhere, is part of the United Nations Framework Convention on Climate Change that was adopted at the Rio Earth Summit in 1992 and has been used since then as a target for limiting future carbon dioxide emissions and their associated global average temperature rises. This limit has a specific definition: it aims to avoid "dangerous anthropogenic interference with the climate system." Although it is commonly accepted as a precise limit for avoiding the worst impacts of climate change, readers should realize that we could pass dangerous tipping points before or after that exact temperature is reached. The history and implications of that limit are analyzed in "Two Degrees: The History of Climate Change's 'Speed Limit,'" by M. Hope and R. Pearce, posted December 8, 2014, on the Carbon Brief blog site.

The shift in the ratio of hot-to-cold extreme temperature events, described in my June 24 journal entry, is discussed in the NCAR/UCAR AtmosNews release "Record High Temperatures Far Outpace Record Lows across U.S.," posted November 12, 2009. This press release is based on research by G. Meehl et al. that was published in *Geophysical Research Letters*.

The accelerated average temperature rise since the 1980s, mentioned in chapter 7, is based on the *Third National Climate Assessment* (2014) and on *The State of the Climate in 2009*, edited by D. Arndt, M. Baringer, and M. Johnson, 2010, produced by NOAA and available on its website; it is also published in the *Bulletin of the American Meteorological Society* 91, S1–S224.

Atmospheric carbon dioxide levels, discussed primarily in the March 7 journal entry, have been carefully recorded since 1958 at NOAA's Mauna Loa Observatory in Hawaii, with results graphed at "Global Greenhouse Gas Reference Network: Trends in Atmospheric Carbon Dioxide," posted on NOAA's Earth System Research Laboratory's website. (That site also includes a simulated "History of Atmospheric Carbon Dioxide from 800,000 Years Ago.") The Environmental Protection Agency's website includes a longer-term graph of emissions; go to "EPA home," search "climate change," then "global emissions." A table of these measurements is posted at "Atmospheric Carbon Dioxide Levels" on the Carbonify website.

The Arctic and worldwide exceedance of 400 ppm of carbon dioxide (mentioned in the July 14 journal entry and chapter 10) are documented in "400 PPM: Carbon Dioxide Levels Cross a Sobering New Threshold" by K. Levin, posted June 5, 2012, on the World Resources Institute's blog site, and in the article "Five Things to Know about Carbon Dioxide" by B. Henson (May 15, 2013), posted on NCAR/UCAR's AtmosNews site. The latter article also compares Chinese and U.S. emissions (included in the March 7 journal entry), as does "CO2 Emissions (Metric Tons Per Capita)," which is posted on the World Bank's Data website. (Note: The 400 ppm level was first passed for an entire month in March 2015.)

"Target Atmospheric CO2: Where Should Humanity Aim?" by J. Hansen et al., a discussion of 350 ppm of atmospheric carbon dioxide as the maximum safe limit (mentioned in chapter 7), was posted at NASA's Science Briefs website in December 2008, with more detailed versions on other websites.

Past and Future Temperatures and Atmospheric Carbon Dioxide

When trying to understand ancient changes in atmospheric carbon dioxide, global average temperature, and global climate, along with future predictions, I benefited greatly from the books *The Long Thaw: How Humans Are Changing the Next 100,000 Years of Earth's Climate* by David Archer (2009, Princeton University Press) and *Storms of My Grandchildren* by James Hansen (2009, Bloomsbury, New York). These books were especially helpful for the April 23 journal entry, where I also describe the climatic stability and importance of the Holocene in human development; E. Arthur Bettis (personal communications, January 2015) was generous in reviewing this section and answering my questions about ancient climate change and human prehistory. Also broadly helpful for ancient climate change were *The Rough Guide* (2011) and *Climate Change—Evidence and Causes* (2014).

The intense planetary warmth of 56 million years ago (March 19 and April

23 journal entries), which is thought to be the best analogue for modern climate change, was informed by the articles "World without Ice," by R. Kunzig, published in the October 2011 *National Geographic* and posted on its website, and "The Last Great Global Warming," by L. Kump, published in the July 2011 *Scientific American* and posted on its website.

Predictions for twenty-first-century rises in temperature and atmospheric carbon dioxide, as presented in the March 7 and 19 journal entries, are from a synthesis of values stated in my major climate-change sources listed earlier, with *Third National Climate Assessment* (2014), *Climate Change—Evidence and Causes* (2014), and IPCC's *Fifth Assessment Report*, vol. 1 (2013) being especially helpful.

A more detailed set of potential increases is included in the November 3 journal entry. That discussion is based on figure 1 in the report *Turn Down the Heat* (2012), with additional information from the *Third National Climate Assessment* (2014). The same journal entry mentions a report on the potential emergence of extreme heat waves by the mid-2000s, which is "The Projected Timing of Climate Departure from Recent Variability," by C. Mora et al., published in *Nature* 502 on October 10, 2013, doi:10.1038/nature12540. Carbon dioxide's long tail, mentioned in the February 11 and November 3 journal entries, is described in "Five Things to Know about Carbon Dioxide" (2013). I also found the EPA's website "Future Climate Change" to be useful. The possibility of mitigating climate extremes is from IPCC's *Fifth Assessment Report*, vol. 3 (2014) and other reports.

The consideration of climate change beyond 2100, discussed in the December 26 journal entry, is based on IPCC's *Fifth Assessment Report*, vol. 1 (2013), and *Climate Change—Evidence and Causes* (2014), as well as *Abrupt Impacts of Climate Change: Anticipating Surprises* by the National Academies' Committee on Understanding and Monitoring Abrupt Climate Change and Its Impacts (2013, published by the National Academies Press and available on its website) and "Climate Change: What Happens after 2100?" by G. Trencher, November 16, 2011, posted on the United Nations University website, Our World.

Arctic and Antarctic Changes

Changes in the Arctic in 2012, discussed primarily in the September 21 journal entry, are covered in numerous articles, reports, and analyses. My sources included "Polar Ice Sheets Melting Faster Than Ever" by I. Quaile, April 2, 2013, in Germany's *Deutsche Welle*; "2012: Record Arctic Sea Ice Melt, Multiple Extremes and High Temperatures," press release 966 of the World Meteorological Organization, November 28, 2012, posted on the WMO website; "Ending Its Summer Melt, Arctic Sea Ice Sets a New Low That Leads to Warnings" by J.

Gillis, September 19, 2012, the *New York Times*; and "The Emergence of Modern Sea Ice Cover in the Arctic Ocean" by J. Knies et al., November 28, 2014, *Nature Communications* 5, 5608, doi:10.1038/ncomms6608.

Changes in arctic algae, described in the August 20 journal entry, are from "Ice Algae Sink onto Seafloor as the Arctic Warms" by I. Quaile, February 26, 2013, *Deutsche Welle*.

Arctic information used for the November 29 journal entry included changes in Canadian snowmelt, from "Variability and Change in the Canadian Cryosphere" by C. Derksen et al., May 9, 2012, doi:10.1007/s10584-012-0470-0, published online by Springer Science Media; and shipping use of the Arctic Ocean, from "Gas Tanker to Cross Autumn Arctic Ocean Carrying Natural Gas to Japan" by C. Schultz, November 26, 2012, posted on the Smithsonian's Smartnews blog.

For changes in Greenland and Antarctic ice cover, described in the May 30 and July 14 journal entries and mentioned in the preface, I used "A Reconciled Estimate of Ice-Sheet Mass Balance" by A. Shepherd et al., November 30, 2012, published in *Science*, doi:10.1126/science.1228102; "Satellites See Unprecedented Greenland Ice Sheet Surface Melt," July 24, 2012, posted on the NASA Science News website; and "West Antarctic Glacier Loss Appears Unstoppable" by C. Rasmussen, May 12, 2014, posted on the NASA Jet Propulsion Lab website.

Oceanic Changes

Modern climate-induced changes in the oceans (discussed primarily in the November 4 and 25 journal entries, also mentioned in chapter 10) are based on the following sources.

For sea level rise: "Hotspot of Accelerated Sea-Level Rise on the Atlantic Coast of North America" by A. Sallenger Jr., K. Doran, and P. Howd, published June 24, 2012, *Nature Climate Change* 2:884–888, and summarized on the USGS Newsroom website as "Sea Level Rise Accelerating in U.S. Atlantic Coast"; IPCC's *Fifth Assessment Report*, vol. 1 (2013).

For rising temperature: IPCC's *Fifth Assessment Report*, vol. 1 (2013); "Climate Change Indicators in the United States—Oceans" on the EPA Climate Change website.

For acidification: "What is Ocean Acidification?" posted on the NOAA Pacific Marine Environmental Laboratory Carbon Program website. The change from an alkaline toward acid pH represents a shift of more than 0.1 pH units since pre-industrial times.

For the effects of oceanic changes: "Extensive Dissolution of Live Pteropods in the Southern Ocean" by N. Bednaršek et al., November 25, 2012, *Nature Geoscience* 5:881–885, doi:10.1038/ngeo1635, a discussion of sea butterflies; "Biotic and Human Vulnerability to Projected Changes in Ocean Biogeochemistry over the 21st Century" by C. Mora et al., October 15, 2013, *PLOS Biology*, doi:10.1371/journal.pbio.1001682, a discussion of human food sources.

Plant and Animal Effects

Patterns of bird distribution and migration are discussed in March 7 and 26, April 25, and August 20 journal entries. Information on the possible effects of climate change was provided by Stephen J. Dinsmore, personal communication (May 19, 2014), and by the National Audubon Society's *Birds and Climate Change Report: 314 Species on the Brink* (2014), available on the web. For Iowa migration patterns, I used "Spring Arrival Dates of Migrant Birds in Northeastern Iowa: A 32-Year Study" by T. Sordahl, 2012, *Iowa Bird Life* 82(4):133–144. For 2012 spring migration patterns, I consulted "Field Reports: Spring, 2012" by M. Kenne, 2012, *Iowa Bird Life* 82(3):90–117, and James Fuller, personal communication (April 26, 2012).

My examples of climate-change effects on other species (April 25 journal entry) include discussion of Wisconsin's springtime (where average March temperatures rose five degrees between the 1930s and 1990s), based on "Phenological Changes Reflect Climate Change in Wisconsin" by N. L. Bradley et al., 1999, *Proceedings of the National Academy of Sciences* 96:9701–9704, and temperature-related sex changes in turtles, based on "Modeling the Effects of Climate Change–Induced Shifts in Reproductive Phenology on Temperature-Dependent Traits" by R. Telemeco, K. Abbott, and F. Janzen, May 2013, *American Naturalist* 181(5):637–648. Changes in tree ranges, as described in the August 20 journal entry, are mapped in the "Climate Change Tree Atlas" of the Northern Research Station, U.S. Forest Service, and posted on the NRS website. My October 1 journal entry mention of ghost moose is from "Ghost Moose: Winter Ticks Take Their Toll" by S. Morse, March 13, 2012, published in *Northern Woodlands* and posted on its website.

The Sixth Extinction by Elizabeth Kolbert (2014, Henry Holt & Company) is a compelling discussion of Earth's current mass extinction and its climate-change connections.

For the influence of climate change on agriculture, covered in the July 18 journal entry and elsewhere, I supplemented information from IPCC's *Fifth Assessment Report*, vol. 2 (2014), the *Third National Climate Assessment* (2014), and *The Rough Guide* (2011) with Iowa reports by E. Takle, namely "Assessment of Potential Impacts of Climate Changes on Iowa Using Current Trends and Future

Projections," October 26, 2011, posted on Iowa State University's Climate Science Program website under Publications, and the report *Climate Change Impacts on Iowa 2010*, which I edited, posted in 2011 on Iowa State University's Climate Science Program website under Publications.

Economics of Climate Change

The costs of 2012 extreme weather events were largely taken from news reports; an economic summary of the year, in chapter 10, is from "NCDC Releases 2012 Billion-Dollar Weather and Climate Disasters Information," undated, posted on the NOAA National Centers for Environmental Information website. Information on 2011 billion-dollar disasters, summarized in the July 2 journal entry, is from *Disaster Resilience: A National Imperative* by the National Academies' Committee on Increasing National Resilience to Hazards and Disasters (2012, National Academies Press, also posted on its website). The July 2 journal entry also includes climate-change costs more generally, for which I used the Executive Summary (posted on the web) of the 712-page *Stern Review: The Economics of Climate Change* by Nicholas Stern (2007, Cambridge University Press). Readers are also referred to reports of the Risky Business Project (posted on the project's website) mentioned in the preface, which focuses on assessing specific economic risks of climate change for the U.S. and its various regions. Additional economic implications are now included in many general climate-change reports.

2012 Extreme Weather Events

Data for the March extreme heat wave, detailed in the March 26 journal entry, were taken from *The State of the Climate in 2012* by J. Blunden and D. Arndt, 2013, produced by NOAA and available on its website, also published in the *Bulletin of the American Meteorological Society* 94, S1–S258. Also useful was the posting "In March 2012, 15,000 Warm Temperature Records Broken in US," by M. Daniel, April 10, 2012, on the EarthSky blog site and two postings on Climate Central's website, "Global Warming May Have Fueled March Heat Wave Odds," March 26, 2012, and "Warmest Ever? You Bet. March Temps Fry All Records," April 9, 2012, both by A. Freedman.

Information about the slowing of the polar jet stream, its implications for extreme weather, and possible connections to several 2012 events—first detailed in the March heat wave discussions (March 26 journal entry)—is based on the research of Jennifer Francis. She explains her theory (as developed in 2012) in excellent YouTube postings, including *Understanding the Jet Stream* (Jennifer

Francis, February 26, 2013) and *Climate Change & Extreme Weather* (Jennifer Francis, February 17, 2013). One of many summaries of Francis's research that I used is "Arctic Warming Is Altering Weather Patterns, Study Shows," (A. Freedman, September 30, 2012), posted on Climate Central's website.

Francis's theory is a subject of ongoing research and debate; see, for example, the discussion in Inquiring Minds 22, "Jennifer Francis and Kevin Trenberth— Is Global Warming Driving Crazy Winters?" (February 21, 2014) posted on SoundCloud.

The June 29 derecho discussed in the July 3 journal entry is described in the U.S. Storm Prediction Center's "The Ohio Valley / Mid-Atlantic Derecho of June 2012," posted on the NOAA website and in multiple other locations.

The drought's national and state trends, discussed throughout chapters 4 and 6 and in the December 16 journal entry and chapter 10, were based on the U.S. Drought Monitor maps archive on the National Drought Mitigation Center's website. These maps show the extent of drought and rate it as moderate, severe, extreme, or exceptional—a relative terminology that I adopted for this book. Drought information also came from assorted news releases. Iowa-specific drought trends and temperatures were from comments by Harry Hillaker, Iowa's state climatologist, in his weather summaries posted on the Iowa Department of Agriculture and Land Stewardship website, in particular his report "The Drought of 2012 in Iowa" (undated), and from *The State Climatologist, 2012 Annual Summary*, vol. 31, issue 1, 2013, published by the American Association of State Climatologists and posted on its website.

Information on the drought's effect on agriculture mentioned in several journal entries was drawn from the USDA Economic Research Service's summary report, *U.S. Drought 2012: Farm and Food Impacts*, dated July 26, 2013, and posted on the USDA website; *Updated Assessment of the Drought's Impacts on Crop Prices and Biofuel Production* by B. Babcock, August 2012, published by the Center for Agricultural and Rural Development at Iowa State University and posted on that center's website; comments in news reports and by Harry Hillaker in "Iowa Monthly Weather Summaries," posted on the IDALS website; and postings on the USDA National Agricultural Statistics Service's website.

The *Third National Climate Assessment* (2014) predicts future precipitation and drought trends for different regions of the country, which are mentioned in the July 7 journal entry.

Hurricane Sandy, described primarily in the November 1 journal entry, was explored in great depth in several reports. I used the National Hurricane Center's *Tropical Cyclone Report Hurricane Sandy (AL182012) 22–29 October 2012*, by E. S. Blake et al., February 12, 2013, and the National Weather Service's *Hurricane/*

Post-Tropical Cyclone Sandy, October 22–29, 2012, May 2013, both posted on the NOAA website; and "Superstorm Sandy and Sea Level Rise" by B. Kahn, November 4, 2012, posted on the NOAA Climate.gov website. I also used "How Does Climate Change Make Superstorms Like Sandy More Destructive?" by J. Romm, October 31, 2012, posted on the Climate Progress blog, and "How Global Warming Made Hurricane Sandy Worse" by A. Freedman, November 1, 2012, posted on the Climate Central website.

I based the statistical summaries of the year's extreme weather in chapter 10 mostly on *The State of the Climate, National Overview—Annual 2012* (2013), produced by NOAA and available on its website. These summary data are reproduced on several websites, for example, NOAA's "National Overview—Annual 2012: 2012 By The Numbers," which I used in my December 16 journal entry.

The report "How Global Warming Is Driving Our Weather Wild" by S. Battersby, July 9, 2012, published in *New Scientist*, no. 2872, and posted on its website, enlightened me about extreme weather of all types.

Iowa-Specific Information

My 2012 temperature and weather information specific to Iowa, used throughout the book, was verified using reports by Harry Hillaker, which are posted on the Iowa Department of Agriculture and Land Stewardship website. These include the "Iowa Monthly Weather Summaries" and preliminary summaries for each month of 2012 and "Preliminary Weather Summary—2012." I also used *The State Climatologist, 2012 Annual Summary* (2013), which has annual summaries for the nation and for each state.

Climate Change Impacts on Iowa 2010 (2011) provided data on Iowa's increasing atmospheric moisture (March 26 journal entry) and increasing frost-free days (May 1 journal entry). I used this Iowa report and the *Third National Climate Assessment* (2014) for discussions of midwestern climate, for example, in the May 1 journal entry. The April 16 journal entry on climate change and precipitation was based largely on the latter report, with input from *The Rough Guide* (2011), *Global Climate Change Impacts in the U.S.* (2009), and IPCC's *Fifth Assessment Report*, vol. 1 (2013). That journal entry includes the increase in very heavy precipitation events, which is documented in the *Third National Climate Assessment* and refers to the "heaviest 1 percent of all daily events between 1958 and 2011."

Iowa's 2008 floods, mentioned in the June 21 journal entry, are discussed in a book that I edited, *A Watershed Year: Anatomy of the Iowa Floods of 2008* (2010, University of Iowa Press), which describes many aspects of midwestern flooding including its climate-change connection. Data on the intense rainfall in our woodland in April 2013, described in chapter 10, from the Iowa Flood Center, University of Iowa (personal communication, Witold Krajewski).

Information on Iowa's geological past and prehistoric ecosystems, discussed in April 23 and August 20 journal entries, and midwestern natural history, which forms the spine of my journal chapters, came from personal knowledge and my book *The Emerald Horizon: The History of Nature in Iowa* (2008, University of Iowa Press). Jean Prior's book *Landforms of Iowa* (1991, University of Iowa Press) was a trusted reference for geological change.

The Environmental Movement and Environmental Changes

My history of the environmental movement, which strings through chapters 3, 5, 7, and 9, was based on personal experience, environmental textbooks from decades past, and the Environmental Protection Agency's websites for history of environmental legislation and its effects. In particular, I referred to "Progress Cleaning the Air and Improving People's Health" and "40th Anniversary of the Clean Air Act" on the EPA Clean Air Act website; the Clean Water Act 40th Anniversary website; and the EPA 40th Anniversary website.

For the increase in fossil fuel use discussed in chapter 7, I consulted "History of Energy Consumption in the United States, 1775–2009," February 9, 2011, on the U.S. Energy Information Administration website. For that chapter's discussion of the ozone hole and Montreal Protocol, I used the above EPA Clean Air Act websites, as well as "The Skeptics vs. the Ozone Hole," J. Masters, circa 2004, posted on the Weather Underground blog site. And for sulfur dioxide mitigation through the cap-and-trade program, also in chapter 7, I relied on data from the EPA's Clean Air Markets, Programs, Acid Rain Program website.

Much of my understanding of the historic development of climate-change science (as included in chapters 5, 7, 9, and the February 11 journal entry) can be attributed to *The Discovery of Global Warming—A History*, an excellent and detailed hypertext created by S. Weart and mounted on the website of the Center for History of Physics of the American Institute of Physics.

My understanding of recent changes in public opinion regarding climate change was greatly expanded by the Yale Project on Climate Change Communication, which posts its research and analysis on its website; this site provided data for the April 19 journal entry.

COP18 and COP19 Meetings

The reports I mentioned in the November 29 journal entry, released during COP18 meetings, include the World Bank's *Turn Down the Heat* (2012), with quotes from that report; the U.N. Environment Programme's *Policy Implications of Warming Permafrost*, K. Schaefer et al., November 2012; the World Meteorological Organization's *Provisional Statement on the State of Global Climate in 2012*, November 28, 2012, with M. Jarraud's quote taken from the WMO's Press Release 966 for that report. And the new study I refer to on Antarctic ice mass is "A Reconciled Estimate of Ice-Sheet Mass Balance" by A. Shepherd et al., November 30, 2012, published in *Science*, doi:10.1126/science.1228102.

The Filipino negotiator's COP18 response to Typhoon Bopha, quoted in the December 8 journal entry, is taken from "Will Philippines Negotiator's Tears Change Our Course on Climate Change" by J. Vidal, published December 6, 2012, in the *Guardian*.

The same diplomat's response at COP19 to the even larger Typhoon Haiyan, quoted in chapter 10, is taken from "Philippines Urges Action to Resolve Climate Talks Deadlock after Typhoon Haiyan" by J.Vidal and A. Vaughan, published November 13, 2013, in the *Guardian*.

Chapter 10 Citations

Information on Iowa's wind power industry, in chapter 10 and mentioned elsewhere, is available on the Iowa Energy Center's and the Iowa Wind Energy Association's websites.

Statistics on wildfire were from the National Interagency Coordination Center, *Wildland Fire Summary and Statistics Annual Report 2012*, undated, posted on the National Interagency Fire Center website.

The increase in registered U.S. vehicles was taken from "Table 1-11: Number of U.S. Aircraft, Vehicles, Vessels, and Other Conveyances: Highway, Total Registered Vehicles" on the U.S. Dept. of Transportation, Bureau of Transportation Statistics website.

Increases in violent behavior associated with higher temperatures were from "Climate Change and Violence Linked, Breakthrough Study Finds" by R. Wilkey, published August 1, 2013, in the Huffington Post. The subject is further discussed in "There's a Surprisingly Strong Link between Climate Change and Violence" by C. Mooney, posted October 22, 2014, on the *Washington Post*'s blog.

Discussion of Boulder's 2013 extreme rainfall is summarized in "Inside the Colorado Deluge," by B. Henson, September 14, 2013, posted on the NCAR/UCAR AtmosNews website.

Chapter 11 Citations

An analysis of net-zero emissions strategies is presented in "Briefing: The 15 Options for Net-Zero Emissions in the Paris Climate Text" by S. Evans, posted on the Carbon Brief blog on February 13, 2013. Note that the IPCC's *Fifth Assessment Report*, vol. 3 (2014), gives multiple mitigation scenarios but states that keeping temperatures below a 3.6-degree rise would require global emissions cuts of 40–70 percent (below 2010 levels) by 2050 and cuts approaching 100 percent by 2100.

For discussion of the need to leave fossil fuels unburned, I used "Global Warming's Terrifying New Math" by B. McKibben, published in *Rolling Stone* on July 19, 2012, and accessible on its website.

The Solutions Project is well described on its own website and many others.

The importance of black carbon is described in *On Thin Ice: How Cutting Pollution Can Slow Warming and Save Lives, Main Report* by P. Pearson et al., 2013, posted on the World Bank website.

General information on the pricing of carbon was found at "World Bank, Pricing Carbon," a website of the World Bank. British Columbia's successful carbon tax is described on the Province of British Columbia's website at "Ministry of Finance, Carbon Tax."

Data on the 2012 percentage of energy from renewable sources is from the U.S. Energy Information Administration's website at "Total Energy, Overview." Information on the growth of renewables in the U.S. was taken from the report *The Outlook for Renewable Energy in America, 2014*, posted on the American Council of Renewable Energy's website.

Information on carbon neutrality at Google, Kohl's, Staples, and Whole Foods was taken from those companies' websites.

The following sources provided information on governmental initiatives to reduce carbon footprints: State of California website, "Climate Change Portal"; the New York State Department of Environmental Conservation website, "Energy and Climate" and "Climate Change"; the Commonwealth of Massachusetts website, "Energy and Environmental Affairs" and "Climate Change"; the Regional Greenhouse Gas Initiative website and The Oberlin Project website. Information on Switzerland's carbon-neutral initiative was taken from "New Renewables on Integration Course" by L. Leiva, posted October 10, 2014, on the Paul Scherrer Institut website, and from Christopher Mutel, personal communication, December 2014. Details of use of renewables in Sweden, Germany, Iceland, Norway, Denmark, and the European Union are readily available on multiple websites.

The recent decline in U.S. carbon emissions is documented at the *U.S. Greenhouse Gas Inventory Report: 1990–2013* on the Environmental Protection Agency's website.

Additional Citations

And finally, the following citations are for details that did not fit into any of the above broader categories.

James Enloe (personal communication, March 2015) provided information on the archaeological features near my home mentioned in chapter 1, particularly Woodpecker Cave adjacent to the Coralville Reservoir.

The high percentage of trained climate scientists who accept the reality and human causation of climate change, given in chapter 1, is from "Expert Credibility in Climate Change" by W. Anderegg et al., July 6, 2010, *Proceedings of the National Academy of Sciences* 107, doi:10.1073/pnas.1003187107.

The social justice aspects of climate change (April 19 journal entry) were taken primarily from *Turn Down the Heat* (2012).

The quote in the July 3 journal entry was by Michael Oppenheimer, as included in "'This U.S. Summer Is 'What Global Warming Looks Like': Scientists" by S. Borenstein, July 3, 2012, posted on the *Phys.org* science news website.

The climate skeptic who refuted his former stance, as I describe in the July 28 journal entry, is Richard Muller, a physics professor at the University of California Berkeley, who wrote about his turnaround in the *New York Times* op-ed piece "The Conversion of a Climate-Change Skeptic," July 28, 2012.

The ozone hole study described in the July 26 journal entry was "UV Dosage Levels in Summer: Increased Risk of Ozone Loss from Convectively Injected Water Vapor" by J. Anderson et al., published online July 26, 2012, later in *Science* 337, doi:10.1126/science.1222978. A thoughtful critique of the study appeared on the Climate Central blog site on August 1, 2012: "Like Ozone Layer, Holes in Study on Thunderstorms" by M. Lemonick. Readers should note that these potential ozone holes differ in cause from the extant ozone hole described in chapter 7.

For the effects of climate change on toxic algal blooms and the Great Lakes, mentioned in the September 14 journal entry, I used the *Third National Climate Assessment* (2014); "Impacts of Climate Change on the Occurrence of Harmful Algal Blooms," document EPA 820-S-13-001, published May 2013 on the EPA website; and "How Climate Change Is Damaging the Great Lakes, with Implications for the Environment and Economy" by M. Kasper, posted January 18, 2013, on the ClimateProgress blog.

The perils of climate change for national security and the military, mentioned in the December 3 journal entry, are discussed in the book *Climate and Social Stress: Implications for Security Analysis*, edited by J. Steinbruner et al. and prepared by the National Research Council at the request of the CIA (2013, National Academies Press).

Acknowledgments ∾

THREE PERSONS improved the content of this book tremendously and devoted many hours to helping me navigate this project. Holly Carver, friend, editor, and former director of the University of Iowa Press, believed in my project from its inception and talked me through many knotty problems. Her constant positive support guided me through difficult days, weeks, and months. Robert Henson, meteorologist and blogger at Weather Underground and author of *The Thinking Person's Guide to Climate Change*, taught me details about climate science and generously edited the manuscript for accuracy. His guidance steered me beyond many scientific misunderstandings and mistakes regarding climate change. And Mary Nilsen, author, writing teacher, and founder of Zion Publishing, added depth and complexity to the manuscript, urging me forward with her belief in the book's importance and her enduring friendship. I consider these three to be cocreators of *A Sugar Creek Chronicle*.

My home institute, IIHR–Hydroscience & Engineering in the University of Iowa College of Engineering, provided professional and collegial support during my three years of manuscript writing. Being part of a research institute with colleagues and staff who are interested and helpful, even as they remain respectful of creative exploration, has been a tremendous gift throughout the quarter century I have been at IIHR. In particular, I thank Larry Weber, IIHR director, who has always encouraged meaningful investigation and expression.

Colleagues at the university's Center for Global and Regional Environmental Research, in particular Jerald Schnoor and Gregory Carmichael, likewise have supported me with their interest and belief in this project. In addition, CGRER awarded me a very helpful grant that allowed the project's expansion and completion. Eugene Takle, director of Iowa State University's Climate Science Program, has also unfailingly supported my climate-change writing efforts and offered helpful comments on my manuscript.

Numerous friends discussed approaches or commented on the several manuscript iterations, providing insights when my vision was foggy or my brain was exhausted. These included Katherine Burford, Elizabeth Christiansen, Laurie Eash, Catherine Forman, Nancy Jones, Deb Lewis, Jackie Stolze, and Judith Sutherland. Kelley Donham, James Fuller, Carter Johnson, and Jean Sandrock helped me track 2012 weather events.

Several experts helped review parts of the manuscript or provided valuable content that was integrated into the text. These included E. Arthur Bettis, Stephen Dinsmore, James Enloe, James Fuller, Witold Krajewski, Mark Müller, Christopher Mutel, Robert Mutel, John Pearson, and Jerald Schnoor.

Learning about climate change, struggling to express its complexities in an understandable fashion, and allowing its reality to permeate my innermost being at times exhausted and depressed me. At those times, I needed (and received) the friendship and guidance of those mentioned above and many more who asked how I was doing and gave me supportive hugs. Others offering crucial guidance and support included Diane Baumbach, Lori Erickson, pastors Mark Pries, Jennifer Lutz, and Rob Dotzel, Sister Kathleen Storms, and my husband, Robert, our sons, and their families, who got me to lighten up when I needed to do so. As did our Labrador retreiver Sandy—whose true name was usurped by Hurricane Sandy. (She became "Sidney" in my manuscript without complaint, asking only for puppy biscuits in return.)

The University of Iowa Press shepherded my manuscript through the publication process with dedication, grace, and thoughtfulness. I thank especially Catherine Cocks and Susan Hill Newton for their kindness, emphasis on quality, and sensitivity to the product at hand, and Rebecca Marsh for her detailed wordsmithing and enthusiasm for this project.

This book required me to throw my thoughts about the planet's future to the wind, even as I probed the meaning of the word hope. Doing so required a firm footing. Here I remember family members who taught me the meaning of hope, love, and joy from my earliest days, in particular, my parents, Herbert and Dorothy Fleischer and stepmother BB Fleischer, and my grandparents, Gustav Groth and Alma Fleischer (whom we called Mambie), all now long deceased. Little could they have known how important their lessons would become in my later years. And, of course, I need to remember the natural world and its many inhabitants who—as I write in this book—have always formed the ground base of my life, stretching my curiosity and presenting me with inspiration and visions of abundant beauty.

To all of the above, as well as the thousands of highly trained researchers who have dedicated their lives to probing the complexities of climate change and where it might take us and thousands more who even now are working to stave off climate change's worst expressions, I express my heartfelt appreciation, even as I take full responsibility for any errors or misinterpretations that may remain in my book.

Index ∾

This index is limited to climate-change concepts, features, and remediation efforts, as well as major U.S. weather events for years 2012 and 2013. Daily observations of midwestern natural history and other weather events, and memoir descriptions of my personal life, are included only when they touch upon broader climate-change or environmental-change issues.

OTHER BUR OAK BOOKS OF INTEREST

Between Urban and Wild: Reflections from Colorado
Andrea M. Jones

Booming from the Mists of Nowhere: The Story of the Greater Prairie-Chicken
Greg Hoch

The Butterflies of Iowa
Dennis W. Schlicht, John C. Downey, and Jeffrey Nekola

A Country So Full of Game: The Story of Wildlife in Iowa
James J. Dinsmore

Deep Nature: Photographs from Iowa
Linda Scarth and Robert Scarth

The Ecology and Management of Prairies in the Central United States
Chris Helzer

The Elemental Prairie: Sixty Tallgrass Plants
George Olson and John Madson

The Emerald Horizon: The History of Nature in Iowa
Cornelia F. Mutel

Enchanted by Prairie
Bill Witt and Osha Gray Davidson

Fauna and Flora, Earth and Sky
Trudy Dittmar

Fifty Common Birds of the Upper Midwest
Dana Gardner and Nancy Overcott

Fifty Uncommon Birds of the Upper Midwest
Dana Gardner and Nancy Overcott

Fragile Giants: A Natural History of the Loess Hills
Cornelia F. Mutel

Iowa Birdlife
Gladys Black

The Iowa Breeding Bird Atlas
Laura Spess Jackson, Carol A. Thompson, and James J. Dinsmore

The Iowa Nature Calendar
Jean C. Prior and James Sandrock

Landforms of Iowa
Jean C. Prior

Of Men and Marshes
Paul L. Errington

Of Wilderness and Wolves
Paul L. Errington

Out Home
John Madson

A Practical Guide to Prairie Reconstruction
Carl Kurtz

Prairie: A North American Guide
Suzanne Winckler

The Raptors of Iowa
Paintings by James F. Landenberger, Essays by Dean M. Roosa, Jon W. Stravers, Bruce Ehresman, and Rich Patterson

Restoring the Tallgrass Prairie: An Illustrated Manual for Iowa and the Upper Midwest
Shirley Shirley

Stories from under the Sky
John Madson

The Tallgrass Prairie Reader
Edited by John T. Price

A Watershed Year: Anatomy of the Iowa Floods of 2008
Cornelia F. Mutel

Where the Sky Began: Land of the Tallgrass Prairie
John Madson

Wildflowers and Other Plants of Iowa Wetlands, Second Edition
Sylvan T. Runkel and Dean M. Roosa

Wildflowers of the Tallgrass Prairie: The Upper Midwest, Second Edition
Sylvan T. Runkel and Dean M. Roosa